WOMEN IN AMERICAN HISTORY

Series Editors
MARI JO BUHLE
JACQUELYN D. HALL
ANNE FIROR SCOTT

WINTER FRIENDS

WINTER FRIENDS

Women Growing Old in the
New Republic, 1785-1835

TERRI L. PREMO

UNIVERSITY OF ILLINOIS PRESS
Urbana and Chicago

Library of Congress Cataloging-in-Publication Data

Premo, Terri L.
    Winter friends : women growing old in the new Republic, 1785-1835
/ Terri Premo. — [Rev. & enl. ed.]
        p.   cm. — (Women in American history)
    Originally presented as the author's thesis under the title: Women
growing old in the new Republic.
    Bibliography: p.
    Includes index.
    ISBN 0-252-01656-4 (alk. paper)
    1. Aged women — United States — History — 18th century.   2. Aged
women — United States — History — 19th century.   3. Aged women — United
States — Social conditions.   4. Old age — United States — History.
5. United States — Social conditions — To 1865.   I. Premo, Terri L.
Women growing old in the new Republic. II. Title. III. Series.
HQ1064.U5P683   1990
305.26'082 — dc20   89-4980
                                                                        CIP

For
HELEN WEAVER PREMO
and
ANNA CATHARINE PREMO WILLIAMS

Contents

ILLUSTRATIONS

Abbreviations

AAS	American Antiquarian Society, Worcester, Massachusetts
CHS	Connecticut Historical Society, Hartford, Connecticut
EI	James Duncan Phillips Library, Essex Institute, Salem, Massachusetts
GHS	Georgia Historical Society, Savannah, Georgia
LCP	Library Company of Philadelphia, Philadelphia, Pennsylvania
HSP	Historical Society of Pennsylvania, Philadelphia, Pennsylvania
LCMD	Library of Congress, Manuscript Division, Washington, D.C.
MHS	Massachusetts Historical Society, Boston, Massachusetts
SL	Arthur and Elizabeth Schlesinger Library on the History of Women in America, Radcliffe College, Cambridge, Massachusetts

Acknowledgments

Recapturing the world of aged eighteenth-century women is a daunting task. It can be undertaken only with the aid of experienced archivists and librarians who hold the keys to our past and invariably know which key to try when doors won't open. I am indebted to the staffs of libraries and historical societies from Massachusetts to Georgia who assisted me in locating the voices of these old women. I am grateful, too, to the Taft Foundation of the University of Cincinnati and the Society of the Colonial Dames of America in Ohio for their financial support which helped make such research possible. The Women's Studies Research and Resources Institute of the University of Cincinnati provided additional support for which I am grateful.

Although the journey from research paper to dissertation to publication has been long and sometimes arduous, its passage was made smoother by the good counsel and expertise of many friends and associates. Gene Lewis and Frank Kafker, who read earlier versions, offered thoughtful insights. Robert Atchley awakened me to the concerns of social gerontology and helped me learn to ask the right questions. Nancy Grey Osterud offered useful criticism of early drafts. John Alexander not only guided the earliest efforts but continued to provide support and direction way beyond the call of duty.

As the manuscript matured, I profited from the thoughtful insights of a number of historians. As a friend and colleague, Thomas Cole introduced me to new ideas and perspectives long after I (foolishly) thought my work was done. Joanne Meyerowitz, Kriste Dick, Pat Van Skaik, Janet Reed, and Andrea Kornbluh all raised useful and probing questions. Audrey Borenstein's enthusiastic support of my work helped sustain me during darker moments. Anne Firor Scott, Mari Jo Buhle, Carole Appel, and Jane Mohraz have nudged and prodded me to get the manuscript right. To the extent that it is right, I have all of them to thank.

Finally, I am most appreciative of those who allowed me the time and

solitude it takes to turn a manuscript into a book. Mildred Williams and
Valrea Denlinger offered worry-free child care. Peter Jay Williams and Anna
Catharine Williams gave me valuable "quiet time." But my deepest thanks
go to Jay Williams for his patience, his support, and his infinite faith.

Introduction

Like others who have found their way into new, unchartered academic territories, scholars studying the history of old age have justifiably called themselves "pioneers." Until the past decade, historians largely ignored the social, cultural, and intellectual implications of growing old, despite a quarter-century of solid research on nearly all other aspects of social history. Beyond the obvious need to "fill the historical gap," there were other incentives to investigate the history of growing old. Pointing to current statistics forecasting ever-increasing numbers of old persons in our society, gerontologists, health-care planners, and others have properly cited the need for solid data from the past to help prepare for the future. Growing interest in various stages of the life cycle further supported the conviction held by historians of aging that theirs was an important field. Despite these laudable (and absolutely correct) assumptions, however, scholars and nonacademics alike find this field fascinating and enticing for purely selfish motives. We are all caught up in our own individual history of growing old. We seek guidance, direction, and hope from those who have grown old before us. We search, ultimately, for ourselves.

Women, unfortunately, will need to search longer and harder to find historical patterns of growing old. This is true for a number of reasons. Women's written record is less accessible; most documents written by aging women remain uncollected, unpublished. More to the point, historians have failed to give women equal attention in their studies of old age. While many elements of the aging process are applicable to men and women alike, the history of women growing old is, by and large, a separate story requiring new sets of assumptions and different kinds of questions. By considering women growing old within the context of women's individual and collective history, one can gain new perspectives which both complement and challenge earlier findings.[1]

Growing Old: The Historical Setting

The experience of aging in the past resembles in many ways the process of growing old today. Physical problems associated with aging—reduced

strength, increasing inability to fight infection, and diminished sensory
response — were as familiar to old people two hundred years ago as they
are to twentieth-century Americans. Although fewer people lived into old
age in years past, people then as now associated advanced age with changes
in family status and work capacities. Even images of aging have remained
constant in their reminders that death, the Grim Reaper, was near at hand.
Such images tempered the dreams and future prospects for all people approaching the end of life.[2]

Yet in early America many attitudes about aging differed from those
commonly shared today. Old people in years past seldom felt the need to
deny their age. Supported by a solid religious foundation, aging men and
women earnestly prepared for their final years. Old age, they knew, meant
debility and reliance on their adult children for care and comfort. Yet old
age also held out the promise of veneration and the hope of divine redemption at the end of life. The joyful expectation of a better world to
come eased the fear of death and dismissed as only temporary the declining
physical body. By integrating negative and positive aspects of old age into
an intellectual framework that emphasized natural decline and renewal,
the elderly could treat aging honestly and directly.

This is not to imply, by any means, that a "golden age" for old persons
existed in preindustrial America. Fear of illness or disability, concern over
continued usefulness to oneself and others, and anxiety over declining
mental powers plagued the old of early America. Beyond this, old age when
combined with poverty could, and often did, exact heavy tolls from countless
men and women who left no literary epitaph to document their struggle.
With few institutional supports to provide aid and care in times of need,
poor old people felt the full burden of old age. Nevertheless, for those able
to subsist, old age at least offered the comfort and hope of a quick, "blessed
Release" when life ended.[3]

While neither religious consolation nor filial responsibility totally al-
leviated fear and apprehension in old age, these two support systems remained viable for many older Americans into the first third of the nineteenth
century. Over time, however, societal changes eroded the effectiveness of
this workable, if innately conservative, approach to old age and death.
Increased geographic mobility, significant after the Revolution and even
more consequential by the 1830s, imposed restrictions on an adult child's
ability to care for parents. Changing religious perspectives among clergy and
laity alike altered and eventually reduced the feasibility of a theological
argument based on decay and dependency. As values changed in an indus-
trializing and increasingly mobile society, the organic and redemptive features associated with old age no longer seemed entirely appropriate or reasonable.[4]

By the middle of the nineteenth century, diverging attitudes and behaviors toward the aged signalled the beginning of a new period in age relations. Privately operated institutions for the care of the dependent aged emerged as an alternative to filial duty. Age limits on judicial officeholding were imposed in seven states prior to the Civil War. Such changes, while not necessarily indicative of revolutionary changes in age relations, nevertheless indicate a transitional period in which individuals were forced to develop new ways of coping with old age and new perspectives from which to view it.[5]

A Differing Feminine Perspective

Women and men alike were aware in the fifty years following the Revolution that theirs was a world bent on change. Excitement and opportunity abounded in the new republic, and women, no less than men, wanted the seeds of this new nation to grow and flourish. Unlike men, however, most women were not fully free to explore new options and develop new ambitions. Their worldly aspirations remained, for the most part, confined to sharing in the prosperity (or drawing moral lessons from the failures) of the men in their lives.

In their private worlds, however, women built on established domestic foundations to erect a feminine structure stronger and more resilient than previously known. Most women's lives had long been associated with the duties of maintaining a home and children, but the importance attached to those duties by the early nineteenth century gave new meaning to "domesticity" and the intrinsic values of "womanhood." Within their increasingly separate sphere, women relied on each other for friendship and guidance and for the moral sustenance they believed women uniquely possessed. As time passed, a self-conscious preoccupation with "woman's sphere" gave new significance to the meaning of gender and new power to the notion of home.

The values implicit in the "cult of domesticity" emerging in the early nineteenth century appealed mainly to middle-class men and women or to those who aspired to middle-class status. Poor women and slaves had little opportunity to adopt the norms of domesticity. For such women, the ideals of domesticity only served to alienate them further in an increasingly class-conscious society. Nonetheless, the values associated with feminine domesticity would influence women's roles and the direction of nineteenth-century society.[6]

Integrating Women into the History of Aging

To establish the important link between women's history and the history of aging, I have chosen to examine records from the fifty years following the Revolution, a period traditionally acknowledged as critical in the development of early American society. Historians of women have established the significance of this post-revolutionary period on a number of points: the energizing effect of the Revolution on women's private lives (and its limited impact on their public personae); the channeling of women's political and intellectual ambitions into an ideology of domesticity; and the bonding of women as they attempted to interpret their rights and duties as conservators of domestic harmony and agents of social change. Feminist scholars, however, have not yet acknowledged the effects of these historical shifts on women grown old with the memories and the consequences of such change.[7]

Historians of aging have also designated this period as pivotal in the history of age relations. In his controversial thesis, David Hackett Fischer argued that a "revolution in age relations" occurred between 1770 and 1820. By the end of this period, the "moral authority of old age was seriously eroded," and a cult of youth had emerged. According to Fischer, this radical transformation in age values reflected the "deep change" of the revolutionary era itself.[8]

Other historians disagree with Fischer. Some instead consider the 1830s as the critical period, marking a decline in the traditional mechanisms supporting old-age systems and the simultaneous rise of a romantic tradition which distorted earlier values. Indeed, there can be little doubt that major shifts occurred during this time in the social, economic, and political world of the "common man" which influenced his old age. Yet, because Fischer and others have not examined the feminine context of growing old, their broad theses and sweeping conclusions are, at best, premature.

This study, then, will not use data which imply a standard of power based on political officeholding or possession of property. Such criteria, considered crucial to previous investigations of status in old age, have little relevance to women in a society which denied them political and property rights. Instead, the study examines those aspects of the feminine experience that gave meaning to women growing old, as expressed by old women themselves. Kinship ties, friendships between women, and strong moral and spiritual beliefs comprise the dominant value system of the women studied here. Within their sphere of activity and influence, aging women approached the end of life firm in the conviction that their concerns and values were far from trivial — that, indeed, their perspective (based on both age and gender) uniquely qualified them to contemplate and interpret life's mysteries and to prepare the next generation for its blessings.

My findings convince me that historians can no longer be blind to the presence of women in the history of old age or of old women in feminist scholarship. From these personal documents, we learn the significance of continuity and connection in the lives of aging women; the prospect of change only reinforced their determination to persevere as before. Their model of strength and durability extended to new generations as well, serving to sustain younger women whose own options were as yet limited in the new republic.

For most old women, the post-revolutionary era was a time to appreciate and, most important, to perpetuate their female heritage. Less attracted to the promise of change than their younger sisters, older women began to fear the prospect of a future void of moral and spiritual substance. Their task, as they saw it, was not only to continue serving the needs of family and friends into old age but to act as living reminders of a peculiarly feminine moral order. As the nineteenth century advanced, this moral imperative became synonymous with the broad spectrum of women's issues, becoming the central component of what was considered "female sensibility." Old women in the new republic not only lived in but helped create a cult of feminine morality that would become both the glory and the bane of nineteenth-century womanhood. Yet, in the early years of that century, older women combined this moral strength with enduring feminine ties and continued domestic involvement to secure a remarkable sense of purpose and direction in the final years of life.

Aged women, nonetheless, bore numerous burdens, including the ambiguous legacy of their revolutionary heritage and the rigidity of woman's sphere which supported their old age only to the extent that they embraced its tenets. There is no evidence, however, that women experienced Fischer's "revolution in age relations" in the fifty years following the Revolution. Within their sphere, women continued to work, to pray, and to function effectively. Although some change occurred by the end of this post-revolutionary period, old women usually found strength and comfort in the prospect and the process of growing old.

In many ways, this book is a response to the challenge presented by a number of colleagues and archivists who initially doubted the existence of enough material written by or about older women in this early period to create a well-grounded study. Studies of women's perceptions and attitudes in early America are difficult enough without the additional consideration of age. Illiteracy and a social system that was, at best, uneasy with the notion of a feminine literata prevented most women from pursuing a career in writing. Women essayists remained few in number, and women novelists fought an uphill battle until at least the second third of the nineteenth century. Among women's private writings, however, much valuable material can be found to illuminate the personal and reflective side of women's daily lives. From among the 160 women, both young and old, examined in this study, it was possible to establish a pattern of women's perspectives both from and about old age in the late eighteenth and early nineteenth centuries.[9]

This study has drawn heavily on manuscript material in collections from all sections of the new republic. It also includes published accounts of women's personal writings. The women examined here, however, clearly were not representative of the country's female population in the early national period. Despite an effort at geographic balance, the preponderance of material is from Pennsylvania and New England, regions offering an extraordinary quantity and scope of manuscripts. In addition, most women studied here lived in or near urban areas or in sizeable towns and villages, even though the vast majority of the population remained agriculturalists. The extant sources are overwhelmingly the writings of middle- and upper-class, white Protestant women who were sufficiently motivated to record their thoughts on paper and whose heirs considered those thoughts valuable enough to preserve. Poor or illiterate white women as well as black and Indian women left few traces of the personal, introspective aspects of growing old. It is particularly unfortunate that the views of poor women, who bore the worst burdens associated with old age and no doubt anticipated its onset with considerable trepidation, were not available. Aging non-Protestant women are similarly underrepresented in the surviving source material. Such source problems impose obvious limitations on a study that focuses on educing the *mentalité* of the population. Yet to the extent that women growing old shared a number of characteristic changes in late life, it can be assumed that the attitudes expressed by this sample of women were familiar to many women of the time.

The use of women's diaries and journals requires special care from historians hoping to determine perceptions and attitudes which are both accurate and representative. It is clear from their own writings that women who kept diaries in the late eighteenth and early nineteenth centuries believed their words were being recorded for posterity. Although only women from the most illustrious and powerful families might have expected their private writings to become historically valuable, many women understood their records would be passed down to future generations of their own families. This awareness doubtless affected the content and style of the journals. These diaries often lack the introspective, free-flowing narrative associated with today's private journals, but they do provide a view of what women considered signficant and useful for later generations. Such perceptions help illuminate women's personal values as well as the values of the society.

Women diarists did not, of course, focus entirely on posterity. Many diarists, particularly those within the Puritan tradition, expected their daily entries to provide a spiritual guide for their own improvement and edification, recording in the diary's pages their hopes, failures, and shortcomings. Quaker diarists often used the journal as an ongoing record of their never-ending struggle for purification and redemption. Other women kept more mundane journals that merely served as permanent records of visits and accounts of the weather and expenses. These journals offer a source for determining patterns of work and social activity. They do not, however, provide the introspection and spontaneity necessary for establishing direct, unequivocal responses to problems of growing old. But in their comments about friends and relatives, the acknowledgments of births and deaths, and even the recordings of their own birthdays, the most circumspect diarists offered useful and valuable material.[10]

Letters written by women offer a different perspective from that gained by reading women's diaries. The introspective and religious material so often found in journals appeared less frequently in personal correspondence. While journals tended to reveal personal expressions of an inner, solitary existence, letters exposed the social, interactive side of women's lives. Despite the highly affected, stylized form of much feminine correspondence, letters by women often revealed issues and attitudes not always apparent in diaries. The nature of relationships, for example, is often best gleaned from letters written by women to their friends and relatives. Letters, like diaries, must be used with caution, however. They tend to portray only the best side of a writer anxious to advise and console. Letter writers expected their epistles to be read and reread by many people, both before and after being sent. Such letters were often carefully worded and frequently edited before sending. Nevertheless, they serve as valuable indicators of the values women attached to the events occurring in their daily lives.[11]

Autobiographies and published memoirs pose additional challenges to researchers intent on uncovering the "reality" of lived experience. Such materials (even those intended as family documents) represent carefully selected interpretations of private lives for public consumption. Yet what is lost in terms of spontaneity and candor is often compensated by the integrated vision of past life presented in such works. Autobiographies written in old age often tell us more about the writer's unique old-age perspective than about specific events in life. Even though few women wrote (and fewer published) autobiographies during this early period, this genre remains a distinctively useful source for students of aging.[12]

Taken together, the record of women's private writings during this early period of American history is impressive. What is most striking, however, is the enduring sense of self which rises to the surface in even the most mundane and prosaic entries. The strong presence of these aging women, kept alive and well through their writings, imposed its own format on this

Dr Betton, to my great and sincere comfort, seems decidedly better.

It is now the afternoon of the 17th August. Quite warm, Sunshine and serene. I feel low. I have no one to sustain and comfort me, in the outward, however. I am in the Library by myself. No one in the House but me. I hear the people at work on the farm as they pass and repass with the Cart, but in the interval no other sound, except the loud ticking of my Library clock. On my table, among other Papers is part of Rapin de Thoyras's History of England, which appears to have been Printed in 1732. and Issued in Numbers. There is some account of the author in the Preface. The Good Anthony Benezet told my mother that the Historian De Thoyras was his maternal Uncle. Thoughts, of the Past ___ of the long Past ___ and of the Painful Recent Past ___ of the Sluggish Present ___ and of the (Perhaps never to be experienced in this World) Future, float before the mind's eye. long train ___ often intricate and Involved ___ and yet obliging me to say
_____ "For who would Loose
    "Tho' full of Pain, this Intellectual Being.
    These Thoughts that wander thro' Eternity?"

    Now, I seem a kind of Isolated Being. _____ But I do not dislike to be alone and to feel as I do now.

Well, on Fifth day afternoon, before I had Issued out of my Room, maria Logan called and asked me to go with her to Betsy Robsons to Tea; mary had gone

Pages from the diary of Deborah Norris Logan, courtesy of Historical Society of Pennsylvania. 17 August 1837: "Now I seem a kind of Isolated Being — But I do not dislike to be alone and to feel as I do now."

had *[been]* at meeting, besides taking him to the Public Institutions, and giving all necessary explanation — The General gratefully acknowledged the kindness. And upon returning one of his visits when he happened not to be at home, but nevertheless he went in to the Primitive Cottage-looking habitation of this good man — But was received with great courtesy by his wife, who was a native of Philadelphia, a Plain Friend, and a Preacher in the Society, but withal a real Gentlewoman: The General seated himself in the little back parlour, and after some conversation told Joyce Benezet, that since he had became acquainted with her Husband he had fully experienced the reality of the Apostle Peters declaration: "That in Truth God was no Respecter of Persons, But that in every Nation those who feared Him, and worked Righteousness, would be accepted of Him."

It is now Seventh day, But really what day of the Month I do not know, But I will look and acquaint myself. I am wretchedly fatigued, having exerted myself to the utmost to get this House cleaned and put in pretty good trim to day — I have likened myself to those who live a life of care and Penury in order to put up something of a Store for Old-Age — Old Age may never be ours, but if it does come, Care and Disappointment, and difference from what we expect attends it, and "the cruel something unpossessed" is still flitting before our eyes. What then shall be done? —— I answer Get good Principles, look beyond this narrow scene of things, and let the Soul Plume her wings for her flight to an higher and better World.

Another day in August 1837, two years before her death. Logan described her continuing struggle to "put up something of a store for Old Age." Her answer: "Get good Principles, look beyond this narrow scene of things, and let the Soul Plume her wings for her flight to an higher and better world."

study — one which acknowledged the sources of their strength and identified those forces that gave meaning to their lives. Part 1 addresses those aspects of women's identity gained through connection to others (i.e., husbands, children, grandchildren, sisters, and friends). For women growing old, such connections proved critical — in varying degrees — to achieving a sense of harmony and contentedness in their final years.

Part 2 examines the counterpoint to this necessary web of connection: the singular, personal nature of old age and death. As they looked inward, women growing old relied on traditional metaphors of aging to give direction to their final years. The contradictions between popular images of feminine aging and the reality of women's daily lives presented new, often troubling issues, sometimes threatening individual identity. Ultimately, questions of self and identity would be posed within a framework of spirituality as women prepared to integrate their connected and individual selves at life's end.

If the structure of this study was imposed by the values of the women themselves, it was reinforced by much recent literature on the psychological concepts of self and identity, particularly as applied to questions of morality and values. The work of Carol Gilligan, Carol Ochs, and Robert Jay Lifton — all working from different directions toward different goals — influenced my own approach to this study. So too did the work of Caroll Smith-Rosenberg. Such influence is not taken lightly. By emphasizing the values of connection and commitment, the critical roles of friendship and kin, and the singular strength of women's spirituality, I have aligned myself with what is often termed a "women's culture approach." Within feminist scholarship this imposes a clear and obvious risk. To affirm the strengths and values of nineteenth-century American women may appear at times to deny the existence of patriarchal culture or to minimize its effects on generations of women. It also provides fodder for those who would argue that women's nature and status are "innate" or "natural." I intend to do neither in this study. I believe, however, that the women examined here offer evidence that their world and their "culture" — albeit circumscribed — provided a viable framework for addressing the fundamental issues associated with old age and death. The universal quality of those issues reminds us that we must pursue each and every path to the past if we are to be prepared for our own future.[13]

Old people in the new republic often relied on the Bible for both inspiration and metaphor. They believed, as did the author of the Ninetieth Psalm, that life was a "tale that is told." For them, life's story was complete; the end held no surprises. While we now marvel at that sense of completion, we have yet to understand its full implications. What follows is an attempt both to hear and to interpret the voices of aging women not heard for two hundred years. Theirs is a tale well worth the telling.

NOTES

1. David Hackett Fischer, W. Andrew Achenbaum, and Carole Haber have each published significant monographs on the early history of aging in America. See Fischer, *Growing Old in America,* 2d ed. (New York: Oxford University Press, 1978); Achenbaum, *Old Age in the New Land* (Baltimore: Johns Hopkins University Press, 1978); and Haber, *Beyond Sixty-Five: The Dilemma of Old Age in America's Past* (New York: Cambridge University Press, 1983). Some scholars have acknowledged that historical treatments of old age ignore the experience of women growing old. See Peter N. Stearns, "Old Women: Some Historical Observations," *Journal of Family History* 5 (Spring 1980):44-57; and Janet Roebuck, "Grandma as Revolutionary: Elderly Women and Some Modern Patterns of Social Change," *International Journal of Aging and Human Development* 14:4 (1983):249-66. See also John Faragher, "Old Women and Old Men in Seventeenth-Century Wethersfield, Connecticut," *Women's Studies* 4:1 (1976):11-33.

2. According to Robert V. Wells, life expectancy at birth for eighteenth-century white women was probably about forty years. About thirty percent of these women could expect to reach age sixty-five; most of them would spend the majority of their lives engaged in childrearing. See Wells, "Women's Lives Transformed: Demographic and Family Patterns in America, 1600-1970," in *Women of America: A History,* ed. Carol Ruth Berkin and Mary Beth Norton (Boston: Houghton Mifflin, 1979), pp. 22, 27; and Wells, "Demographic Change and the Life Cycle of American Families," in *The Family in History: Interdisciplinary Essays,* ed. Theodore K. Rabb and Robert I. Rotberg (New York: Harper and Row, 1971), p. 91. John Faragher found that over half of seventeenth-century Wethersfield women lived beyond their seventieth birthdays. See Faragher, "Old Women."

The over-sixty population in late eighteenth-century America has been estimated at less than two percent; at least four percent of the white population was sixty or above by 1830. More than a third of Americans born in that year would survive to age sixty. Although the aged population was only one-third of what it is today, old persons were not rare and men and women could reasonably hope to live to old age. See Fischer, *Growing Old,* pp. 27, 272, 278. John Demos argues that elderly people comprised four to seven percent of the population in established colonial New England communities. See Demos, "Old Age in Early New England," in *Turning Points: Historical and Sociological Essays on the Family,* ed. John Demos and Sarane Spence Boocock (Chicago: University of Chicago Press, 1978), pp. 254-55. Profound changes in the proportion of the aged population occurred only during the twentieth century.

3. Most historians agree that no "golden age" for old people existed in preindustrial societies. See, for example, Fischer, *Growing Old,* pp. 234-69; Achenbaum, *Old Age,* pp. 4-5; and Peter Laslett, "Societal Development and Aging," in *Handbook of Aging and the Social Sciences,* ed. Robert H. Binstock and Ethel Shanas (New York: Van Nostrand Reinhold, 1976), pp. 86-116.

4. See Thomas R. Cole, "Past Meridian: Aging and the Northern Middle Class, 1830-1930" (Ph.D. dissertation, University of Rochester, 1980), pp. 93, 156, 201.

5. Among the earliest institutions devoted specifically to the care and shelter of old women, Philadelphia's Indigent Widows' and Single Women's Society was founded in 1817 to meet the needs of "poor but respectable old ladies." See Carole Haber, "The Old Folks at Home: The Development of Institutionalized Care for the Aged in Nineteenth Century Philadelphia," *Pennsylvania Magazine of History and Biography* 101 (April 1977):240-57.

6. Aileen S. Kraditor first articulated the phrase "cult of domesticity" in her introduction to *Up from the Pedestal: Selected Writings in the History of American Feminism* (Chicago: Quadrangle Books, 1968).

7. Many scholars have contributed substantially to our understanding of this critical period of women's history. See especially Mary Beth Norton, *Liberty's Daughters: The Revolutionary Experience of American Women, 1750-1800* (Boston: Little, Brown, 1980); Linda K. Kerber, *Women of the Republic: Intellect and Ideology in Revolutionary America* (Chapel Hill: University of North Carolina Press, 1980); and Nancy F. Cott, *The Bonds of Womanhood: 'Woman's Sphere' in New England, 1780-1835* (New Haven: Yale University Press, 1977).

In Audrey Borenstein's extensive examination of women and aging in twentieth-century America, she addresses the necessity for feminists to adopt a multigenerational focus. "Until now," she argues, "the great social movement of feminism has been, above all else, a declaration of our common sisterhood. Henceforth, it may be a declaration of our common daughterhood as well." See Borenstein, *Chimes of Change and Hours: Views of Older Women in Twentieth Century America* (Cranbury, N.J.: Associated University Presses, 1983), p. 100.

8. Fischer, *Growing Old*, pp. 77-112, 153.

9. Although not all women studied here were themselves old, women who thought themselves "growing old" proved the most valuable sources for the purpose of this investigation. Yet defining who was "old" among these women is considerably complicated by the looseness with which old age was defined. Most women thought themselves old by their sixties, but some described themselves as "old" even in their early fifties. Grandmothers have been defined here as "aging women" even though they may still have been in their forties. Borrowing from their own common assumptions, this study considers "old" women to be in their sixties or older.

10. See Margo Culley's useful introduction to the functions and forms of women's diaries in Culley, *A Day at a Time: The Diary Literature of American Women from 1764 to the Present* (New York: Feminist Press at CUNY, 1985), pp. 3-26.

11. For discussions on the uses of women's personal writings in eighteenth- and nineteenth-century America, see Nancy Cott, *The Bonds of Womanhood*, pp. 9, 16-17; and Marilyn Ferris Motz, *True Sisterhood: Michigan Women and Their Kin, 1820-1920* (Albany: State University of New York Press, 1983), pp. 53-81.

12. In the past decade, the distinctive qualities of women's autobiographical writing have received increasing scholarly attention. See, for instance, Estelle C.

Jelinek, ed., *Women's Autobiography: Essays in Criticism* (Bloomington: Indiana University Press, 1980). See also the essay discussing the relationship between autobiography and old age by Thomas Cole and T. Premo, "Aging in American Autobiography: Meaning, Selfhood, and History," *Human Values and Aging Newsletter* 8 (May/June 1986):3-5.

13. Carol Gilligan, *In a Different Voice: Psychological Theory and Women's Development* (Cambridge: Harvard University Press, 1984); Carol Ochs, *Women and Spirituality* (Totowa, N.J.: Rowman and Allanheld, 1983); Robert Jay Lifton, *The Broken Connection: On Death and the Continuity of Life* (New York: Simon and Schuster, 1979); Carroll Smith-Rosenberg, *Disorderly Conduct: Visions of Gender in Victorian America* (New York: Alfred A. Knopf, 1985). On the inherent problems of using the terms "women's sphere" and "women's culture," see Ellen DuBois, Mari Jo Buhle, Temma Kaplan, Gerda Lerner, and Carroll Smith-Rosenberg, "Politics and Culture in Women's History: A Symposium," *Feminist Studies* 6 (Spring 1980):26-64; and Linda K. Kerber, "Separate Spheres, Female Worlds, Woman's Place: The Rhetoric of Women's History," *Journal of American History* 75 (June 1988):9-39.

Recent work in related fields of autobiography, reminiscence, and life review argues convincingly that such life records should be viewed, in James Olney's phrase, as "metaphors of self." Much fine popular literature written by older women in recent years reiterates the need to focus on women's lives as they themselves would interpret them. See James Olney, *Metaphors of Self: The Meaning of Autobiography* (Princeton: Princeton University Press, 1972); Marc Kaminsky, ed., *The Uses of Reminiscence: New Ways of Working with Older Adults* (New York: Haworth Press, 1984); Florida Scott-Maxwell, *The Measure of My Days* (New York: Knopf, 1968); and May Sarton, *Journal of a Solitude* (New York: W. W. Norton, 1973).

PART ONE

Identity through Connection

The quality of women's lives can be interpreted on many levels, none of which can stand alone in any definition of status or power. Today, for instance, we celebrate the solid achievements made by women in the labor force. Indeed, over half of American women are now working outside the home. Yet working women remain reluctant to identify themselves solely within the narrow confines of their professional relationships. Their public/working personae continue to be tightly intertwined with long-established patterns of family obligation, personal ties, and an ethic of care and responsibility (both in the workplace and at home) deviating from traditional, typically "male" models. Similarly, old women today cannot be identified merely through longevity statistics or Social Security rolls. Family association, commitments to people and places, and women's unique historical experience all contribute to the distinctive identity of aging women today.[1]

Certainly no less can be said for women in past centuries. Despite the negligible public presence of women in the new republic, women forged a strong sense of identity through a complex weaving of kinship ties, moral fortitude, and an increasing devotion to gender. As women aged, this sense of identity held firm, fortified by the ethic of care and the emphasis on connection that remained valid, if modified, as age advanced. To interpret the perspective of women growing old in the new republic, we first examine these webs of connection which bound women to their families, to others, and most important, to a continuing sense of self.

1. In her interpretation of feminine ethics and morality, Carol Gilligan emphasizes an ethic of care and mutual obligation as a critical element in women's moral development. Although Gilligan's work focuses on findings in developmental psychology, her conclusions illuminate and reflect women's historical experience as well. While her work has spurred considerable debate within academic and feminist circles, her findings, as they relate to women's past lives, suggest strongly the enduring qualities of feminine values and morality. See Gilligan, *In a Different Voice: Psychological Theory and Women's Development* (Cambridge: Harvard University Press, 1982).

The Old Age of Wives, Widows, and Spinsters

This day Is forty years sinc I left my father's house and . . . I think in
every respect the state of my affairs is more than forty times worse than
when I came here first, except that I am nearer the desierered haven."
                    — Molly Cooper, Oyster Bay, New York, 13 July 1769,
                            on her fortieth anniversary

I can safely say, that tho' I loved him with the utmost tenderness in
our youth, yet the bond seems strengthened and consolidated with advancing years, and added to its tenderness esteem, respect, and the purest
friendship.
                    — Deborah Norris Logan, Philadelphia, 6 October 1822,
                            reviewing her forty years of married life

When fifty-five-year-old Molly Cooper scribbled these pathetic lines com-
memorating forty years of marital misery, she saw no need to hide the hard
work and pain that characterized her daily life in colonial Long Island.
Living with Joseph Cooper for four decades yielded six children and numerous grandchildren but little in the way of warmth or enduring "friendship" with her mate. Her dreams were not of "mutuality" or "companionship" in marriage. She just wanted "won minutts rest." More than fifty
years later, however, Deborah Logan looked back on what she regarded as
forty rewarding years of marital happiness.[1] Her occasional frustrations with
George Logan were more than balanced by shared interests and mutual high
regard. In her old age, she would continue to extol the virtues of George

Logan and the institution of marriage itself. After George Logan died, she did not long for "rest," as had Molly Cooper, but for her husband's friendship that had grown for nearly a half-century.[2]

Most women's married lives were neither as miserable as Molly Cooper's nor as idealized as Deborah Logan's. After the Revolution, however, expanding hopes and opportunities changed the nature of women's expectations in and out of marriage. While many women would continue to work as long and hard as Molly Cooper, their dreams broadened to encompass the aspirations of a new society. In time it would become clear to most women, however, that any dreams of emancipated womanhood—or of unchanging marital bliss—would need to be tempered with a good dose of reality.[3]

The rising aspirations that inspired Deborah Logan's generation to help create and sustain a new government and a new society were not mirrored in the political and legal reality of women's lives after the Revolution. Indeed, the common-law apparatus shaping the life of Molly Cooper and other colonial women remained virtually in place throughout the early federal period. The restrictions imposed by their *feme covert* status denied married women a legal identity of their own. Even women without husbands who "enjoyed" *feme sole* status quickly discovered that their lives remained circumscribed by cultural and economic barriers that functioned nearly as effectively as coverture itself.[4]

Nevertheless, young women began to marry with increasing hopes of finding in their husband a companion and a friend. While marriage still signified the end of carefree youth, it promised new possibilities for mutual sharing and growth. And, of course, it offered the additional promise of children and a home of one's own. For most women, marriage still provided the best, perhaps the only, chance of improving their social and economic positions and building new family units which would, in time, define new roles and identify new options.[5]

As the dreams and visions of young revolutionary brides like Deborah Logan matured over the years, goals were revised, expectations reappraised. Some women were fulfilled in their relationships with their husbands; others chafed under a system that afforded them little hope for independence or autonomy. As widows, Logan and other women engaged in creative and independent action, often for the first time. Such action was necessarily circumscribed, however, by the confines of woman's sphere. Ironically, it was within the context of this sphere—a sphere structured and dedicated to the promotion of the conjugal union—that women would find many of the elements favorable to successful aging. As they grew older, women discovered that many of the basic attributes of that sphere—domestic employment, active childrearing, strong friendships between women, and an abundance of moral rectitude—were conducive to a satisfying and productive old age. For those women able to fit themselves comfortably within the confines of this sphere, old age could be viewed with some reassurance. For those who failed to "fit," however, old age might signify fear, alienation, and an unwelcome end to youthful dreams.[6]

Marriage: A Compromise in Dependency

For some women, growing old with one's mate was its own reward. Women like Deborah Logan believed that time actually enhanced the quality of marital relationships, giving them a depth and resonance unequaled in earlier years. The great friendship between Abigail and John Adams continued to grow in old age, despite problems associated with poor health and constant concern for their children. Long separated during the Revolution, they especially cherished their later years together. Mercy Warren, nearing fifty, equated her future happiness with the continued company "of that man of whose friendship I have had more than 20 years Experience & without whom *life* has no charm for me." The Philadelphia Quaker Rebecca Shoemaker, who already saw herself "in the decline of life" at fifty-four, hoped only to spend the remainder of her life with her then-exiled husband.[7]

These and other women who enjoyed the company and affection of their mates nonetheless acknowledged that their relationships in law, and sometimes in practice, were based on dependency. For women totally at ease within the confines of their sphere, such dependency remained acceptable, even agreeable. "I have no independent fortune," wrote Elizabeth Drinker in 1796, "nor do I wish for one, unless it was in case of necessity, which I trust is not like to be the case." Because Henry Drinker ranked among Philadelphia's leading merchants, his wife saw no need to secure her own separate estate. (Apparently short on memory, Elizabeth Drinker failed to recall the "necessity" known to other prominent Quaker women less than twenty years earlier when denied the support of Loyalist husbands.)[8]

Women such as Elizabeth Drinker accepted financial dependency as a permanent element within a fixed constellation of gender-based duties and responsibilities. As such women aged, they were likely to appreciate increasingly the comfort and familiarity of the domestic world they knew so well. Because a woman's domestic responsibilities remained essentially unchanged over the years, her purview stayed largely intact as she grew older. Already beyond middle age when the last of her children left home, she could reasonably anticipate the continuation of her maternal role with the arrival of a third generation. Indeed, continuity signified well-being to many wives growing old.[9]

Although many of a woman's daily domestic chores remained the same as the years passed, circumstances often forced new emphasis on age-old roles. As nurses and caretakers, women in old age frequently faced the added responsibility of caring for elderly mates at a time when their own health and physical capacities were declining. The Quaker preacher Elizabeth Collins nursed her invalid husband into old age, finding in this role a rationale for her own advanced age. Yet the continuous nursing of an old and disabled husband could be both demanding and lonely. Elizabeth Farmer lived alone with her feeble husband in the Pennsylvania countryside. Nearly seventy and often lonesome, Farmer fervently attempted to maintain some contact with the outside world through letters to her nephew. "Pray let me hear from you frequently," she wrote in 1789, "for I have nobody but you." Her husband, she wrote, "feels himself older and can[']t help freting at things going." She seldom went out and clearly felt the strains of her situation. Growing old without children or friends and increasingly infirm herself, she yearned for a taste of life beyond her own home. Although her marriage provided a focus for her care and attention on a daily basis, it did not in itself create an entirely satisfying and fulfilling world.[10]

Indeed, long-term marriages presented ample opportunity for increasing demands on time and energy, particularly when the infirmities of age implied reduced economic power. For the vast majority who were without a substantial income, survival would depend on the growing interdependence of husband and wife. When men were too old to work, their wives did what they could to make ends meet. Ann Livingston's 1784 description of a poor old woman and her disabled husband provides a case in point. "The wife . . . gathers wild herbs & carries them on her head to the market which is five miles from where she lives in order to get a living—I asked her what she lived on, she said a little bread when she could get it." While the lives of most poor old women in similar circumstances went undocumented, it is apparent that many such women bore a heavy burden in providing daily sustenance.[11]

The infirmities accompanying advanced age were well known to many older women who could not expect, except in rare cases, any relief through pension plans or old-age insurance. Women with disabled husbands usually continued to nurse and assist them, but economic necessity sometimes forced separations on an older pair. Because her husband was nearly blind, Elizabeth Prescott found herself dependent on the care of her daughter while her husband was "comfortably provided for by friends at private lodgings." Seeming to take these circumstances in stride, Prescott acknowledged that her husband was unable to contribute to her support. In her adversity, this New England matron revealed the flexibility which older women needed to cope with the problems associated with the failing health of a spouse. Such dependence on family and friends during difficult periods was familiar to many older women whose income had always derived from the continued activity and good health of a husband.[12]

Older married women who were relatively free from financial worries and the burdens of caring for an aging husband nonetheless faced numerous small but nettlesome problems with their elderly mates. Poor communication between couples could persist despite years of familiarity. Such was often the case in the comfortable (if occasionally strained) Quaker household of Elizabeth and Henry Drinker.

Despite forty years of marriage, Elizabeth Drinker found living with Henry could be frustrating and annoying. Her Quaker reticence notwithstanding, Elizabeth revealed in her diary numerous points of friction between them, points which, in fact, seem to have increased over time. Much of this friction centered around his distancing himself from his family. Although she never expected her husband to retire completely from his business and civic responsibilities in his old age, Elizabeth Drinker apparently had hoped her life with Henry would settle down after their five children had reached adulthood. Henry, however, continued to work as a successful merchant, keeping so busy, in fact, that Elizabeth referred to him in 1798 as "one of the greatest Slaves in Philadel'a." Although he often worked at home, he seemed inaccessible to Elizabeth. "[He is] always at home, and never at home," the sixty-four-year-old Elizabeth remarked later that same year.[13]

Even when Henry Drinker was nearby, he often failed to communicate effectively with his wife. In 1796, for instance, he sold their country property without considering that Elizabeth and their son William relied on the clean air of Clearfield to restore their health. Frequently, Henry's stubbornness or lack of attention forced Elizabeth to act herself. When her old and ailing friend Susanna Swett asked to move into the Drinker home, Elizabeth found her husband unwilling to discuss the situation. Concerned for her friend's well-being, Elizabeth consented on her own. "I have many and many times experienced the great inconvenience of not understanding or fully knowing his mind," she wrote with obvious frustration after thirty-eight years of marriage to Henry Drinker.[14]

Despite these tantalizing suggestions of discord in the Drinker household, Elizabeth Drinker's extensive diary provides few glimpses into her marital relationship. Indeed, married women's journals and correspondence during this period often give little indication that they were, in fact, married. In long letters to friends, women correspondents say little or nothing about their spouses. On the other hand, expressions of concern for children and grandchildren fill both journals and collections of letters. To some extent, this may simply reflect the difficulty of maintaining a candid diary (or keeping copies of letters) intended to be passed down to future generations.

For many women, however, it appears that maternal responsibilities gained priority as the years passed while marital relationships were put on a back burner. As the Virginia matron Fanny Bernard wrote to her son, "[Your father] has so little to say that interests me," admitting that the feelings of her children were more "congenial." Reasons for this shift of interest may be as simple and obvious as the changing nature of human relationships over time, dulled naturally by years of sameness and continuity. Yet the tone and content of women's writings strongly suggests the increasing influence of the maternal role, even after children grew into adulthood. For many women such as Elizabeth Drinker, relationships with husbands occupied less of their time and attention than the ties they maintained with their adult children. Accustomed to their own separate sphere, older women sought to retain the "congenial" bonds that had provided comfort and support for so many years.[15]

Being married was not necessarily accorded the same value as the institution of marriage. This is strikingly revealed in the reluctance of widowed women to find another mate. Despite their loneliness and economic hardship, widows seldom considered remarriage a viable option. "A second marriage never once entered my head," wrote Eliza Lucas Pinckney, echoing the thoughts of many widows. Although their reluctance to remarry might also suggest a lack of opportunity, widows often expressed a certain intolerance toward other women who married more than once. When her neighbor chose to remarry after *only* two and one half years of widowhood, one Quaker woman responded with incredulity: "It seems to me astonishing," she wrote. "I would as soon commit suicide." Although few women responded as radically, such sentiments indicate the degree of hostility remarriage could engender.[16]

Older women who chose to remarry did so for a variety of reasons. Elizabeth Murray Smith Inman, who was widowed twice, apparently believed that husbands provided not only companionship but also the opportunity to share the burdens of business management, burdens which this successful Boston merchant often felt keenly. When she considered marriage to Ralph Inman in 1771, her friend Christian Barnes counseled her. "Retirement and ease is what you at present stand in need of," she wrote. "You must fix upon some worthy Person who will releve you from the fetigues and cares of life or at least share them with you." Elizabeth, then forty-five years old, heeded her friend's advice but found, as Christian Barnes had warned, that "the remedy may be as bad as the disease."[17]

While most widows apparently did not actively search for new husbands, some found pleasure in relating stories of "snares" they had set for unwitting old men. Elizabeth Putnam, writing to her brother in 1810, described her fruitless efforts to entrap the unsuspecting Samme Allen. "You will see by this that all my matrimonial strings are snapt short off," she wrote. "It is a difficult matter to new string an old, cracked, worn out instrument," she added. The following year, her plans to catch the reluctant Mr. Coolidge were foiled. "I have seen him long enough to admire him," she wrote, "but despair of being able to captivate him." Although she apparently enjoyed ruffling her straitlaced brother with tales of her exploits, Elizabeth Putnam was motivated by a desire to establish her sons securely in the world. With that accomplished, she prophesied, "my face should not be long, though I should not get married." Financial security rather than romantic attachment appears to have underscored her quests in the marriage market.[18]

Elizabeth Putnam's treatment of remarriage as a subject for humor may indicate the peculiar sensitivity aroused by such an equivocal issue. Because a woman's identity in both law and custom was so clearly associated with her husband's, remarriage provided the best opportunity to recast another comfortable, if symbiotic, relationship. Often burdened with financial liabilities, many widows might have been tempted to remarry with the hope of eliminating both poverty and loneliness. Some might have wished to marry again but could find no likely candidate. No doubt an abundance of widows in some densely populated areas diminished opportunities for remarriage. A scarcity of men, however, does not explain the overwhelming reluctance of most widows to wed again. Instead, a deeply ingrained preference to maintain one's established identity prompted most older women to reject second marriages. Long-term marriages, although not always rich and fulfilling, provided a family orientation that was the nexus of women's lives. This focus would continue into widowhood as adult children and other relatives moved in to fill the void. Women already accustomed to depending on their children and other women for emotional support and security seemed unwilling to cast aside past allegiances for the uncertain prospects of a new spouse.[19]

Successful marriages, like successful aging, seemed to depend on a woman's willingness to conform to the confines of her sphere and, indeed, to enjoy the rewards of family, friendship, and moral sustenance which that sphere implied. Some women, however, attempted to expand the limits of their world; others simply felt alienated within a rigid and inflexible domestic culture. To the extent that women departed from the dictates of sphere, they risked censure and unhappiness, both of which might appear increasingly inappropriate and undesirable as old age advanced.

Censure might accrue from the most innocent of undertakings. In a world where husbands handled business affairs, for example, a wife's active interest in economic and business activities could yield unpleasant results. Anna Thornton of Washington, D.C., for example, experienced the chilling "taunts" of society because she apparently ventured too far in advising her husband on business matters. Angered because William Thornton was considered "henpecked," she countered that "if a husband was applauded & respected as much for being influenced by his wife . . . as he is jeered at for it, there would be less unhappiness & misfortune in married life." No doubt Anna Thornton realized that her husband's penchant for speculation would eventually be his undoing, as indeed it was. Yet her own attempts to set things right—at the risk of stepping beyond her bounds—created further frustration and discord within her own household and contributed to many unsettling memories which would plague Anna Thornton years after her husband's death.[20]

Some women pushed beyond the confines of their domestic sphere in an attempt to achieve financial security and independence. For such women, marriage could prove problematic indeed. Already twice widowed, Elizabeth Murray Smith understood the importance of prenuptial agreements by the time she married Ralph Inman in 1771. A successful Boston businesswoman, she learned to her dismay that her own energies and courage far surpassed those of Ralph Inman. Nevertheless, she professed to blame herself for any disharmony in her marriage. "If I am not a happy wife," she wrote, "it is my own fault—no one has more of their own will and few so much. . . ." Because she had amassed considerable property of her own which she had protected in her marriage agreement, Elizabeth Inman could approach old age with an uncommon amount of power and control. In her will, as provided for by her prenuptial agreement, she distributed her estate as she saw fit, leaving her husband a sizeable annuity which was, nonetheless, inferior to those she provided for others. Apparently fearing just such a settlement, Ralph Inman pressed his wife for a better financial provision while she lay on her deathbed in 1785. Ironically, during the last days of her life, her secure and independent financial position may have subjected her to considerable stress and unhappiness. Nearly sixty when she died, Elizabeth Inman illustrates all too well the ambiguous nature of late-life marriages when a woman had power of her own.[21]

Elizabeth Inman died before the tenets of domesticity became firmly entrenched in the early nineteenth century. By that time, women who lived outside the model of true womanhood risked a greater chance of alienation, one which could increase with age. Some women quite obviously had little opportunity to indulge in the promises of domestic ascendency, needing instead to concern themselves more properly with day-to-day survival. Yet affluent women could also feel themselves beyond the pale of woman's sphere. For these women, old age could only exacerbate their sense of failure and loss. In the late-life memoirs of Louisa Catherine Adams, we can trace the sorrowful reflections of a talented, spirited woman obsessed with her perceived failings as a wife and mother in the new republic. Ultimately, she came to believe that it was her inability to become the American domestic ideal — as epitomized by her mother-in-law Abigail Adams — that secured her fate.[22]

Born in Britain to an English mother and an expatriate American father, Louisa Catherine Johnson had been raised in a privileged environment and was prepared for a life of "ornamental" duty but little else. Her father, Joshua Johnson, a successful merchant, doted on his daughters and became, in turn, the single object of their love and admiration. In her old age, she revelled in her tranquil, highly romanticized recollections of childhood, which contrasted sharply with her memories of events occurring after her marriage to John Quincy Adams.[23]

Her marriage to John Quincy Adams got off to an ominous start. Shortly after the ceremony, publicity surrounding her father's financial collapse reached both sides of the Atlantic. This, and her father's continuing financial embarrassments, created a burden of guilt and suspicion she never lost. Indeed, over time her uneasiness appears to have grown, as she increasingly doubted the forgiveness and goodwill of the Adams family and most especially her husband. Although John Quincy Adams was a difficult and ill-tempered man in the best of times, Louisa Catherine Adams remained convinced that he never forgot this early embarrassment and never accepted her as a "suitable" wife. "Forty-three years since I became a Wife," she wrote, "and yet the rankling sore is not healed. . . ." She continued to believe (and indeed became fixated on the notion) that he would have been better off if he had broken his engagement to her. Yet, as one examines her memoirs, it becomes clear that her notion of "suitability" extended beyond her marriage and carried far more damaging weight in later life than any lingering doubts about those awkward and discomfiting early years.[24]

On almost every count, from Louisa Catherine Adams's late-life perspective, her marriage was ill-starred and destined for disappointment, if not failure. "To a man in a public career in this Country," she recorded, "a woman should be like Caesar's wife." But Louisa Catherine Adams was no American Calpurnia. Although she understood well the American concept of woman's sphere, she never felt herself a part of that sorority. Rather than enjoying a sense of camaraderie and community in her adopted home of Quincy, Massachusetts, she was convinced of the "contempt" of her neighbors for her perceived lack of "responsibility." Her attempts to keep busy within the household met with failure. "[I tried] to work, as they call it," she bitterly recalled, but she felt herself untrained and unfit for the task. Separated from her children years earlier while she accompanied John Quincy Adams on diplomatic missions abroad, she remained guilt-ridden, never seeming to come to terms with the consequences of those earlier choices.[25]

Other aspects of woman's sphere eluded her as well. She apparently gained little encouragement or strength from her contacts with other American women. The bonds between women that offered support and nourishment for those firmly settled within their sphere failed to extend to a woman who felt herself an outsider and seemed to view most women as hostile or uncaring. Life among the Quincy gentry was particularly painful in this regard. "Forty-three years in America is equal to a century any where else," she recalled, "and do what I could there was a conviction on the part of others that I could not *suit*, however well inclined. This I necessarily *felt.*" Never completely at ease with Abigail Adams, she typically felt much closer to the male members of the Adams clan.[26]

Ironically, Louisa Catherine Adams qualified in many ways to serve as the perfect mate to John Quincy Adams. Bright, well-read, and articulate, she was more than capable of keeping up with his renowned intellect. Accustomed to high society and familiar with the machinations of court life, she played well her role as diplomatic wife in many European courts. Never as straitlaced as her husband, she could enjoy dancing at court balls until three in the morning and often did so. Yet once in America, she found little encouragement for those qualities, either at home or in the restrained society of early nineteenth-century Massachusetts. By 1840, when she compiled her memoirs, she saw failure and disappointment at every turn, consistently (although indirectly) pointing to her marriage as the pivotal turning point from which all later misfortunes emanated. Yet it was, she seemed to suggest, a peculiarly American dilemma. The demands of American domesticity, as she interpreted them, were too stringent to afford her any sense of accomplishment or even contentment in old age.

The unhappy reflections in Louisa Catherine Adams's late-life memoirs reveal the unsettled and unsettling perspective of one woman unable to make peace in her own world. Yet in her failures she tells much about the nature of long-term marriage in the new republic. Unlike her native-born American sisters who had come to demand much of the institution of marriage but expect less of their mates over time, Louisa Catherine Adams came of age with a highly romanticized notion of connubial bliss, one which set her up for years of disappointment. While her American counterparts concentrated their efforts on developing their role within the various components of the woman's sphere, she continued her one-to-one struggle with her husband and failed to build the female network which would have helped sustain her over the years. As American women, long trained for their domestic roles, enjoyed the fruit of that training in old age, Louisa Catherine Adams remained an outcast, an "ornament" grown old.

Even women born in American society, of course, could come to regard long-term marriages with a certain degree of ambivalence. If nineteenth-century marriages were "relationships of power," as Carl Degler has described them, then the potential for conflict might have increased as the years passed. While a woman's domain remained essentially unchanged as she aged, her husband might find the domestic arena increasingly unfamiliar and uncomfortable as ill health and reduced responsibilities forced him to spend more time at home. Although men were seldom pushed to retire from their public duties, they nonetheless understood that a curtailment of activities was considered appropriate and necessary in old age. Their continued presence in the home, however, interfered with their wives' patterns of activity and intercourse. Although not all women would have agreed with Molly Cooper's dour assessment of her forty years of married life, neither could many confirm from their own experience Deborah Logan's conviction that time had only "strengthened and consolidated" her relationship with her husband. Yet because marriage was only *one* (albeit the primary) aspect of a woman's sphere of activity and influence, aging women could look beyond the conjugal bed to locate a personal sense of fulfillment and growth in old age.

The Discontinuity of Widowhood

The death of a spouse abruptly disrupted and substantially altered the course of a woman's life. Without husbands to serve as the critical link to the public world, newly widowed women faced challenging, sometimes frightening prospects of independence and self-reliance. With no mate to help complete her sense of identity, an older widow was forced to confront the shape of her new self and to determine her future. Widowhood not only marked a change in legal status for women but also provided women with the opportunity to reevaluate their dependence on others and on themselves.[27]

Because few widows remarried, women could reasonably anticipate ending their lives as widows. Yet few were prepared for life alone. Restricted by financial pressures and lack of management skills, some women entered widowhood on the defensive, seeking to survive through continued dependency on others. Others settled into lonely and retrospective lives, dwelling on the past and avoiding the future. Still others remained active and productive throughout widowhood, devoting themselves to family and friends and to the maintenance of their own homes or businesses. Regardless of circumstances, widows quickly learned both the limits and the rewards of the sphere that continued to define their lives.[28]

"[It is] the most Forlorn and Dismal of all states," wrote Abigail Adams to her friend Mercy Warren in 1778. Her assessment of widowhood was shared by most women of the time. Widowhood elicited anger, loneliness, and depression; it was often considered the point at which life began to decline. Because of their subordinate legal and social position and their obligatory reliance on men, women in post-revolutionary America faced widowhood with considerable fear and trepidation.[29]

Confronting the loneliness of widowhood could be a long ordeal and often grew worse as other friends and relatives died, leaving widows further isolated and alone. Rebecca Shoemaker, despite daily visits from family and friends, complained in 1805 that she spent "very many hours alone." Writing to her daughter, Anna Holyoke Cutts mourned not only the death of her last old friend but also her own loneliness. "I feel desolate," she admitted. Maria Montgomery, writing to her cousin in 1833, reviewed her widowhood. "Now all is gone," she wrote. "Time is passing away, and every earthly form I loved are quickly [s]liding too." Loneliness was a fact of widowhood seldom denied.[30]

Since most widows remained unmarried, they soon faced the full implications of their newly regained *feme sole* status. Some, like Deborah Norris Logan, recoiled from the prospect of an independent existence and longed for the emotional dependency to which she was accustomed. Viewing herself as a "clinging vine," Logan felt she had lost "the support of the venerable tree to which it [the vine] clung and which lay supine and bruised around the Root from which it was torn." Despite the consolation she gained from such a metaphor, Deborah Logan did not consistently maintain this passive, dependent role. Over the years she came to believe that women must possess their own property and urged her niece and other women to secure their possessions before marriage. Such a change, however, reflected the effects of widowhood rather than marriage. During her marriage, Logan considered dependency and marital bliss as one and the same.[31]

Although the initial shock and loneliness of widowhood might entail months or years of emotional recovery, many women were not granted the luxury of time to cope with new and pressing financial problems. These problems were only exacerbated by the legal position in which newly widowed women found themselves. The economic dependency imposed on women newly freed from their *feme covert* status offered an ironic twist to the promise of widowhood. Even after the settlement of a husband's estate, a newly widowed woman often became encumbered by financial pressures. Although her "widow's third" entitled her to a lifetime interest in one third of the estate left by her husband, a woman was often placed in an inflexible and dependent position, since property was generally intended to serve as part of a son's eventual inheritance upon the death of his mother. Even in cases where additional property settlements had been provided, women frequently were surprised at the size of the debts left by their husbands. Widows with farms often were short of labor and unaccustomed to handling all aspects of property management. Forced once again to rely on others, such older women inherited a burdensome, unenviable position.[32]

Feme sole status could indeed become a double-edged sword for newly widowed women. While it enabled women to make contracts and conduct their own business, it also exposed them to the difficulties of financial responsibility. Often unacquainted with the true state of their household finances, widows needed to learn quickly how to keep books and manage affairs. Anna Thornton's husband left debts of $25,000 or more when he died in 1828. Anna Thornton not only confronted creditors but also attempted to assuage family members who contested her share of her husband's property. In addition, she repeatedly petitioned the State Department for the salary her husband never received while he served as superintendent of patents. Anna Thornton was perhaps better acquainted with her husband's financial affairs and misfortunes than many women, but she nonetheless found a heavy burden in *feme sole* status.[33]

Widows often felt ill-equipped to handle their own financial matters. Admitting "very bad sucses in my affairs," Mary Hopkinson, widow of a well-known Philadelphia jurist, was forced to borrow money to pay her rent. A widow's ignorance of her financial position could surprise family and friends alike. Margaret Bayard Smith expressed concern that her widowed sister Maria Boyd seemed so "free from anxiety," considering her obvious financial plight. "I cannot help wondering at it," she confided to another sister in 1839. "May it not partly proceed from her being kept in ignorance of the real condition of the estate—I cannot understand it," she concluded. Yet Boyd's inability to understand her new financial status was not unusual during a period when women's focus was often narrow and sometimes shortsighted. Few widows, however, could maintain their ignorance for long.[34]

The financial plight of widows resulted from a combination of factors. Poor planning, unsettled accounts, and prior debts incurred by a late husband might give a widow little hope of ever rectifying her dubious legacy. Lack of confidence, coupled with a gnawing sense of impropriety, could weaken a woman's chance of boldly taking hold of her property and her finances. Women whose dower rights only entitled them to restricted use of property sometimes had strained relations with designated heirs. Or, relying too heavily on the continued assistance and managerial skills of her adult sons, a widowed mother could find herself "re-widowed" if her sons died or moved away. Many of these situations became familiar, in fact, to Deborah

Norris Logan, whose widowhood serves as sad testimony to the strains and pressures of her newly regained "freedom."

When George Logan died in 1821, Deborah Logan inherited an impressive estate. Nevertheless, although her late husband was a noted agricultural economist, he did not bequeath an estate free from debt or anxiety. A variety of property holdings in addition to her substantial farm in Germantown, Pennsylvania, enabled her to sell some lands to pay her most demanding creditors. Yet, when she recorded in her diary in 1827 that she was "very low just now, as to both spirits and cash," Logan merely repeated a sentiment she had felt and would continue to feel throughout her widowhood.[35]

As a widow the last eighteen years of her life, Deborah Logan fought to hold on to Stenton, the Logan family estate, and to keep it in the family after her death. Although ultimately successful in this goal, she had many doubts along the way. "I have been unwise in desiring to be left this property," she wrote in 1826, "and to continue to live here with all this establishment, of which I feel the expense and burthen—I have at present a discordant family [of household help]. Repairs wanting all around me, and I feel weak and inadequate to any exertion." Although her unmarried son Algernon continued to live with her and assisted in managing Stenton, she bore the ultimate burden of financial success or failure. Despite sustained frugality, her debts grew. By 1828 she had determined to borrow on her "little property" to maintain some sense of comfort at Stenton. By then, anxiety over meeting her financial obligations caused countless hours of worry and many sleepless nights. While she had hoped to set aside time to write, she noted in 1829 that the pressure of mounting debts prevented her from such nonessential pursuits. "When I am alone," she concluded, "how constantly I am sitting on Committees of Ways and Means!"[36]

By 1833, at the age of seventy-two, Deborah Logan acknowledged financial insecurity to be one of her greatest sources of anxiety. Wanting desperately to pay her debts before her own death, she had tried unsuccessfully to sell some property. "The weakness of declining years demands quiet and Repose," she wrote, expressing the hope that she could be free from the "harassing thoughts and perplexities which I now sensibly feel." Yet three years later she seemed even more troubled, blaming herself and her lack of management skills for her financial woes. Describing herself in 1836 as "oppressed and unhappy," Logan admitted, "I am sensible I have not managed my affairs to the best advantage, and indeed I seem incapable of it." With the death of her son and companion Algernon the previous year, she was forced in her seventy-fourth year to undertake management decisions on a scale previously unknown to her. "I have debts to pay and money is wanting—What to do, I know not." To a certain degree, her own failing health soon demanded that decisions be made by others. By the end of 1838, she finally admitted she could no longer manage Stenton. Acquiescing to another son's offer to move in and assume the business of the estate, Logan acknowledged her loss of both physical and fiscal power. She died within months of that final decision.[37]

Deborah Logan's example in widowhood is important despite the fact that she did not typify most older women of her time. Her struggle was familiar to many women, regardless of economic or social status. Although she had been born into wealth and continued to live comfortably, if modestly, after her marriage to George Logan, she relied heavily on male protection and direction. She enjoyed living under George Logan's "protective wing" and was unprepared for an independent existence after forty years of marriage. Yet because she spent nearly eighteen years as a widow, she made decisions and accepted responsibilities in late life in ways previously unknown to her. The extent of her continuing discomfort with her newly enlarged sphere reveals the reluctance of some bright and talented women to move beyond their established purview. It also indicates, however, the tenacity and strength with which older women could pursue their goals, despite anxiety and self-doubt. Still dependent on her sons and eventually her grandsons for help in running Stenton, Deborah Logan nonetheless bore the weight of fiscal responsibility herself. Her achievements were like those of other women, the result of hard work and self-sacrifice coupled with the perpetual nagging doubt that a man could do better.

Women like Deborah Logan attempted to balance their continued reliance on others with active participation in the work and management of their households. Others, however, ignored the financial pressures of widowhood by succumbing completely to the care and support of an adult child or other relative. In these cases when women donned their widow's weeds, they merely shifted their base of dependency. The legal support formerly provided by their husbands was supplanted by the morally sanctioned support of their children or even their grandchildren. Some women found this continuation of support both agreeable and well deserved. Alice Shippen, who had raised her grandson William Shippen III, appeared quite comfortable in reminding William that "your dear Grandfather left me to your care." When Thomas Ward and his wife reassured his mother that she would be provided for, Elizabeth Denny Ward responded with gratitude, admitting that their readiness to help "takes away anxious care that might otherwise arise, and distress the mind."[38]

While some women expressed the desire to continue their dependency, others dwelt on the past. Such preoccupation with a past identity was particularly intense for women who equated their own success with their late husbands' achievements. Widowhood for such women could abruptly

Deborah Norris Logan (1761-1839) by Charles Willson Peale, circa 1822, courtesy of the Commissioners of Fairmount Park. Deborah Logan never liked this portrait and refused to have it completed until 1825. By then she was amused at the idea of "a Dame of 64" painted by an artist of eighty-two.

signal a change in personal identity and status, one which they might attempt to deny for as long as possible.

Biographical sketches and memoirs helped some women confirm their late husbands' achievements. Women whose husbands served in the formation of the new republic were often among those who worked hard to preserve the memories and the images of a happy marriage. Mary Palmer Tyler, for instance, clearly revered her late husband Royall Tyler while only occasionally showing an awareness of his faults and imperfections. Anna Thornton, Deborah Logan, and others wrote reminiscences of their husbands to ensure their mates' posterity and, no doubt, their own as well. Women's desire to retain an attachment to the revolutionary generation, particularly during the increasingly nationalistic period of the early nineteenth century, should not be confused, however, with the durability and strength of marriage over time. Such reminiscences and biographical sketches tend to reveal marriage as it was idealized, not as it was practiced.[39]

A late husband's achievements unfortunately offered no guarantees for a widow's prosperity. In an eight-page letter to her friend Mercy Warren in 1780, Hannah Winthrop vividly described her anger when John Winthrop's position at Harvard was "usurped" after his death. "Ah, must the place, the person, the services, the attainments be oblivioned! Forbid it," she mourned. Clearly equating her own loss in status with her late husband's, Hannah Winthrop later described her existence as "treading the darksome maze of widowed life" toward a future filled with pain and devoid of human joy.[40]

"I am like a being who does not belong," wrote Deborah Logan in 1821, a testament not only to her love of the past but to her fear of the future as well. Because their self-perception typically mirrored their husband's well-being, newly widowed women often regarded the death of a spouse as the start of their own inevitable decline. Widowhood imposed a sense of discontinuity which became particularly stressful in old age, when years of comfortable sameness might be abruptly ended. Widows throughout this period often described themselves as living in a "different world" and frequently expressed the desire to return to the past.[41]

While some widows remained tied to a dependent posture associated with past identity, others came to see the potential of independence in their widowhood. "Dependence, surely, is one of the capital evils, inflicted on the human species," remarked a Virginia widow in 1789. Whether independence in widowhood took the form of independent living arrangements or simply learning the business and chores of daily living, women alone in old age often revealed considerable strength and flexibility.[42]

From the revolutionary period into the mid-nineteenth century, widows consistently expressed the desire to maintain their own homes. Hannah Emlen Logan of Philadelphia declined to give up her family home after her husband's death in 1776. Seventy years later, Sally Richmond expressed similar determination to keep her home. "I sometimes think my home a Paradise on Earth," wrote the old woman. "I endeavor to make my House pleasant to relations & friends," she wrote, adding smugly that "they all visit me with pleasure, and leave with regret." Whether animated by pride or merely the need to feel self-sufficient, many widows during this time worked hard to maintain separate, independent living arrangements.[43]

Hannah Carter Smith of Boston was one of a number of widows who struggled to remain independent despite great financial obstacles. Writing the news of her late husband's insolvency to her son in 1816, she refused to express fear or uneasiness about the future. "I do not feel anxious," she wrote, "but that I can provide for myself & my rents are paid punctually." After boarding in homes for a number of years, however, she realized the value of maintaining an independent living arrangement. "It is important that I should have a house of my own on moderate terms," she wrote her daughter in 1828, "even if there are some inconveniences." Like other women, Hannah Carter Smith eventually found it necessary to live with her children. Such choices were not easily made. "I prefer to be at House-keeping," wrote Anna Cunningham to her cousin in 1835 after moving into her daughter's home, "although I am as pleasantly situated as I could be out of my own house."[44]

Many women, anxious to lead productive and useful lives, found it difficult to maintain completely independent living arrangements. Like Anna Cunningham, women sought compromises in which their own needs and those of others were equally addressed. Usually residing with children or grandchildren, they helped with domestic duties. Permanent arrangements, however, were not always possible. Some travelled frequently between the homes of brothers, sisters, and friends. "I am grown weary of my life," wrote Elizabeth Putnam in 1811 as she anticipated another trip to Boston to visit her sister. "This wandering about does not suit old folks," she concluded. While circumstances forced some widows to be "footloose," they were seldom "fancy free."[45]

When widows decided to live with their adult children, they often found themselves leading equally nomadic lives, residing with those who had room or whose need was greatest and relocating when situations changed. A widow since 1804, Alice Izard lived at her son's house until his remarriage in 1814. While there, she was careful "to interfere as little as possible with the management of the family, and would never take the head of the table." Clearly feeling her position tenuous, she agreed in 1814 to move to Phil-adelphia to be near her daughter. The move, however, would be made on her terms, which included having a separate residence. She also insisted that her granddaughter reside with her in Philadelphia. While past experience had taught her the value of having her own home, Alice Izard was unwilling to live alone and was skeptical of other women who professed a desire to live by themselves.[46]

Indeed, living independently did not always mean living alone. Residing with grandchildren or friends eased the loneliness of widowhood and appeased the concerns of friends and relatives who believed women should not live alone. When Margaret Bayard Smith learned in 1838 that her recently widowed sister Jane Kirkpatrick was planning to live by herself, she was appalled. "How is it possible she can live alone—alone!" she repeatedly asked another sister. When writing to Kirkpatrick the next month, Smith directly confronted the issue. "You *must* not live alone," she wrote in no uncertain terms. To Smith's great relief, Kirkpatrick apparently agreed and eventually arranged to live in her own "independent establishment" next door to her daughter. While such happy compromises were not the rule, they illuminate the conflict faced by many widows who sought to retain close ties with family and friends but were equally anxious to maintain an independent existence.[47]

After years of married life, women widowed in old age quickly learned the price of dependency. Some, comfortable in that dependency, would continue to rely on others for support and aid after the death of a husband. Women who narrowly defined their options within the woman's sphere and perceived their identities as inseparable from their late mates would continue to live in the past, fearing the future. Other women, accustomed to making their own decisions, persisted in building an independent existence as widows.

For most women, however, a spirit of compromise prevailed in achieving economic and emotional stability after a husband's death. Although most women expressed the desire to live independently, many were persuaded to reside with children or other relatives. Few women indulged in completely dependent or retrospective lives. Most widows desired to remain useful to their family and friends and proceeded successfully to reorganize their lives despite loneliness and persistent grief. Those patterns of compromise, in which the maintenance of past identities merged with a reawakened spirit of independence, predominate throughout the period. Daughters of the Revolution, grown old in Jacksonian America, responded to widowhood with the same ambivalence toward dependency that their mothers and grandmothers had known. Neither geographic nor regional differences altered the consistency of these patterns of compromise. Within a society that continued to define women's status in terms of affiliation rather than achievement, widows with family and friends could continue to give and receive comfort and care. On the other hand, by forcing older women to examine their values and their goals, widowhood allowed some women the opportunity to stretch beyond the limits of confined domesticity and achieve, however modestly, a new sense of self. For these women, the death of a spouse provided the chance for renewal and redirection in old age.

"Old Maids" in the New Republic

"How sad . . . to see a woman singel above fifty and not married," wrote the spinster Rebecca Dickinson in 1788, herself fifty. "Something is the matter. . . ." While older women with husbands or memories of departed husbands approached old age with some hope of familial companionship and filial care, women who never married anticipated growing old from a different perspective. Married women might attempt to ignore their advancing age; single women found their status as "spinsters" reaffirmed with each passing year. During a period when the expectation of filial support in old age eased the prospects of widowhood or infirmity for married women, spinsters looked to the future with apprehension and believed, like Rebecca Dickinson, that something was the matter. Yet during this same period, the number of spinsters increased and the stigma attached to spinsterhood began to diminish. The problems faced by older single women were not, however, easily resolved within a society dedicated to exalting women's role within the conjugal setting. Women who remained single by either choice or necessity were still obliged to adopt a mode of dependency strikingly similar to what their married sisters knew.[48]

"The appellation of Old made has always appeard to me very Formidable, and I don't believe one of our Sex wou'd Voluntarily Bare that Title if by a proper opportunity they could avoid it," wrote the young Sarah Hanschurst in 1762. Like other pre-revolutionary young women, she hoped to avoid the life of a spinster. According to historian Carol Berkin, social disapproval of unmarried women increased as women aged in colonial America. While single women in their mid-twenties might be viewed with both "alarm and pity," a thirty-year-old New England spinster would be openly labeled a "thornback." Often forced to rely on brothers and other relatives for support in late life, single women faced bleak prospects of dependency and financial insecurity. While some attitudes toward spinsters changed after the Revolution, most of the difficulties associated with spinsterhood remained.[49]

The pressure caused by financial insecurity created obvious problems for single women. Although most unmarried women were not confronted with the sudden shock of fiscal responsibility experienced by many widows, spinsters often anticipated long lives of penury and economic uncertainty. Some received adequate compensation from the estates of parents or the continued support of other guardians. Most, however, found it difficult to make ends meet. For even the most remarkable women, spinsterhood could signal the onset of a life of never-ending frugality and hard work.[50]

Hannah Adams's experience provides an excellent example of the difficulties faced by single women forced to make their own way. Raised in a cultured but impoverished household, Adams inherited a love for books but little else. To maintain herself and her older sister, she made lace during the Revolution and tried her hand at spinning, weaving, and braiding straw. During summer months she "kept school" at a neighboring town. Having been educated "in the habits of debilitating softness," she spent many years summoning the courage to become a professional writer and historian. Despite her extraordinary intellectual gifts, she found it difficult to earn a living. Near the end of her life she conceded that poverty was the main, perhaps the only, inducement for undertaking a career in writing.[51]

Even after establishing herself as a competent interpreter of historical and religious material, Hannah Adams faced a future of financial insecurity. Problems with publishers and publication rights plagued her for many years. "At length I saw old age approaching," she recalled, "without any provision for it. . . . My mind was at times depressed by this gloomy prospect." Finally, a lifetime annuity arranged by a number of prominent friends allowed her to live out her last years in relative comfort. Hannah Adams continued to write and publish into her seventies. Yet, after her death, the publishers of her memoirs described Adams as a "poor old woman," a description with which she would probably have concurred.[52]

Because Hannah Adams was among the first American women to make a living by writing professionally, her achievements certainly are not typical. Most unmarried women had neither the ability nor the encouragement necessary to undertake a literary career. Her example is useful precisely because of the perpetual financial difficulties she encountered *despite* her unusual talent and determination. Even the granting of an annuity by a group of friends reveals the precarious state of her financial situation. For single women without family or independent wealth, survival became a lifetime struggle. The anticipation of old age seemed indeed a "gloomy prospect" for all women in similar positions.

Despite the problems imposed by financial insecurity, some young women born during or after the revolutionary era considered spinsterhood a viable alternative to marriage. Ann Livingston, arguing that "single Blessedness is attainable," estimated that she knew of "about three hundred single ladies" in Philadelphia in 1787. Nearly fifty years later, Harriet Drinkwater wrote her nephew that "quite a number" of unmarried women remained in her Massachusetts town. (Such women, she claimed, were consoled by the fact that "the cheapest generally go first.") In the 1830s, women's magazines reflected this emerging trend, professing that no marriage might be preferable to an unhappy one and trying, in the process, to remove the stigma from being an "Old Maid."[53]

Women alone nonetheless confronted the frightening prospect of "doing something" with their lives. Catherine Sedgwick found this to be "the only reproach for a single life": spinsters, she argued, were "generally condemned to uselessness. . . ." Although Catherine Sedgwick was able to overcome this obstacle through a productive literary career, most women who faced the future alone had to find other ways to prove their usefulness to themselves and others. For some, willing to exemplify their common title as "spinsters," textile work in the homes of siblings or other relatives provided a useful and necessary outlet, although one whose importance diminished with the growing demand for factory-finished textiles. Other single women dedicated themselves to raising nieces and nephews and caring for sick or elderly parents and friends. Spinsterhood could thus provide a satisfying if sometimes lonely mode of existence for women who kept busy and believed they contributed to the well-being of those around them.[54]

Because women focused their attention almost exclusively on the family, it is not surprising that women without husbands or children still devoted themselves to the idea of family life. The Philadelphia Quaker Sally Wister was described by her nephew as having been "eminently conspicuous for her devotion to her mother. . . ." Older women without parents often dedicated themselves to other members of the family. For many single women, these attachments proved as significant and meaningful as conjugal ties, demonstrating once again that women could be thoroughly dedicated to the tenets of their sphere without the presence of a husband.[55]

The life of Eunice Paine illustrates the overarching importance of family ties to single women in the eighteenth century. Born in 1733 to a well-known Massachusetts family, she suffered from failing health throughout her seventy years. She never married despite having the opportunity to do so. Over the course of her life, she developed a symbiotic relationship with her brother Robert Treat Paine, a relationship which both supported and crippled her. The correspondence between Eunice Paine and other family members, in fact, reveals her growing dependency on her brother for advice, companionship, and financial security. Although he consistently and eagerly doled out advice to his younger sister, he was less generous with his time and money. Because she had tied her own fortunes so exclusively to those of her brother, her spinsterhood bears no resemblance to the life of freedom and independence to which some later aspired.

Eunice Paine's dependency on her siblings began at an early age. Motherless and with her father living abroad, young Eunice learned early how insecure her home life would prove to be. Her married sister reluctantly took her in after their father's departure. "I hope it will be for the best," wrote Abigail Paine Greenleaf to her brother Robert in 1749, "but I fear the consequences will be bad."[56]

Eventually Eunice Paine took separate lodgings. Dependent on her brother to help pay her rent, she was continually forced to live in rooms she found cold and unpleasant. Her brother's responses to her pleas for improved living arrangements appear far from sympathetic. Writing to the "Dear Old Maid" in 1758, Robert Paine tried to cajole his sister. "Forc'd to lay alone these cold Nights, I don['] pity you in yr cold chamber," he responded after her request for new lodgings. Many years later, Mary Palmer Tyler recalled her childhood visits to Eunice Paine who was then living in a room at the Palmer family home. Believing that Paine might have been cheated by her brother out of her share of the inheritance, the Palmer family gave her special treatment. They provided her with the best room in the house, where she was "waited upon like a queen," wrote Mary Tyler. Despite spending pleasant years in the Palmer household, Paine lived most of her late life under a shadow of insecurity and doubt.[57]

In 1759 Eunice Paine found an opportunity to break away from the sibling dependency that had characterized her life. Receiving an offer of marriage she seemed anxious to accept, she turned to her brother, as her guardian, for his consent. Robert Paine's eight-page reply provides an outstanding opportunity to examine the machinations employed by some men to promote an unmarried sister's dependency and subservience.

Initially reminding her that he had "forsook my own Plan of life to promote yours" and had "voluntarily undertaken the anxious charge" of being her guardian, Robert Paine proceeded to belittle and deride her, her proposed mate, and her prospects for a happy marriage. Suggesting that her poor health would eliminate any hopes of physically consummating her marriage, Robert Paine wondered how she would endure "the chilling indifference of ungratified Love. . . ." He further argued that her suitor, being only a sailor, would not be satisfied with mere platonic love. He also condemned any hope she may have had for raising healthy children. "What think you of cursing yr Infants with a crazy Constitution & bringing a Race into the World to be miserable on many accts," he asked her. As Paine warmed to his subject, it became clear that class consciousness lay behind many of his accusations. Should she marry this sailor, he warned, she could expect neither the respect nor notice he had formerly paid her. "You have hitherto been of my Rank, but if you descend below it you can['])t expect me to follow you," argued this future signer of the Declaration of Independence. Warning her of "widowhood, decay'd circumstances & many other evils," Paine concluded his threatening epistle with a dagger aimed directly at the heart. "If in *him* you think you can find a friend that is nearer than a Brother," he thrust, "may Heaven bless the Alliance." Although it is difficult to know which—if any—of these arguments favorably impressed her, her decision not to marry was no doubt gratifying to her undeniably forceful brother.[58]

It is hard to determine the exact nature of the relationship between Robert Paine and his sister, but this letter reveals much of the underlying balance of power between this successful "patriot" and his spinster sister. Determined to keep his sister under his wing, Paine willingly destroyed what he surely knew to be the sanctified rights of every eighteenth-century woman: the right to marry and to bear and raise children. Stripping her of these basic functions, Robert Paine offered her the grand booby prize of spinsterhood—enduring brotherly love. Remaining chaste and at a distance, Eunice Paine would continue her dependency on her brother for another half-century. While she continued to express concern and disappointment over her brother's apparent disregard for her welfare, she accepted his dominant role in her life, extending it to other women as well. Paine's wife, she wrote, should be treated no differently. "You are her Overseer," she wrote him in 1771. "Take care that she performs. . . ." Dependency, in any form and at all costs, had become the hallmark of Eunice Paine's life.[59]

Brothers often played a vital role in the lives of their unmarried sisters. Most post-revolutionary women, however, experienced healthier relationships with their male siblings than Eunice Paine did. Rebecca and Bridget Noyes, for instance, continued to live in the homes of their brothers, moving from the residence of one brother to that of another in 1811. Rebecca's diary reveals a no-nonsense approach to the debts she owed her brothers. Each year she duly recorded her payment to her brother for the cost of residing with him. When her brothers owed her money, she similarly noted receipt of payment. She seldom indicated any misgivings about paying her own way.[60]

Although Rebecca Noyes apparently conducted her business with her brothers in a straightforward, business-like manner, she nevertheless maintained strong emotional attachments to them. This became especially evident in times of illness and death. Other brothers and sisters felt similar bonds which sometimes seemed as close as those of husband and wife. "I can never love anybody better than my Brother," wrote Catherine Sedgwick in 1813, adding that she fully expected to remain a sister rather than becoming a wife. Such women apparently preferred to confine their affections to the men they had long known and trusted rather than risk disappointment outside their family.[61]

As the years passed, single women devoted themselves almost exclusively to family ties. The effects of time and the infirmities of old age only enhanced the bonds between siblings and other relatives. The late-life diary of the Connecticut spinster Rebecca Noyes, for instance, spans more than thirty years, revealing a pattern of family visits and concerns which reads like that of the stereotypical southern diarist. Although declining health forced her to curtail extended journeys to visit relatives, she continued to focus almost exclusively on her brothers and their families and especially on her sister Bridget, with whom she had always lived. Her constant companion, Bridget was also her best friend. When Bridget was sick or ill, Rebecca invariably felt "low spirited" herself. Although her contact with other family members declined considerably in the final years of her life, Rebecca remained closely tied to her siblings, living with Bridget in the home of her brother.[62]

Like Rebecca and Bridget Noyes, many spinsters lived together or with married sisters. Mary Sandwith lived permanently in the home of her sister, Elizabeth Drinker, and increasingly took over responsibility for looking after the family. This allowed Drinker more leisure time for "reading and doing such work as I like best." Hannah Adams, who became a well-known historian in late life, worked for many years to support an aged and infirm spinster sister. Susan Assheton lived with her sister Frances until Frances's marriage; when her sister Maria died in 1807, Susan moved to Maria's home where she helped raise her nieces and nephews for the next four years. Sororal bonds, indeed, could extend even beyond death.[63]

The ties between unmarried women and their families were undeniably influenced by their need for a place to live. When their parents were alive, single women usually resided at the family home, often taking care of an ever-increasing share of the domestic chores as well as the care of aged and infirm parents. Such living arrangements were mutually beneficial in many respects, but they could pose strains on all sides. When her seventy-nine-year-old mother returned to Hatfield, Massachusetts, to reside with her once again in 1787, the spinster Rebecca Dickinson could muster little enthusiasm. "One time more," she wrote in her diary. "How we are to live i cant see." At another time, Dickinson noted the difficulty of living with an old woman unable to care for herself. "In a puzzling fit [she] broke my specticles," she wrote with obvious frustration.[64]

When parents died, aging single women often chose to reside with a sibling and share in the domestic work of that household. Such women, not wanting to be a "burden" on other family members, often found it difficult to move into the home of a brother or sister. Some, like Eunice Paine, were clearly not invited to share their siblings' hearth and home. Most unmarried women with brothers and sisters, however, could realistically expect they would be welcome. For those without a family, boarding houses proved a last resort. According to her friend Hannah Lee, Hannah Adams "had not even a home" she could call her own. Indeed, at a time when the notion of home increasingly signified a protected, feminized sanctuary, most spinsters were unable to enjoy a home of their own.[65]

Because the lack of a home came to symbolize the fragility and dependency of their spinster status, single women struggled to maintain a place to live, although they seldom enjoyed a sense of permanency in their living arrangements. A change of residence produced anxiety and occasionally depression among unmarried women. In 1804, when Rebecca Noyes was forty-five, she and her sister Bridget agreed to leave the family seat and move in with their brother and his family. "It is very hard for us," Noyes confided, "to leave a place that we are so much attach'd to." At that point, however, she believed that, if things did not work out, she and her sister could return to the family homestead "where our *Parents* has made provision for us." Neither sister ever exercised that option, however. When another move became imminent in 1811, the sisters considered a number of possible living arrangements, including living by themselves. They eventually decided to move in with another brother and his family. Throughout this period of uncertainty, Rebecca Noyes expressed considerable apprehension in her diary. She hoped for "more resolution" in reaching such an important decision, and she worried for an entire month. Yet, after deciding to make the move, she still seemed uncertain. "Where I shall be a year from this," she wrote on Thanksgiving Day, "I know not!" Despite such anxiety, they remained in this brother's home for the remainder of their lives.[66]

When single women did live alone, they faced many problems. Such women felt besieged with the prospect of being sick with no one to help and no one to care. Throughout the year 1787, the forty-nine-year-old spinster Rebecca Dickinson articulated this fear. "How sad to be sick — no one to doe the least kind offis," she bemoaned. Denied the comfort of a close friend or sister, women like Rebecca Dickinson remained lonely and frightened as they aged.[67]

The ease with which single women settled into their lives alone depended greatly on their self-perceptions. Eunice Paine, for all her loneliness and anguish, maintained a perspective and a sense of humor which allowed her to overcome many difficulties. Noting in 1791 how noise and quick motions increasingly irritated her, this aging spinster added with obvious irony, "A Spinning wheel of all things distress's me!" Indeed, a positive perception of spinsterhood is evident in a number of women's writings. The Pennsylvania poet Susanna Wright, for instance, extolled the virtues of her friend Elizabeth Norris in a revolutionary era poem that celebrated her friend's determination to remain single. Because Elizabeth Norris never yielded to the "chain," she was indeed a "queen," free to reign over her own independent thoughts, wrote the similarly single and aged Susanna Wright.[68]

While spinsterhood was occasionally exalted, it did not always inspire the healthiest self-concepts. In a curious inscription on the inner cover of her diary, for example, Rebecca Noyes described a wallflower as an "ill-suited ornament" whose decay over time was "rendered but more conspicuous. . . ." Years later, characterizing herself as "poor *me*," Noyes confirmed this tendency toward depression and self-doubt. Rebecca Dickinson revealed a similar lack of self-esteem. Alone at home, she wrote, "I lited no candel for the Darkness of my mind was far beyond the Darkest Dunjon — there was no hope for me in the things of time." Although evidence of such intense unhappiness among spinsters is uncommon, Dickinson's entries reveal a depth of sorrow which was probably familiar to many.[69]

As single women grew older, they faced greater potential for economic hardship and loneliness than their married or widowed sisters. Nonetheless, as their numbers increased, single women appeared more comfortable in their *sole* status. Eighteenth-century spinsters such as Eunice Paine had largely relinquished all control over their lives, preferring to remain deferential and subordinate to male relatives who supported them. In Jacksonian America, however, single women such as Rebecca Noyes took greater charge of themselves. Although both women depended heavily on the continued goodwill of a brother, Noyes engaged in none of the self-debasing, ego-destructive exchanges that characterized Eunice Paine's relationship with her brother. Noyes understood her role within the family and contributed her fair share, as she saw it, to its well-being. Unlike Eunice Paine, Rebecca Noyes gained comfort and emotional support from her sister, revealing a bond which reflected, in part, the growing interdependence of women in the early nineteenth century. While Paine and Noyes might not have been typical spinsters, they illustrate well the direction of change in the early republic.

Such changes, however, did not improve the economic status of single women. Writers such as Hannah Adams enjoyed some opportunities for self-sufficiency; yet even Adams relied on financial assistance from friends. Most women lacked her degree of talent, and few had such generous friends. For these women, growing old alone remained difficult despite its greater acceptance over time. Even by 1835 it was clear that, since most women were denied the opportunity to earn their own living, unmarried women would be unable to exercise fully the freedoms their independent status implied.[70]

Whether as wives, widows, or spinsters, most women in the early national period grew old, like their grandmothers before them, dependent on men for their legal identity and economic support. Ignored by the revolutionary fathers doling out the fruits of Independence, women remained locked into a legal system that effectively prevented them from entering the public domain. It was only in the private sphere that women could consolidate their power and confirm their identity.

Over time, as women's experience became increasingly defined within a discrete and distinctive feminine arena, women both young and old began to view their world as equal and in certain respects superior to its male counterpart. This separate sphere, characterized by domestic mastery, active childrearing, strong feminine bonds, and abundant moral rectitude, provided an environment that proved both comfortable and meaningful to many old women. In this respect, despite the denial of the promises of Independence, aging women found new opportunities for developing strong and purposeful identities in old age. While men might have undergone a "revolution in age relations" threatening their status in old age, old women in the new republic experienced no such loss of esteem. Within their sphere, aging women could continue many of the familiar tasks of a lifetime, comfortable in the knowledge that their skills and values might be of service to yet another generation.

Undoubtedly, marriage served as the nexus for the promotion and survival of the woman's sphere. Even those women who devoted themselves to "single Blessedness" supported the bonds of womanhood, with the family continuing to serve as the social and cultural center of post-revolutionary society. While young women of marriageable age demanded more from their prospective mates in terms of companionship and affection, however, older women expected less from their husbands per se and more from those other elements of their sphere which promised to continue providing support and purpose to the end of life. To the degree that women extended themselves into the full reaches of their domain, their old age could be regarded as satisfying and meaningful regardless of their marital status.

This is not to say that aging women did not suffer from the conditions imposed on them by law and tradition. Their lack of confidence and ignorance in business matters, their fear of dependency on other family members, and their loneliness and guilt when marriages ended (in apathy or death) were all symptomatic of the limitations under which they continued to live. While most women survived hard times by turning to others and to their God for comfort and guidance, some of the most talented and self-sufficient old women of the period endured substantial pain and hardship. Married women such as Louisa Catherine Adams, whose expectations and background failed to prepare her for either marriage or the reality of the woman's sphere, suffered an unhappy old age. Widows like Deborah Norris Logan, who had relied too heavily on male "protection" throughout her life, adjusted with difficulty to her new *sole* status. Spinsters such as

Hannah Adams never felt completely relieved from the burdens of financial hardship.

Despite such adversity, aging women in the new republic attempted to conquer their fears and their dependency. Women's lives in old age extended beyond the society and opinions of men. As they grew older, women increasingly turned to sisters and female friends to fill out and enrich the patterns of their lives established by male relatives. And, as woman's sphere became increasingly identified with childrearing and moral development, aging mothers discovered new directions in which to continue, and sometimes expand, the critical role of motherhood.

NOTES

1. Molly Cooper, *The Diary of Molly Cooper: Life on a Long Island Farm, 1768-1773*, ed. Field Horne (Oyster Bay, N.Y.: Oyster Bay Historical Society, 1981), pp. 4, 15; Deborah Norris Logan, Diary, 6 October 1822, HSP. Note also Caroline Gilman's poem on "The Fortieth Wedding Day," *The Rose Bud or Youth's Gazette* (Charleston, S.C.), 6 October 1832, which concentrates not on the happiness of a long marriage but on loneliness and spiritual preparation.

2. Mary Beth Norton discusses the nature of Molly Cooper's domestic life in *Liberty's Daughters: The Revolutionary Experience of American Women, 1750-1800* (Boston: Little, Brown, 1980), pp. 11-12, 34, 45. Deborah Norris Logan's life is well documented through both letters and her seventeen-volume diary. For an extended examination of her life and diary, see Marleen S. Barr, "The 'Worthy' and the 'Irrelevent': Deborah Norris Logan's Diary" (Ph.D. dissertation, State University of New York at Buffalo, 1980).

3. Women's aspirations in post-revolutionary society mirrored new ideas about the value of education, the family, and women's roles. Within the family, the relatively new notion of companionate marriages promised women a greater share in decision making and marital satisfaction. However, as Susanne Lebsock argues, marriage remained "fundamentally asymmetrical. Men retained the upper hand in almost every aspect of marriage; mixed with the new ideal of mutual affection and respect were substantial elements of male dominance and coercion." See Lebsock, *The Free Women of Petersburg: Status and Culture in a Southern Town, 1784-1860* (New York: W. W. Norton, 1984), p. 18. Beyond new notions about marriage, the political dialogue begun during the Revolution thrust the question of woman's role into public debate for the first time. As the terms of that debate increasingly focused on republican motherhood as the appropriate role for women, the possibilities for change in women's lives narrowed yet simultaneously expanded to include the notion of women as "keepers of the nation's conscience." See Mary Beth Norton, "The Evolution of White Women's Experience in Early America," *American Historical Review* 89 (June 1984):593-619, quote on 617.

4. See Linda K. Kerber, *Women of the Republic: Intellect and Ideology in Revolutionary America* (Chapel Hill: University of North Carolina Press, 1980),

pp. 139-55; and Norma Basch, *In the Eyes of the Law: Women, Marriage, and Property* (Ithaca: Cornell University Press, 1982).

Women's legal status remained inextricably tied to their marital status, forming in law a dependency which both mirrored and propelled their inferior position in the larger society. While single women (*femes sole*) could act as independent agents in the conduct of their own business, married women (*femes covert*) became the legal appendages of their mates. *Femes covert* were unable to sue or be sued, to sell or buy property, or to make contracts or wills. Wages earned by married women legally belonged to their husbands. Except when modified by a prenuptial agreement, a woman's personal estate at the time of her marriage came under her husband's supervision. Even women's dower rights began to erode during this period. Married women's property legislation was not actively promoted until the 1850s.

5. Because only a small percentage of women obtained divorces, they are not represented in this study. See, for example, Nancy F. Cott, "Divorce and the Changing Status of Women in Eighteenth Century Massachusetts," *William and Mary Quarterly* 33 (October 1976):586-614; and her article, "Eighteenth-Century Family and Social Life Revealed in Massachusetts Divorce Records," *Journal of Social History* 10 (Fall 1976):31.

6. While distinct gender roles certainly existed prior to the nineteenth century, the notion of "separate spheres" is considered a nineteenth-century phenomenon, the result of the separation of home and workplace along with the increasingly middle-class aspirations of the period. During this time, women and men defined themselves and each other in restrictive, mutually exclusive terms. Within this sphere, the "cult of domesticity" flourished. Women's roles as wives, mothers, and mistresses of their households received new emphasis to the exclusion of other roles. Not all women, of course, fit neatly into such patterns. Free blacks and slaves (and certainly native American women) had little opportunity to adopt these norms.

7. *The Book of Abigail and John: Selected Letters of the Adams Family, 1762-1784,* ed. L. H. Butterfield (Cambridge: Harvard University Press, 1975), p. 354; Mercy Otis Warren to ?, 14 June 1777, Mercy Otis Warren Papers, MHS; Rebecca Shoemaker to Samuel Shoemaker, 29 December 1784 and 12 March 1785, Shoemaker Papers, HSP. For an example of the effective model that successful marriages offered young women, see Sarah Connell Ayer, *Diary of Sarah Connell Ayer, 1805-35* (Portland, Maine: Lefavor-Tower, 1910), pp. 155-56, 305-6.

8. Elizabeth Drinker, Diary, 13 October 1796, HSP.

9. Scholars of aging have suggested a positive relationship between women's domestic purview and successful aging. See, for instance, Peter Stearns's comment that women may have had "less emotional vulnerability than men in confronting the sufferings of old age" because they were "cushioned by ongoing housekeeping routines." Stearns, "Old Women: Some Historical Observations," *Journal of Family History* 5 (Spring 1980):51.

10. Elizabeth Collins, *Memoirs of Elizabeth Collins of Upper Evesham, N.J.* (Philadelphia: N. Kite, 1833), p. 120; Elizabeth Farmer to Jack Halroyd, 22 April 1789, 26 July 1787, and 26 June 1788, Elizabeth Farmer Letterbook, HSP.

11. Ann Livingston, Diary, 1 September 1784, Shippen Family Papers, LCMD.

12. Elizabeth Prescott to Nancy Shaw, 27 August 1837, Shaw-Webb Family Papers, AAS.

Private relief programs for widows and minor children existed in Philadelphia early in the eighteenth century. Similar benevolent societies within occupational groups provided help for individuals and their families in case of accident or death. In later years, pension plans were provided for widows of Continental Army officers who had enlisted and had served for an extended period after the war. The first comprehensive pension plan to include widows became effective in 1832. See the extensive microfilm collection of pension applications at the National Archives, M-804, which includes considerable material on elderly widows. For descriptions of early public and private relief programs that provided for widows, see Gary B. Nash, *The Urban Crucible: Social Change, Political Consciousness, and the Origins of the American Revolution* (Cambridge: Harvard University Press, 1979), pp. 182, 188, 195-96; Carl Bridenbaugh and Jessica Bridenbaugh, *Rebels and Gentlemen: Philadelphia in the Age of Franklin,* rev. ed. (New York: Oxford University Press, 1962), pp. 236-43; John C. Dann, ed. *The Revolution Remembered: Eyewitness Accounts of the War for Independence* (Chicago: University of Chicago Press, 1980), pp. xv-xxii; and John K. Alexander, *Render Them Submissive: Responses to Poverty in Philadelphia, 1760-1800* (Amherst: University of Massachusetts Press, 1980), pp. 122-41.

13. Elizabeth Drinker, Diary, 14 August and 8 September 1798, HSP. See also ibid., 12 December 1795.

14. Ibid., 2 December 1799. See also ibid., 30 November 1795 and June 1796.

15. Fanny Bernard to David M. Bernard, September 1837, quoted in Lebsock, *The Free Women of Petersburg,* p. 161. See, for example, the vast correspondence of Margaret Bayard Smith, whose letters often read as though written by a widow. Despite the fact that Samuel Smith was very much alive, she seldom mentioned him in her correspondence. See Margaret Bayard Smith Papers, especially Vol. 13, LCMD. Carroll Smith-Rosenberg introduces but does not fully develop this notion of intergenerational ties in "The Female World of Love and Ritual: Relations between Women in Nineteenth-Century America," *Signs: Journal of Women in Culture and Society* 1 (Autumn 1975):16-17, 22-23.

16. Eliza L. Pinckney to Mrs. Evance, 13 April 1761, *The Letterbook of Eliza Lucas Pinckney,* ed. Elise Pinckney (Chapel Hill: University of North Carolina Press, 1972), p. 167; Deborah Norris Logan, Diary, 3 January 1833 and 22 March 1822, HSP. Susan Grigg's study of remarriage in Newburyport, Massachusetts, suggests that few old women were likely to remarry in seventeenth- and eighteenth-century New England. While Julia Cherry Spruill claims that no woman in the colonial South was "too old to marry," she does not indicate the rate of remarriage, although it was no doubt considerably greater during the early days of settlement. Robert V. Wells's study of eighteenth-century women also supports the contention that few old women remarried. See Grigg, "Towards a Theory of Remarriage: Early Newburyport," *Journal of Interdisciplinary History* 8 (Autumn 1977):183-220; Spruill, *Women's Life and Work in the Southern Colonies* (New York: W. W. Norton, 1972), p. 160; and Wells, "Women's Lives

Transformed: Demographic and Family Patterns in America, 1600-1970," in *Women of America: A History*, ed. Carol Ruth Berkin and Mary Beth Norton (Boston: Houghton Mifflin, 1979), p. 17.

17. Christian Barnes to Elizabeth Murray Smith, 5 August 1771, *Letters of James Murray, Loyalist*, ed. Nina Moore Tiffany (Boston: Gregg Press, 1972), p. 142.

18. Elizabeth Putnam to Samuel Ward, 6 February 1810 and 2 September 1811, Chandler-Ward Family Papers, AAS.

Remarriage could be viewed from a different perspective outside "mainstream" American society. The elderly Moravian deaconess Anna Catharine Ernst, for example, felt it her duty, as defined by her church, to *remarry* three times; she was sixty years old at the time of her fourth and final marriage. See Adelaide L. Fries, *Road to Salem* (Chapel Hill: University of North Carolina Press, 1944).

19. Alexander Keyssar discusses the relationship between population and remarriage in "Widowhood in Eighteenth Century Massachusetts: A Problem in the History of the Family," *Perspectives in American History* 8 (1974):96-98. Quaker women, according to Mary Maples Dunn, were less likely to remarry than others. See Dunn, "Women of Light," in *Women of America*, ed. Berkin and Norton, p. 127.

20. Anna Thornton, "The History and Life of Dr. William Thornton," n.d., reel 7, William Thornton Papers, LCMD.

21. Elizabeth Murray Smith Inman to ?, n.d. [1771], James M. Robbins Papers, MHS. See also Mary Beth Norton, "A Cherished Spirit of Independence: The Life of an Eighteenth-Century Boston Businesswoman," in *Women of America*, ed. Berkin and Norton, pp. 48-67, especially 56-57.

22. Louisa Catherine Adams, "The Adventures of a Nobody," reel 269, Adams Papers III, MHS (microfilm edition at the University of Cincinnati).

23. A certain amount of sentimental affection for childhood is to be expected in late-life memoirs of this period; the degree of anger, hostility, and guilt in Louisa Catherine Adams's reflections on later life poses an unmistakable and very suggestive contrast.

24. Louisa Catherine Adams, "Adventures," pp. 23, 36.

25. Ibid., pp. 122, 125.

26. Ibid., pp. 121, 185. See also Katharine T. Corbett, "Louisa Catherine Adams: The Anguished 'Adventures of a Nobody,' " in *Woman's Being, Woman's Place*, ed. Mary Kelley (Boston: G. K. Hall, 1979), pp. 67-84.

27. Alexander Keyssar's important study of widowhood in eighteenth-century Massachusetts has contributed much to our understanding of the relationships between widowhood, property, and dower rights. His work, however, does not explore women's emotional responses to widowhood. See Keyssar, "Widowhood in Eighteenth Century Massachusetts," pp. 83-119.

28. Only ten percent of Keyssar's sample was known to have married more than once. Keyssar found women's average age at widowhood was 55.4 years, revealing that "widowhood, as a social issue, involved the accommodation of middle-aged or elderly women to a set of new roles in the family and society." Ibid., p. 90.

29. Abigail Adams to Mercy Otis Warren, 10 December 1778, *Adams Family Correspondence*, 3 vols., ed. L. H. Butterfield (Cambridge: Harvard University Press, 1963), 3:132.

30. Rebecca Shoemaker, Journal, 6 December 1805, Rawle Family Papers, HSP; Anna Holyoke Cutts to daughter, 30 October 1808, Cutts Family Papers, EI; Maria Montgomery to Rebecca Nicholson, 9 March 1833, Shippen Family Papers, LCMD. See also the diary of Anna Blackwood Howell, 4 February 1832, AAS; and Jane Howell to Thomas Chandler, 22 August 1837, quoted in Marilyn Ferris Motz, *True Sisterhood: Michigan Women and Their Kin, 1820-1920* (Albany: State University of New York Press, 1983), pp. 113-14. See chapter five, below, for a more extensive discussion of depression in old age. Richard A. Kalish describes the impact of deprivation in widowhood in "Death and Dying in a Social Context," in *Handbook of Aging and the Social Sciences*, ed. Robert H. Binstock and Ethel Shanas (New York: Van Nostrand Reinhold, 1976), p. 502.

31. Deborah Norris Logan, Diary, 19 August 1821 and 4 April 1835, HSP.

32. Keyssar, "Widowhood in Eighteenth Century Massachusetts," pp. 96-116; Norton, *Liberty's Daughters*, pp. 145-46. Robert J. Gough has uncovered four methods most commonly used for distributing property to widows among the Philadelphia elite in the late eighteenth century. Widows were provided with one of the following: (1) use during the course of their lifetime; (2) outright bequest; (3) property willed to a child with provision for the mother's care; (4) no provision because of independently owned property. See Gough, "Towards a Theory of Class and Social Conflict: A Social History of Wealthy Philadelphians, 1775 and 1800" (Ph.D. dissertation, University of Pennsylvania, 1977), p. 239. See also the 11 May 1827 letter of Sarah Washington to her niece Rebecca Nicholson, Shippen Family Papers, LCMD, which reveals a family torn by demands for property. Slaveholding women did not, in most cases, share the problems of labor shortage and were sometimes familiar with the techniques of managing plantations. The letters of Eliza Lucas Pinckney, for instance, reveal her considerable management capabilities. See Pinckney, *Letterbook*, passim.

33. Anna Thornton to Dr. Ed. Stevens, 28 December 1828, William Thornton Papers, LCMD. Anna Thornton seemed ready to take on anyone, including "presidents, Secretaries, Congress" whom she claimed had misused her husband. Yet she acknowledged that her husband's passion for horses was his weakness. See her "History and Life of Dr. William Thornton," n.d., reel 7, William Thornton Papers, LCMD. See also Mary Beth Norton, "Eighteenth-Century American Women in Peace and War: The Case of the Loyalists," *William and Mary Quarterly* 33 (July 1976):386-98. In this essay, Norton examines the extent to which married women remained ignorant of the financial interests governing their lives.

34. Mary Johnson Hopkinson to children, 27 January 1785, Hopkinson Family Papers, HSP; Margaret Bayard Smith to Jane Kirkpatrick, 19 December 1839, Margaret Bayard Smith Papers, LCMD.

In his discussion of women's property rights, Keyssar notes, "Widows . . . possessed property which, without family labor, was difficult to utilize and which, because of legal restraints, they could not sell." See Keyssar, "Widowhood in Eighteenth Century Massachusetts," p. 109. In the South, as suggested by

Suzanne Lebsock in her study of Petersburg, Virginia, widows over time became increasingly effective in utilizing the legal system to protect and even accumulate property. See Lebsock, *The Free Women of Petersburg*, pp. 129, passim.

35. Deborah Norris Logan, Diary, 9 August 1827, HSP. Deborah Logan was nearly sixty years old when George Logan died. See also ibid., 21 July 1825.

36. Ibid., 11 February 1826, 29 September 1828, and 14 February 1829.

37. Ibid., 2 October 1833 and 2 November 1836.

38. Alice Shippen to William Shippen III, 2 August n.d., reel 3, Shippen Family Papers, LCMD; Elizabeth Denny Ward to Thomas Ward II, 24 February 1836, Ward Family Papers, AAS. See also Deborah Norris Logan, Diary, 25 October 1826, HSP. For a discussion of filial support, see chapters two and three, below.

39. Mary Palmer Tyler, *Grandmother Tyler's Book: The Recollections of Mary Palmer Tyler (Mrs. Royall Tyler)*, ed. Frederick Tupper and Helen Tyler Brown (New York: G. P. Putnam's Sons, 1925), pp. 217-18. Examples of such biographies by wives include Deborah Logan's *Memoir of Dr. George Logan of Stenton*, ed. Frances A. Logan (Philadelphia: Historical Society of Pennsylvania, 1899); and Anna Thornton's "The History and Life of Dr. William Thornton," n.d., reel 7, William Thornton Papers, LCMD.

40. Hannah Winthrop to Mercy Otis Warren, 20 April and 1 September 1780, Warren-Winthrop Papers, MHS. See also ibid., 9 January 1778. Robert C. Atchley argues that twentieth-century widows with a traditional orientation suffer similar changes in self-identity. See Atchley, *Social Forces and Aging*, 4th ed. (Belmont, Calif.: Wadsworth, 1985), p. 225. See also Helen L. Lopata, "Role Changes in Widowhood: A World Perspective," in *Aging and Modernization*, ed. Donald Cowgill and Lowell Holmes (New York: Appleton-Century-Crofts, 1972), pp. 275-303.

41. Deborah Norris Logan, Diary, 7 September 1825 and 1 January 1823, HSP. See also Maria Montgomery to Rebecca Nicholson, 9 March 1833, Shippen Family Papers, LCMD; Hannah Winthrop to Mercy Otis Warren, 9 January 1778, Warren-Winthrop Papers, MHS; and Mary Andrews to Nancy Shaw, 13 June 1823, Shaw-Webb Family Papers, AAS. Women writing for a larger public voiced similar views. See Caroline Gilman's comments on widowhood in her Charleston, S.C. publication, *The Southern Rose*, 25 June 1836.

42. Mary Armistead to Jane Armistead, 9 April 1789, quoted in Norton, *Liberty's Daughters*, pp. 146-47.

43. Sarah Logan Fisher, Diary, n.d. (1:31), HSP; Sally Richmond to Nancy Shaw, 18 February 1846, Shaw-Webb Family Papers, AAS. Peter Laslett has observed in his studies of preindustrial England that "widows and widowers . . . lived for the most part where they were before they were widowed." See Laslett, "Societal Development and Aging," in *Handbook of Aging and the Social Sciences*, ed. Binstock and Shanas, p. 107. Marilyn Motz's study of nineteenth-century Michigan women supports the argument that elderly women wanted separate, independent residences. See Motz, *True Sisterhood*, p. 114.

44. Hannah Carter Smith to Thomas Carter Smith, 24 November 1816, Smith-Townsend Family Papers, MHS; Hannah Carter Smith to daughter, 19 July 1828, Smith-Carter Family Papers, MHS; Anna Cunningham to Nancy Shaw, 14 January

1835, Shaw-Webb Family Papers, AAS. See also Deborah Norris Logan, Diary, n.d. September 1818, HSP.

Pride in owning one's own property was not merely a function of middle-class values. The "white Indian" Mary Jemison, an octogenarian, had lived as a Seneca since childhood and fully identified with that culture. Nonetheless, as she described in her 1824 memoir, "I live in my own house, and on my own land. . . ." See Jemison, *A Narrative of the Life of Miss Mary Jemison,* ed. James E. Seaver (Canandaigua, N.Y.: J. D. Bemis, 1824), p. 143.

45. Elizabeth Putnam to Dorothy Chandler Ward, n.d. 1811, Chandler-Ward Family Papers, AAS. See also Maria Montgomery to Rebecca Nicholson, 9 March 1833, Shippen Family Papers, LCMD. According to Robert V. Wells, "Old age, without family, was not common before 1800." See Wells, "Demographic Change and the Life Cycle of American Families," in *The Family in History: Interdisciplinary Essays,* ed. Theodore K. Rabb and Robert I. Rotberg (New York: Harper and Row, 1971), p. 91.

46. Alice Izard to Margaret Manigault, 8 May, 19 October, 17 November, and 15 December 1814, Izard Family Papers, LCMD.

47. Margaret Bayard Smith to Maria Boyd, 23 September 1838, and Margaret Bayard Smith to Jane Kirkpatrick, 26 October 1838 and 9 February 1839, Margaret Bayard Smith Papers, LCMD. See also Elizabeth Drinker's comments on widows alone in her Diary, 19 December 1795, HSP.

48. Rebecca Dickinson, Diary, September 1788, quoted in June Sprigg, *Domestick Beings* (New York: Alfred A. Knopf, 1984), p. 22. The role of single women in American society has only recently received careful historical consideration. In her study of early nineteenth-century spinsters, Lee Chambers-Schiller examines a select group of post-revolutionary women who regarded marriage as an obstacle to self-development and achievement. Motivated by their search for autonomy, these spinsters represented one way in which, says Chambers-Schiller, "women internalized the individualistic ethic that grew from changes in the structure and values of the early modern family." Her work, however, focuses largely on mid-nineteenth-century sources and fails to consider fully the critical transition from earlier values or the continuing dependence which characterized much of single livelihood in this early period. See Chambers-Schiller, *Liberty, a Better Husband: Single Women in America, the Generations of 1780-1840* (New Haven: Yale University Press, 1984), quotation on p. 1.

Robert V. Wells has found in his sample of Quaker women in eighteenth-century America that the percentage of single women living at age fifty rose from 9.8 percent of women born before 1786 to 23 percent among those born in 1786 or after. Such figures indicate a dramatic rise which was evident, to a lesser extent, among non-Quaker women as well. See Wells, "Quaker Marriage Patterns in a Colonial Perspective," *William and Mary Quarterly* 29 (July 1972):425-27, 433-34.

Many historians agree the number of never-married women increased substantially in the years following the Revolution and offer a number of possible reasons for this phenomenon. Some point to the changing sex ratio within settled communities. Others speculate that revolutionary ideology helped free women by providing options beyond marriage and family. While both reasons no doubt contributed to the rising number of spinsters, most aging unmarried women revealed little sense of "liberation" in the fifty years following the Revolution. They were, after all, growing old when the concept of motherhood was increasingly extolled and virtue was becoming synonymous with domesticity. See Daniel Scott Smith, "Parental Power and Marriage Patterns: An Analysis of Historical Trends in Hingham, Massachusetts," *Journal of Marriage and the Family* 21 (August 1973):419-28; and Norton, *Liberty's Daughters,* pp. 240-41.

49. Sarah Hanschurst to Sally Forbes, n.d. 1762, Miscellaneous Manuscript Collection, LCMD; Carol Ruth Berkin, *Within the Conjurer's Circle: Women in Colonial America* (Morristown, N.J.: General Learning Press, 1974), p. 4.

50. In his study of Philadelphia wills, Robert Gough noted a common practice among fathers which formalized the bonds of dependency between married brothers and unmarried sisters. Among the wills Gough examined, he found that men often stipulated that their sons pay a specific annuity to an unmarried sister out of their own legacies. Gough also indicates that men's wills often made equal, if not superior, provisions for daughters. See Gough, "Towards a Theory of Class and Social Conflict," pp. 236-38.

51. Hannah Adams, *A Memoir of Miss Hannah Adams, Written by Herself* (Boston: Gray and Bowen, 1832), pp. 2, 22, 68.

52. Ibid., p. 35; introduction.

53. Ann Livingston to her uncle, [9] December 1787, Ann Livingston's Letterbook, Shippen Family Papers, LCMD; Harriet Drinkwater to Joshua Adams Gray, 22 March 1834, Hooker Collection, SL. See also Elizabeth Smith to Hannah Carter Smith, 23 April 1792, Smith-Carter Family Papers, MHS; and Mary Sever to ?, 6 March 1810, Chandler-Ward Family Papers, AAS. Note also Barbara Welter's comments in her *Dimity Convictions: The American Woman in the Nineteenth Century* (Athens: Ohio University Press, 1976), p. 37.

54. Catherine Sedgwick to Frances P. Watson, 25 March 1816, Catherine Maria Sedgwick I Papers, MHS. See also Nancy Cott's note on the term "spinster," indicating that its original meaning ("female spinner") changed during the seventeenth century to become the legal term for unmarried women. Some men as well as women altered their views toward spinsters by the late eighteenth century. Thomas Gisborne, for instance, argued that "the present age has abated much of the ridicule of the spinster." See Cott, *The Bonds of Womanhood: "Woman's Sphere" in New England, 1780-1835* (New Haven: Yale University Press, 1977), p. 27; and Gisborne, *An Enquiry into the Duties of the Female Sex,* 2d ed. (London: T. Cadell, 1797), pp. 407-8.

55. Quoted in Elizabeth Evans, *Weathering the Storm: Women of the American Revolution* (New York: Scribner, 1975), p. 151. See also the journal of Susan Assheton, a spinster who helped raise her late sister's children, in "Susan Assheton's Book," ed. Joseph M. Beatty, *Pennsylvania Magazine of History and Biography* 55:2 (1971):174-86.

56. Abigail Paine Greenleaf to Robert Treat Paine, 15 November 1749 and 9 February 1747, Robert Treat Paine Papers, MHS.

57. Robert Treat Paine to Eunice Paine, 18 November 1758, Robert Treat Paine Papers, MHS; Mary Palmer Tyler, *Grandmother Tyler's Book*, pp. 61-62.

58. Robert Treat Paine to Eunice Paine, 6 May 1759, Robert Treat Paine Papers, MHS.

59. Eunice Paine to Robert Treat Paine, 5 October 1771 and 30 August 1772, Robert Treat Paine Papers, MHS.

60. See, for instance, Rebecca Noyes, Diary, 6 April 1805 and 9 December 1806, CHS.

61. Rebecca Noyes, Diary, 10 September 1827, CHS; Catherine Maria Sedgwick to Robert Sedgwick, 15 August 1813, Catherine Maria Sedgwick I Papers, MHS.

62. Rebecca Noyes, Diary, passim, CHS. For a more extended examination of Rebecca Noyes's visiting patterns, see T. Premo, "Women Growing Old in the New Republic: Personal Responses to Old Age, 1785-1835" (Ph.D. dissertation, University of Cincinnati, 1983), pp. 84-86.

63. Elizabeth Drinker, Diary, 1 January 1802, HSP; Hannah Adams, *A Memoir*, introduction; Susan Assheton, "Book," pp. 174-86; Rebecca Noyes, Diary, 13 February 1830, CHS.

According to Lee Chambers-Schiller, "Sisterly love enabled women to develop and express self-love and self-respect." See Chambers-Schiller, *Liberty, a Better Husband*, p. 134.

64. Rebecca Dickinson, Diary, 26 October 1787, in *A History of Hatfield, Massachusetts, 1660-1910*, ed. Daniel White Wells and Reuben Field Wells (Springfield, Mass.: F. C. H. Gibbons, 1910), p. 207. See also Deborah Norris Logan, Diary, 15 August 1831, HSP.

65. Hannah Lee in her emendation to Hannah Adams's *A Memoir*, p. 58. While Hannah Adams considered residing with her brother, she feared her presence would be a burden.

66. Rebecca Noyes, Diary, 15 April 1804 and 28 November 1811, CHS. See also ibid., 13 and 15 February 1804 and 4 March to 3 April 1811.

67. Dickinson, Diary, n.d. 1787 and 13 August 1787, pp. 206-7. See also Elizabeth Drinker, Diary, 30 November 1795 and June 1796, HSP.

68. Eunice Paine to Robert Treat Paine, 21 December 1791, Robert Treat Paine Papers, MHS; Susanna Wright, "Elizabeth Norris — at Fairhill," in Pattie Cowell, " 'Womankind Call Reason to Their Aid': Susanna Wright's Verse Epistle on the Status of Women in Eighteenth Century America," *Signs: Journal of Women in Culture and Society* 6 (Summer 1981):800.

Women's courtesy titles may reveal a similar positive change. "Mrs." could be a title of respect for an elderly woman. See *New Letters of Abigail Adams, 1788-1801*, ed. Stewart Mitchell (Boston: Houghton Mifflin, 1947), p. 64, note; and Elizabeth Ambler to Nancy ?, 10 October 1798, Letters of Elizabeth Jacquelin Ambler, LCMD.

69. Rebecca Noyes, Diary, [1805], inner leaf of second volume, and 10 October 1825, CHS; Rebecca Dickinson, Diary, 12 August 1787, p. 206. See also Rebecca Dickinson, Diary, 2 September 1787, p. 206, for a description of intense loneliness when, wrote Dickinson, "[I] cryed myself Sick."

70. It is difficult to draw conclusions concerning geographic variations in spinsters' attitudes and responses to growing old. The small number of extant sources from literate aging spinsters during this period distorts any attempt at geographic balance of sources. The conclusions presented here are based on a preponderance of New England sources.

Mothers and Adult Children

In the fall of 1834, Anna Cunningham left the comfortable if frenzied household she shared with her daughter and eleven grandchildren to spend several weeks with her ninety-year-old mother. "I never enjoy'd her Society more," Cunningham wrote in a letter to her cousin. Despite advanced age, her mother managed her own home and continued to maintain complete charge of her dairy, "and [she] does it with as much good judgment as ever she did," marvelled this aged daughter. "I can say with truth that my mother is more endeared to me in every year of my life, and some of my happiest moments are spent with her."[1]

The friendship and love between these two old women is *not* the stuff of headlines today, nor was it one hundred and fifty years ago. Anna Cunningham and her mother enjoyed each other's company during their remaining years together in ways that neither altered the course of women's history nor, by themselves, sustained the new republic. Yet a few quiet revelations emerge from this letter: maternal affections may not only continue but expand with age; commitments to both past and future generations coincide as women themselves grow older; and, at a time when youthful motherhood was exalted, aged motherhood (and aged daughterhood) possessed its own delights.

It is not surprising that ideas about motherhood at this time focused on youthful mothers. From prescriptive literature to maternal associations, concerns about motherhood concentrated largely on those aspects of infant and child care that addressed the needs of the newly empowered young mother charged with the moral and civic development of the nation's future citizens. Mothers were encouraged to forge new and tighter bonds with their children and to rule with love and compassion. With husbands often

removed, both physically and emotionally, from day-to-day household activities, women gained increasing control over their sphere. Yet they carried
a heavy burden. Establishing the right balance of affection and respect,
enthusiasm and control, self-respect and moral virtue required unremitting
vigilance. It is little wonder that babies and youngsters, not grown offspring,
were the subjects of most that was said, written, and pondered about motherhood.[2]

Older women's experience with motherhood was, of course, different
from that of young women about to give birth or even middle-aged mothers
with numerous children still at home. Aging mothers no longer had to
confront the day-to-day responsibilities of guiding the physical and moral
growth of still-undeveloped minds and bodies. Instead, their focus was now
redirected from the perspective of advancing age—both their own and their
children's. Over time, adult children and their aging mothers engaged in
an increasingly *interdependent* relationship as both parties attempted to
support and sustain one another. Only in extreme old age or debility would
compulsory filial duty impose a new kind of dependency on the mother-
child connection.

As the concept of woman's sphere developed in the early nineteenth
century, changes occurred in the nature of the bonds between women and
adult children. Most notably, as the tenets of domesticity were reaffirmed,
mother-daughter ties increasingly formed the central, critical connection
within a complex network of family and friends. Although relationships
between mothers and sons were often close and mutually supportive, maternal expectations differed for sons and daughters. These differences could
become critical to an aged mother's sense of identity and security in her
final years.

In other ways, too, the expansion of woman's sphere influenced the
lives of aging mothers. Because women increasingly viewed themselves as
the prime promoters of moral order, old women appeared doubly fortified—
by gender and by age—to assume enhanced responsibility for moral direction
and leadership. In their relationships with their children, particularly their
daughters, such aging women might serve as models of both spiritual and
feminine strength, models which remained viable for as long as women
continued to regard themselves as ethically and morally distinct from men.

Mother-Daughter Ties

Motherhood in the new republic held many of the same rewards and
invited many of the same frustrations as it does today. Relationships between
mother and child, then as now, represented a complex weaving of biology,
culture, and personality. Yet the role of gender, as it became increasingly

viewed as a criterion for separateness and distinctiveness, added new dimensions to the mother-child relation. A special kind of bond developed between mothers and daughters, altering and enhancing the lives of both generations. Today, as well as two hundred years ago, these feminine ties remain central to the well-being of many aging mothers.[3]

In the early years of the republic, the concept of gender separation encouraged female children to follow their mothers' examples. Whereas mothers prepared their sons for participation in a world markedly different from their own, women raised their daughters to continue the traditions and values which had been passed down to them by their own mothers. Despite the obvious limitations of living within a separate sphere largely outside the public domain, women within the family were able to maintain ties of deep affection, clearly enriching the quality of their circumscribed existences.[4]

The functional and emotional rewards of mother-daughter relationships during this time were manifold. Unable to partake of the expanded opportunities eagerly sought by their brothers, young girls developed within a female network a lasting sense of identity and dignity. Early training in housewifery and motherhood prepared girls for later marriage and parenting. The affection and friendship which united mother and daughter did not end with the completion of this training period. As trainees became companions and friends, the bonds tightened. Separated by their daughters' marriages, mothers often maintained an active interest in all aspects of their daughters' new lives. Similarly, mature daughters expressed their continuing love and devotion to their mothers, as evident in the substantial correspondence which often flowed between the two generations.[5]

"I love the society of my Daughters," wrote Alice Izard to her daughter Margaret Manigault in 1814. "I have every reason to be satisfied with my sons; but they are not like Daughters," she confided. Alice Izard was enormously devoted to her entire family. Yet her correspondence with Manigault, in particular, traces the unusual depth and intimacy of a mother-daughter relationship which spanned both miles and years. "I am most truly your affectionate Mother and delighted friend," Izard typically wrote when signing letters to her daughter. Manigault always responded in kind. When her mother became ill in 1814, Manigault grew despondent: "How could I bear the idea of being separated forever, in this world, from such a mother!" Alice Izard's strong ties with Margaret Manigault and her other daughters reveal the extent to which mothers and daughters relied on each other for advice, comfort, and self-affirmation. Through an active correspondence, Alice Izard maintained in her old age the sense of closeness and immediacy with her daughters which characterized their earlier relationship at home.[6]

As Alice Izard's letters illustrate, separation from a daughter did not appear to reduce the emotional commitment which mothers maintained, even at long distances. The pain of separation at the time of a daughter's marriage was usually eased by the expectation of long visits back home or extended stays at a daughter's new location. Preparation for eventual separation, in fact, often began early. During summers, young daughters frequently lived with other family members, serving to broaden their experience away from home while, at the same time, preparing mothers for a life apart from them.

Connection rather than separation, however, remained central in a woman's relationship with her children. Societal and institutional changes could be interpreted as a threat to that sense of connection. With the spread of female academies after the Revolution, for instance, girls from middle- and upper-class families might spend several years away from home. While such schools provided the opportunity for young women to develop new skills and make new friendships, such early academies sometimes met with disapproval from mothers and grandmothers who resented their intrusion into family life. Arguing that "people are in a great hurry. . . to get rid of their Children," Elizabeth Drinker expressed concern, perhaps alarm, when informed that her granddaughter Eliza Downing would be sent to boarding school. "Had I a doz'n daughters and health to attend to them, not one should go there, or any where else from me," she concluded. Such comments reflect not only the pain which social change could inflict on older generations but the values which such women placed on home training and instruction, especially for girls.[7]

Over time, opportunities for young women expanded in ways which pulled at the ties between mothers and daughters. Some young unmarried women began brief but satisfying careers as teachers, often residing away from home. Attracted by promises of employment and the lure of quasi-independent living arrangements, large numbers of young women began moving to factory towns by the 1830s. Yet thoughts of home were never far away:

> I want to se[e] you more I think
> Than I can write with pen an ink

These lines written by "Lowell girl" Sarah Hodgdon to her family in 1830 suggest the pain accompanying separation, pain sometimes eased by the prospect of personal earnings and by the temporary nature of factory work itself.[8]

Most mothers accepted the notion of separation from children who had come of age, especially when weddings were in the offing. Marriage was seen as a logical, natural step in a daughter's development. It not only enabled young women to utilize those skills long taught at home but also confirmed those values passed on by generations of mothers. Under usual circumstances, relationships between mothers and newly married daughters generated warmth and, no doubt, a few words of maternal wisdom. Unapproved marriages, however, could strain the closest connections. Molly Drinker Rhoads's elopement in 1796 distressed the entire family. Henry Drinker seemed especially unwilling to yield to his daughter's actions, and he imposed a complete moratorium on all visits and communication. Elizabeth Drinker, who keenly felt the strain of the broken relationship with her youngest daughter, vowed not to leave the house until she could visit Molly. "I went . . . without leave, and no reason giving why I should not," she recorded in her diary after calling on Molly. "I feel best pleased that I went," she added. In her willingness to persist despite the objections of her husband and other Quaker friends, Elizabeth Drinker illustrates the importance older women typically attached to maintaining close ties with their married daughters. In time, Molly and her new husband reconciled with Henry Drinker.[9]

When daughters married, the nature of the maternal relationship changed. Young women often grew closer to their mothers, becoming better friends and companions while remaining dutiful daughters. Margaret Bayard Smith noticed a remarkable change in her daughter Julia's demeanor after Julia's marriage in 1836, a change which enhanced their own relationship. "A kind of new relation takes place between a married daughter and her mother which dictates new interests and emotions," Margaret Smith wrote. "Julia is sensible to this and says she never before felt for me as she now does. She loves so, she says, to be alone with me." Many older women noticed, too, that this bond grew with years and maturity. This continuous bonding was especially evident in Anna Cunningham's late-life friendship with her ninety-year-old mother, noted earlier. As adult daughters came increasingly to share with their mothers the experiences, joys, and burdens which only women knew, they appreciated to a greater degree the common ties which united them.[10]

As bonds strengthened over time, so too did the potential for loneliness when circumstances forced married daughters to live far from their mothers. With the increased pace of frontier settlement in the early nineteenth century, young married women often found themselves hundreds of miles away from maternal support. The anguish of separation was most keenly felt when disaster struck. Elizabeth Denny Ward expressed her loneliness and frustration when her daughter Sarah Putnam was widowed while living in Marietta, Ohio, in 1825: "Seldom do I enter my room without calling you to mind," she wrote. She hoped Putnam would return home to Massachusetts. "May it be so in kind providence that I may soothe your Grief and you in turn comfort me," she concluded. Elizabeth Ward believed, as did many other mothers, that adult children could always return home. In her desire for mutual support, she expressed as well her perception of a natural alliance between mother and married daughter, an alliance strengthened by their common understanding of grief and pain.[11]

Such shared experiences ended abruptly, of course, when death intervened. The sense of loss when mothers died often seemed to overwhelm the bereft daughter, and it continued to be felt for many years. It has been "39 years since the loss of my dearest and nearest female friend," noted an aging Quaker matron, revealing a loneliness for her mother lasting throughout her adult life. Because mothers and daughters shared much of their lives within the family homestead, the loss of a mother was often most keenly felt in the domestic domain. "I miss my dear Mother in every part of the house," Lucy Tappan Pierce wrote to her husband after her mother's death in 1826. Weltha Stetson, writing to her aunt, noted the same sense of protracted grief. Although her mother had died three years before, "the time has not worn away my grief for her who was my nearest and Dearest friend on Earth—there is still a void which nothing can fill."[12]

The maternal tie was not always broken in an orderly, predictable way. Adult daughters sometimes died before their mothers, leaving older women with the pain of loss and the guilt of survival. Elizabeth Drinker never fully recovered from the shock of her daughter Sally's death in 1807. At age forty-six, Sally Downing had survived the most dangerous years of childbearing and had been enjoying with her mother newly found bonds of maturity. Drinker was wholly unprepared to lose her. "Oh! What a loss to a mother near 72 years of age, my first born darling . . . 'tho I have been supported far beyond my expectations, [I am] a poor feeble old woman." Although other children had died in infancy and early childhood, Sally's death hit hardest. For nearly a half-century she had enjoyed the friendship and intimacy of her daughter. With Sally's death, Drinker found herself inconsolable, unable to regain a zest for life. Poor health, exacerbated by her depleted will, quickly ended the life of this self-described "old woman." By equating the loss of her daughter with her own "poor feeble" and "old" condition, Elizabeth Drinker signalled the end of a long and productive life.[13]

The death of a grown daughter often shook the very foundation of a mother's faith. When Margaret Bayard Smith's daughter Anna died in 1837, Smith tried to understand the reasoning behind her child's death and her own survival. In God's will alone, she argued, would she find comfort and enlightenment. Yet yielding herself to God's higher authority during times of such immense pain created a sense of self-doubt and insecurity regarding her own faith. "Darkness and doubt chill my very soul," she wrote in 1838.

To carry on the maternal bond missing after Anna's death, Smith redirected her focus. Telling her son Bayard that he had replaced the deceased Anna in her thoughts, she concluded, "You and she are *now* one and the same." To be such an obvious second choice was no doubt as difficult for Bayard as Anna's death would prove to be for his mother, who continued to long for the special mother-daughter relationship.[14]

Love, Honor, and Filial Duty

The affective ties between aging parents and their children in the early republic reflected traditional concepts of duty and obligation. Mary Beth Norton, in her study of the revolutionary experience of American women, stresses the seemingly unending round of filial responsibility imposed on children as their parents grew older. While sons could exercise a number of options to discharge these duties, they usually considered financial support their most appropriate contribution. Daughters, on the other hand, believed they had a special obligation of care and service to their aged parents. Indeed, parents fully expected their daughters to attend to them in times of need in old age. Despite the strain which obligations might entail, the companionship between mothers and daughters was considered vital to both old and young women alike. If daughters suffered from the pressures of filial responsibility, they were nonetheless often motivated by a sense of love and compassion and the fulfillment of what was considered a moral obligation.[15]

Women acknowledged their unique obligations to aging parents throughout the post-revolutionary era. Some, such as this devoted daughter in Utica, New York, expressed filial duty through poetry:

> When thou are feeble, old and grey
> My healthy arms shall by thy stay
> And I will soothe thy pains away
> My mother.

Women frequently shared similar sentiments in letters to family members. Elizabeth Phoenix, in an 1818 letter, underscored the responsibility for care incumbent on daughters. Her parents, she argued, were "too feeble to be left without a daughter." Nearly twenty years later, Margaret Bayard Smith echoed the same sentiments. Describing the plight of "poor Mrs. Clay," she lamented that "in her declining age [she] is left alone & bereaved of the support & comfort which daughters & only daughters can afford." Older women without children often turned to a "near female friend" to assist them in their final years. Throughout this period, younger women as well as their mothers and grandmothers expected to uphold well-accepted notions of women's filial duties.[16]

Duty to aged parents, particularly among youngest daughters, often precluded all other options. Malenda Edwards, who worked in Nashua, New Hampshire, and cared for her parents in a nearby town, admitted that filial devotion kept her from pursuing her dreams out West. "Were it not for my father and mother I would be in the far west ere this summer closes," she wrote in 1845. Lydia Sigourney, as a young woman, decided to avoid "serious advances" from male admirers. "My mind was made up never to leave my parents. I felt that their absorbing love could never be repaid by the longest life-service." Sigourney believed she alone could provide quality care to her aging parents. "I had seen aged people surrounded by indifferent persons who considered their care a burden, and could not endure the thought that my parents should be thrown on the fluctuating kindness of hirelings and strangers." Although she did eventually marry, Lydia Sigourney and her husband shared their Connecticut home with her aged parents in their final years.[17]

Parents and children alike seemed confident that filial obligations were indeed justified. Most believed that a reversal of roles in the parent-child relation provided the just reward for years of parental care and support. Catherine Maria Sedgwick, at a surprisingly early age, understood the notion thoroughly. In 1801, eleven-year-old Sedgwick assured her father that she would never abandon her parents. "Do you think my Dear Papa that I could leave my Dear parents in their old age," she wrote. "No I should be happy in reflecting that I could in a measure reward them for all their kind care to me when I was young." The concept of filial care as repayment for past services is found throughout women's writings during this fifty-year period. Some parents, in fact, considered their own efforts and sacrifices as parents too great to ever be justly repaid. Children, as Sarah Logan Fisher noted in 1790, "certainly bring a great weight of care, & constant anxiety of mind which all their most dutiful, tender and affectionate Behaviour, can scarcely ever sufficiently repay." Bearing the weight of responsibility for childrearing, women appreciated more fully than men the energy and commitment necessary to raise children. Women's domestic training also prepared them for the nurturant duties which might accompany the care of aged parents. As the final extension of their own domestic responsibilities, women's special duties to parents seemed both deserved and appropriate.[18]

Filial obligations, nonetheless, could impose difficulties. Adding parental cares to their own more immediate duties strained many women, both physically and emotionally. When her aging mother became debilitated with rheumatism, Mary Manning recognized her obligation to help. "But with all the personal sacrifices I can possibly make," she admitted, "I cannot do for her as I wish to do while I have so many other cares." If aging parents appeared to grow melancholy or depressed in old age, daughters could feel particularly frustrated, sensing that their best efforts were simply not enough. Roxana Bolles spent all her time with her aging mother, she wrote, but was unable to cheer or amuse her. Grateful when her mother visited other relatives, Bolles admitted that "it is considerable relief to me for when I am alone with her she is constantly longing for something new, wishing to see someone that will divert her a little." Saddened by her mother's changed, unhappy state, she found her devotion could not resolve her mother's many problems. Patty Rogers openly admitted the negative aspects of filial responsibility, which she experienced all too sharply. "Wonce I could go abroad every day & have company," she wrote in 1785, "but now not a moment can I be absent." It is significant, however, that women expressed such negative responses to filial duty only occasionally.[19]

Older women, too, understood the stress and strain that filial duty imposed on younger daughters. Margaret Bayard Smith's response to a friend's clearly burdensome filial obligation illustrates her ambivalence toward un-swerving sacrifice in the care of aging parents. Writing to her sister in 1834, the fifty-six-year-old Smith expressed the fear of becoming a "burthen" to her own children. Her fear was sparked by the dismal circumstances of her friend Anna Thornton. Despite the fact that Thornton's mother experienced a "new lease on life" in her old age, the physical strain of caring for the old woman took its toll on Thornton. "I truly think long life is not a blessing," wrote Smith. A year later she noted that her friend continued to suffer from the exertions of caring for her mother. The old woman's pro-pensity for visiting particularly distressed her daughter. "She rides almost every afternoon, and often spends the evening out," Smith recorded. "All this is very annoying to [her daughter] Mrs. T. But what can she do? The old lady has always been accustomed to having her own way." Obviously, according to Margaret Smith's interpretation of events in the Thornton household, duty to an aged parent could be immeasurably complicated when the parent failed to behave appropriately.[20]

Margaret Smith was not insensitive to the problems of the old woman. She appreciated her zest for life and her struggle with a variety of health problems. Her sympathy, however, lay with Anna Thornton, whom she regarded "as much a prisoner to the house as her mother." Writing to Thornton, Smith chastized her friend for indulging in a useless "hurtful melancholy" which did not help either her mother or her. Urging Thornton to care for her own health, Smith strongly suggested that she divert her thoughts "from the painful object on which they are continually fixed."[21]

By witnessing the self-imposed misery Anna Thornton maintained in her constant vigil over her mother, Margaret Smith acknowledged the complex reality that could accompany filial obligation. Anna Thornton's sense of duty to her mother, as Smith saw it, exceeded the limits of good sense. Yet Smith admired her friend for her devotion and faithfulness to duty, and she continued to believe that "daughters & only daughters" were appropriate helpmates at the end of life. Nevertheless, Anna Thornton's depressing situation made a firm and long-lasting impression. Unwilling to have her own children put in a similar position, Smith failed to reconcile her long-ingrained belief in filial obligation with the reality of the potential hardships the system could inflict on daughters. Smith's own rather melancholy final years attest to the pain she derived from this dilemma.[22]

Despite the problems inherent in a system dependent on sacrifice and a sense of obligation, women generally responded favorably to a mother's call for help. By caring for and supporting an aged parent, many women affirmed their own sense of domestic mastery and completion while providing an example their own children might follow in later years. The general insecurity of older women's position within society, especially when they were widowed, reinforced women's determination to regard filial duty as their special domain. Often without any financial resources of their own and reliant on a reasonable settlement or at least their widow's third after their husbands' demise, older women were unaccustomed to settling financial affairs and were often surprised at the degree of indebtedness left to them. The moral obligation to which children responded reflected a very real need, felt especially by older widows. Women young and old understood this fear of insecurity and fortified themselves through their reliance on the mother-daughter network. It was, as Margaret Smith described so well, a situation which "daughters & only daughters" understood.[23]

Sons and Mothers

Sons, of course, manifested their own sense of duty and obligation to aged mothers. Although they shared fewer common concerns with their mothers than did their sisters, men perceived that years of early devotion should be rewarded by grateful children as parents grow old. Sons, however, frequently discharged their duty through financial contributions, an avenue seldom open to daughters. Sons were often less skilled in providing emotional support to their aging mothers, but their greater ability to secure the physical comforts necessary in late life was often critical to mothers growing old.[24]

As women contemplated old age, their uneasiness about the future is strikingly revealed in the frequency with which they reminded their sons of their duty to aging parents. Rebecca Shoemaker, thirty-five years before her death, wrote her son Edward in 1784 that she hoped he would be "a Blessing in our Declining years." Elizabeth Izard reminded her son of his own obligations in only slightly more subtle fashion. Describing a neighbor's plan to buy a farmhouse for his mother, she continued, "Good excellent

son he is—he says he never can rest in peace until his Mother is fixed
comfortably for the residue of her days." The uncertainty of this sort of
old-age insurance, however, was evident at every turn. Young men who
joined the patriot cause during the Revolution could, as one woman noted,
"blast" the hopes of aging loyalist parents for support in old age. An epidemic
of yellow fever, as another recorded, could destroy a poor Irish widow's
plans for security. Sheer neglect, despite one's expectations, could bring old
women to what was described as "a state truly deplorable." Regardless of
the risks, older women continued to rely on their sons' sense of duty and
found comfort in knowing that their daughters, too, might reap the benefits
of that same devotion. "What a happiness it is for you that you[']r Blist
with . . . three promising boys that I hope will be a comfort to you in your
old days," wrote Margaret Murray to her stepdaughter Dolly Forbes, trans-
mitting this search for security to yet another generation.[25]

Relationships between aging mothers and sons naturally extended beyond the expectations of financial support in late life. Mothers encouraged
their sons' success and continued to guide the moral development of their
male offspring. Many mothers recognized a special duty to direct their sons
along a road of moral rectitude. Once sons passed through the difficult
teenage years, however, relationships changed. Older women enjoyed friendships with their sons based often on mutual respect but also tinged with a
gnawing uncertainty over changing roles and responsibilities.[26]

Deborah Norris Logan's relationship with her two grown sons provides
an extensively documented illustration of an older woman's devoted, though
sometimes ambivalent, connection to her sons. By the time Logan became
a widow in 1821, her older son Albanus was married and the father of
four. Algernon, her only other surviving child, still lived at home with her.
She depended on Albanus for advice and support and looked forward to his
Sunday visits. But Algernon provided more regular and much needed company and friendship. "I love him I think better than I love my life," she
wrote of Algernon in 1825, adding almost as an afterthought, "as I also do
my other son." In time, Algernon in many respects came to take the place
of her deceased husband. She noted in 1831, for instance, that she felt "as
if I had just parted with his Father," when Algernon set off on a trip. Because
Algernon was unmarried, he seemed to require special care from his mother,
who admitted that her only fear of death was leaving Algernon. "Albanus
has an amiable wife and fine children," she wrote, "to live with him and
cherish his happiness—his brother, only myself."[27]

Deborah Logan was not, however, entirely comfortable in her dealings
with her children. Still a devoted mother who worried about her sons'
welfare, she was at times unsure how to reconcile her concern for their
well-being with the obvious fact that they were grown men. "I think I do

not say enough to them in the way of caution and advice," she wrote in 1822 when both sons set off on a journey, "but I fear to make them shun my company if precise and lecturing." Over time, she increasingly felt deprived of her children's companionship. "They are too sparing of this company to one who loves them as I do," she wrote in 1828.[28]

As an archetypical "Republican Mother," Deborah Logan had raised her sons to become virtuous republican citizens. Although neither son equalled his father's stature in public service or renown, Deborah Logan regarded both as models of integrity and virtue. In her old age, she relied on her sons for guidance and support as well as financial and managerial assistance in the continued operation of her Germantown property. Her friendship with Algernon was steadily reinforced by a growing interdependence. Yet she acknowledged implicit limitations to such relationships. Still dependent on men for protection and direction, she grew in time to realize her own capabilities and the problems which accompanied male protection. Without daughters of her own, Deborah Logan increasingly turned to other female relatives and friends for the companionship and attention she needed. These two elements were best found within the woman's sphere.[29]

Extending the Role of Mother

The pleasures and pains of motherhood extended beyond relationships between mother and child. Nieces and nephews frequently formed part of the family circle, usually (but not always) on a temporary basis. Most women with or without families of their own paid close attention to their siblings' children. In many cases, older women became surrogate mothers for their nieces and nephews, bringing to that role many of the same responsibilities and expectations which accompanied raising their own children. As Carroll Smith-Rosenberg has pointed out, such extended female networks wherein aunts and female friends actively assisted in childrearing may have diffused and eased mother-daughter relationships. They also provided a wider range of contact and companionship for women in their old age.[30]

The extent of older women's involvement with their nieces and nephews varied, but many women routinely cared for their sisters' and brothers' children, especially during summer months. As aunts grew older, they often continued to care not only for their own nieces and nephews but for the next generation as well. Typically, aunts responded to periods of illness and crisis in much the same manner as mothers, offering care and shelter when needed. Young persons, recuperating from illnesses which might have threatened large numbers of siblings in their own homes, frequently spent extended periods of time with their aunts.[31]

The fine line between motherhood and aunthood became imperceptible when aunts completely took charge of their nieces and nephews. Sarah Fisher noted in her diary that Sally Lewis had been left with "the weighty charge of four little children to educate at the advanced time of Life about 70 years." Not all aunts, of course, felt this sense of duty. When her niece was in need of a home, Elizabeth Putnam acknowledged that "some of my friends think I ought to send for her." Yet Putnam's own advanced age, she determined, prohibited such an arrangement. "I think it my duty not to incumber myself with any trouble I can avoyd," she wrote in 1794, indicating that for some old women family obligations could indeed be set aside.[32]

Although bonds between nephews and their aunts could be strong and enduring, the heightened commitment and interdependency between nieces and aunts often resembled the relationship between mothers and daughters. This is especially evident in the sense of responsibility nieces frequently felt toward their aging aunts. Sally Logan Fisher, a devoted diarist, dropped her household duties and her diary during the winter of 1791 while caring for her aged and dying aunt. She found in her aunt's final days both inspiration and pause for reflection. "May my latter end be like hers," she recorded after her aunt's death. In her old age, Nancy Shaw enjoyed an active correspondence with many nieces. Her great-niece Rachel described how fondly her own late mother had regarded her "dear aunt": "Oh! how my mother loved you," she wrote in 1837. As daughters often grieved long after their mother's death, nieces too felt the loss of a close and caring aunt for many years. "Three years have passed since her last day," wrote Louisa Adams Park of her aunt in 1800. "It seems to me ten," she mournfully concluded. Surrogate daughterhood, like surrogate motherhood, could create the same strong bonds characteristic of mother-daughter relationships.[33]

Moral Motherhood

The enduring connection between elderly mothers and their adult female children reflected the experience of feminine bonding in post-revolutionary America. Such bonding represents, in part, a triumph of necessity, as women's limited access to the public sphere forced them together in ways which seem, from a twentieth-century perspective, artificially imposed. Yet few women of the time would have acknowledged either the imposition or the unnaturalness of this gender separation. Instead, such bonding would have been interpreted as a natural component of women's peculiar moral and ethical predisposition. Women were predisposed, they believed, to a heightened sensitivity regarding questions of morality—both temporal and spiritual. They thought and spoke in that "different voice" with which, Carol Gilligan informs us, women today continue to frame their moral decisions. This voice was heard not only in matters of religious or spiritual authority (over which women held an increasingly strong reign within the domestic sphere) but also in the daily world of family and friends, where a feminine morality of connectedness and caring promoted both stability and continuity. As women aged, they continued to develop both the spiritual and temporal aspects of this moral predisposition, anticipating their final years as a last chance to consolidate their efforts and confirm their influence.[34]

The instrumental association of motherhood with morality was not new in the early nineteenth century. Moral guidance and religious training comprised a major part of a Puritan mother's duties, concepts strengthened and fortified with each wave of awakenings and revivals throughout the eighteenth and nineteenth centuries. By the early nineteenth century, however, spiritual guidance as part of the maternal role gained authority and credence as it developed within new organizational frameworks. Maternal associations, which fostered the concept of a mother's obligation to moral training within the home, grew in popularity and prominence throughout the 1820s and 1830s. As the Second Great Awakening encouraged women's membership in organized churches, mothers increasingly controlled the religious allegiances of their children. Young mothers predominated in carrying out much of this new organizational work, and their growing influence served to reinforce the notion that women held peculiar sway over the moral development of younger generations.[35]

This growing association of women with issues of morality and spirituality favored aging mothers as well as younger ones. Women growing old regarded themselves (and were considered by others) as major players in an ongoing spiritual struggle for resignation and preparation for the end of life. This struggle demanded even greater strength and moral energy with each passing year. Witnesses to this highly personal confrontation with the future regarded the process with considerable awe and admiration. Older women who were "upborne by this inward spirit of peace," as Ann Page described her mother in 1805, offered adult children a vigorous model for spiritual aging. For older sons, such models might serve as vigilant reminders of their own moral conflicts in the broader public domain, not known for its adherence to a strict moral code. It was from their female offspring, however, that aging women expected to reap their greatest rewards. "Boys are a cause of great anxiety to parents," wrote Mary Few in 1846. "They have more temptations than girls—and their position is certainly less favourable to preparation for a better world—and after all that is 'the One Thing.'" Male children were undoubtedly in danger of losing their moral way; daughters, on the other hand, were considered by their very nature to be less likely to succumb to the "temptations" of the outside world and were, as a result, more capable of developing their spiritual nature, the "One

Thing" which ultimately mattered in a society increasingly structured by male definitions of success.[36]

Feminine morality was not confined to issues of spiritual redemption and preparation for the end of life. Morality also pertained to the here-and-now, the daily, ongoing business of caring for the physical well-being of friends and loved ones. This aspect of moral commitment found especially fertile ground in motherhood. Advancing age only added new dimensions to the maternal nature of woman's morality.[37]

After watching her ill daughter all night, sixty-year-old Elizabeth Drinker asked wearily, "How many solemn hours of watching have I had in the coarse of my life?" In 1795, the following year, Drinker confessed that she had grown "blunted and callous" after so many vigils, wondering if so much "pain and experience caused resignation?" During the summer of 1797 she assisted two daughters in childbirth. Her son's wife also had a child, and another daughter was ill in bed. "How many anxious moments has an Affectionate Mother," she wrote with typical Quaker restraint. Her daughter Molly Rhoads, who always experienced particularly severe reactions from childbirth, created special anxieties. "How often have I suffer'd Labour pains in my mind for my daughter," she wrote with obvious empathy in 1798 when Molly was a month late in delivering. By the time of her oldest daughter Sally's fatal illness in 1807, old age and infirmities finally imposed some restraints on Elizabeth Drinker's capacity to continue nursing her children. Unable to leave her home, the seventy-three-year-old woman persuaded her daughter to stay with her. Fittingly, Sally Downing died under her mother's roof. "Those who have children and love them—especially married children, have many cares," Drinker wrote, summarizing the experiences of many older women whose commitment to their children and to the ongoing ethic of caring extended far beyond the normal years of childrearing.[38]

Many practical aspects of caring did not diminish as years passed. Older mothers often found that their expertise in nursing and their long-developed skills in coping with death would continue to be employed in old age. During their daughters' confinement both preceding and following childbirth, older women not only nursed their daughters in what was still considered a risky undertaking but also often took charge of other children, freeing the expectant mother from anxieties over her household duties. Women relied heavily on their mothers to help care for ailing children, particularly those with a large number of siblings. When illnesses continued despite a young mother's best care or a doctor's close attention, women frequently returned home for reassurance, advice, and care. During a period when primitive professional medical treatments were often more harmful than the illness itself, older women served to promote the use of older, traditional remedies. They also offered a secure and nurturing environment within which family members could regain their strength.[39]

This extensive, continuous commitment of aged parents to the needs of their grown families did not go unnoticed or unappreciated. Adult daughters, in particular, valued such steadfast services since they recognized the reciprocal nature of feminine filial duty. Eleanor Parke Lewis understood her own maternal duties best, she wrote, when she considered the models of caring within her own family. She could not fail to carry on this tradition of continuing service, she insisted, "when I have such an example constantly before me — when I remember the care, the anxiety, the unremitted attention and affection of my revered Parent to me." Such models became vital to the transmission of a feminine morality from one generation to the next.[40]

As women aged, the importance of intergenerational ties added a new dimension to their evolving perceptions of moral duty. Although long aware that their world derived much of its meaning and value from the connections of family and friends, older women perceived with new appreciation the need for continuity in a world of rapid change. They understood, as well, that they served as a vital link between generations. As repositories of family histories, women attempted to affirm those ties and keep alive those traditions which had sustained them throughout the years.[41]

Many older women who saw themselves as linkages between past and present had witnessed their own mothers perform that same function. Mary Tyler, whose reminiscences written during her eighties provided her family with a rich deposit of family anecdotes and geneological data, adopted a form of expression previously used by her own mother, Elizabeth Hunt Palmer. Margaret Manigault, whose frequent letters to her mother formed a valuable family record, was following a pattern established years before by her grandmother, Elizabeth Colden DeLancey. The values implicit in these records extended beyond the concerns of their immediate families. At a time when heightened geographic mobility was coupled with the gradual displacement of an age-ordered power structure, family ties were often strained. As conservators of the family memory, older women eased the transition from traditional to modern family, functioning as a cohesive, conservative force during a period of dynamic family change.[42]

Early Challenges to the "Empty Nest"

Because motherhood was such a significant component of woman's sphere as it was redefined and enlarged in the early years of the nineteenth century, it might be expected that a child's departure from home upon reaching adulthood would have produced a sense of loneliness and even futility among aged mothers. The "empty nest," as it has come to be known in the twentieth century, has been considered an almost universal symbol of women's diminished usefulness and lack of meaningful occupation in old age. When options outside the domestic sphere are severely limited, as they were in the new republic, the vision of a land littered with empty nests looms large indeed. But before such assumptions about our early foremothers can be made, we should first examine their own responses to the departure of their adult children.[43]

Undoubtedly, the strong attachments between mothers and their children in these early years made separation difficult, often painful. Nonetheless, the duties of motherhood were clear. A mother's obligation at such times was to smooth the transition and help facilitate this important step in her children's lives. Elizabeth Cranch Norton fully understood the appropriateness of her son Richard's departure for college in 1808. She realized, too, the necessity for containing her feelings so she would not distress her son. Even after he left, she struggled to keep herself actively engaged in "domestic business, in order to prevent myself from indulging in too tender feelings—they must be reserved for a solitary hour." Norton, like other mothers, felt the pain of separation, but she also acknowledged an obligation not to inflict that pain on others.[44]

"I feel *too much* alone tonight even to enjoy reading," wrote sixty-four-year-old Anna Blackwood Howell during a stormy night in 1831. "My children, where are they?" A widow who successfully operated fisheries in New Jersey, Howell visited her children at least annually, but she found the period between visits increasingly long and hard. Although she enjoyed being alone and preferred, in fact, her own company to that of most others, Anna Howell clearly felt isolated when separated from her children. This sense of loss did not stem from a lack of occupation or diminished sense of purpose. She merely (but profoundly) missed the companionship and friendship her children had provided. She recorded this loneliness in the privacy of her diary. Once children were gone, mothers (and especially widows) could feel lonely indeed.[45]

Such loneliness did not imply that older women were ready to pull up stakes and move in with their sons and daughters. A fondness for independent living arrangements often overrode a woman's longing to be near her children. "I can't describe to you how I miss you," Elizabeth Dunbar wrote her daughter in 1797. To emphasize the extent of her loneliness, Dunbar added that she would "*almost* give up a home of my own to pass the remainder of my life with you." Almost, but not quite. Anna Cunningham cited a similar reluctance to sacrifice independent living. Nonetheless, because her daughter was ill, Cunningham agreed to move in and help nurse her and care for the grandchildren. "I have felt in Abby's sickness that I could be more usefull here than anywhere," she wrote in 1835. "I think we ought to make ourselves usefull as long as we can...." It is notable, too, that Anna Cunningham expressed no desire to reside with her own mother who was in her nineties and still enjoying an independent existence.[46]

If, as it appears, women willingly risked loneliness to promote the independent welfare of their adult children — and might refuse to jeopardize their own independent existence by residing with married offspring — to what extent did women maintain active ties to their mature children? Did these reformulated ties confirm or deny the presence of an "empty nest" in the lives of these aging and aged mothers?

The diaries of three elderly mothers were examined closely over specified month-long periods in an effort to determine the degree of contact older women maintained with their adult children and to establish visiting patterns. The patterns that emerged are less than definitive, yet the overall findings are clear: aged mothers in the new republic maintained close, active ties with adult children and would have been puzzled indeed by the concept of an "empty nest."[47]

The adult children of Elizabeth Drinker, Rebecca Shoemaker, and Deborah Norris Logan visited their mothers regularly and frequently. Only two of their eleven surviving offspring did not come by regularly. A number of children visited daily, often bringing grandchildren with them. Sometimes the visits involved family business, but they usually consisted of the mundane and familiar activities of everyday life ("helped with curtains," "dined," etc.). Interestingly, no clear gender patterns emerged from these visitations. Elizabeth Drinker's daughters, for example, made every effort to see their mother; Rebecca Shoemaker's sons visited twice as often as her daughters. This, of course, could be explained by the ease with which young men, perhaps already away from home during the business day, could drop by to see their mother. Young women at home with children might find such visits more difficult.[48]

According to the patterns revealed in these three journals, grandchildren maintained contact with grandparents just as their parents did. In several cases it appears that grandchildren carried on the functions of their parents when the middle generation was unable to do so. Such close contact across generations reinforced family bonds at all levels. As might be expected, not all visits were greeted with equal enthusiasm. As Elizabeth Drinker pointed out, having her grandson for the entire day was a "troublesome bargin."[49]

The most singularly consistent feature observed in comparing the visiting patterns of these three diarists is how *infrequently* these aging mothers visited their children. Quite obviously, except in times of illness or childbirth, mothers preferred to be visited than to visit. Initially, mothers may have been reluctant to impose themselves on their children's families. In addition, the declining health of older women might have created difficulties with walking and prolonged visiting. The three women examined here, however, were usually capable of going out. Thus, they appear to have responded to their own well-entrenched beliefs in filial duty in which adult children were obliged to confer special care and affection on their aging parents. Since these duties clearly rested with the younger generation, older women were relieved of the need to go out of their own home to find a child's continued devotion. In addition, these three women all accepted the notion of retirement as an appropriate response to old age. Such retirement, demanding fewer contacts with the outside world while promoting solitude and introspection within the home, reinforced and no doubt helped perpetuate the concept of filial duty and, accordingly, meant fewer visits outside the home.[50]

From the material examined, the concept of an "empty nest" appears inappropriate in describing reactions to child-leaving in post-revolutionary America. The extended period of childrearing prevented any chance of an empty nest for nearly forty years in many cases. While the launching of children into a separate adult sphere occasioned pain and loneliness among a number of women, such initial sorrows were often appeased by continued close contact with married children or those living independently. In addition, grandchildren often played a constant if not daily role in the lives of their grandmothers, and together they could form a mutually rewarding relationship, as will be seen. Adult children, too, might continue to live under the maternal roof. As long as mothering was perceived as an active and viable role for aging women, children's departure from the home did not produce a psychological crisis. Yet without frequent contact with their adult children, older women such as Anna Howell could experience real and prolonged loneliness.[51]

Aging mothers in the new republic were not wholly relieved of the cares and burdens of old age by virtue of their motherhood. Such women knew the loneliness of departure and separation from loved ones, the fears of dependency on adult sons or daughters, and even the prospect of alienation from the younger generation. Nevertheless, rewards of maternal affection and responsibility appear to far outweigh the deficits inherent in highly invested, personal relationships. Motherhood enhanced one's chances of happiness and comfort in old age. It provided not only a traditional (although unreliable) old-age insurance in the form of filial duty but also — perhaps more significant — the promise of continuing service and meaning in old age.

Yet, even in the twentieth century, it is not surprising to find that motherhood adds a substantial, often rewarding dimension to the final years of life. What is significant in these findings is the importance both mothers and children placed on continuing maternal engagement into old age. The expanding scope of the maternal role during those years — both in terms of strengthened mother-daughter bonds and in the spiritual and temporal guidance aged mothers provided to younger generations — offered older women the opportunities for increased self-esteem, support, and companionship in old age. Far from feeling alienated within a "new hierachy of generations," aged women maintained active and satisfying roles as both mothers and daughters in multigenerational settings within the new republic. With their heightened sensitivity to the values of connection and continuity, aged mothers would direct their energies and their hopes to yet a third generation, the ramifications of which we will next explore.[52]

NOTES

1. Anna Cunningham to Nancy Shaw, 14 January 1835, Shaw-Webb Family Papers, AAS.

2. See Nancy F. Cott, *The Bonds of Womanhood: Woman's Sphere in New England, 1780-1835* (New Haven: Yale University Press, 1977), pp. 47, 87; Mary Beth Norton, *Liberty's Daughters: The Revolutionary Experience of American Women, 1750-1800* (Boston: Little, Brown, 1980), pp. 236-38; Linda K. Kerber, *Women of the Republic: Intellect and Ideology in Revolutionary America* (Chapel Hill: University of North Carolina Press, 1980), pp. 269-288; and Mary P. Ryan, *Cradle of the Middle Class: The Family in Oneida County, New York, 1790-1865* (Cambridge: Cambridge University Press, 1981), pp. 89-103.

3. See, for instance, E. M. Bromberg, "Mother-Daughter Relationships in Later Life: Negating the Myths," *Aging* 340 (Fall 1983):15-20; and A. M. Lang and E. M. Brody, "Characteristics of Middle-Aged Daughters and Help to Their Elderly Mothers," *Journal of Marriage and the Family* 45:1 (1983):193-202. Margaret Mead has speculated that "deep biochemical affinities" may exist between mothers and female children. See Mead, *Male and Female* (New York: Morrow, 1975), p. 61.

4. Nancy Chodorow examines mother-daughter ties in her cross-cultural study and maintains that a girl's "final role identification is with her mother and women . . . the person or people with whom she has had the earliest relationship of infantile dependence." Her close tie to her mother is "a personal identification with her mother's traits of character and values." See Chodorow, "Family Structure and Feminine Personality," in *Women, Culture, and Society,* ed. Michelle Zimbalist Rosaldo and Louise Lamphere (Stanford: Stanford University Press, 1974), pp. 43-66, quotes on p. 51.

5. See Carroll Smith-Rosenberg, "The Female World of Love and Ritual: Relations between Women in Nineteenth-Century America," *Signs: Journal of Women in Culture and Society* 1 (Autumn 1975):10-22.

6. Alice Izard to Margaret Manigault, 18 February 1814, and Margaret Manigault to Alice Izard, 21 August 1814, Izard Family Papers, LCMD. See also Ann Lowndes to Rebecca Nicholson, 8 November 18??, Shippen Family Papers, LCMD.

7. Elizabeth Drinker, Diary, 1 June 1800 and 15 March 1806, HSP.

8. Letter of Sarah Hodgdon, undated [ca. 1830], quoted in Thomas Dublin, ed., *Farm to Factory: Women's Letters, 1830-1860* (New York: Columbia University Press, 1981), p. 45.

9. Elizabeth Drinker, Diary, 16 October 1796, HSP.

10. Margaret Bayard Smith to Maria Boyd, 23 June 1836, Margaret Bayard Smith Papers, LCMD. See also Mary P. Ryan, *Cradle of the Middle Class*, p. 193. Contemporary studies also suggest that daughters tend to draw closer to their mothers when they reach middle age. See Corinne Azen Krause, *Grandmothers, Mothers and Daughters: An Oral History Study of Ethnicity, Mental Health, and Continuity of Three Generations of Jewish, Italian, and Slavic-American Women* (New York: Institute on Pluralism and Group Identity of the American Jewish Committee, 1978), pp. 148-50.

11. Elizabeth Denny Ward to Sarah Putnam, April 1825, Ward Family Papers, AAS. Martha Brewster's poem on the departure of her daughter provides an early example of this same loneliness. See Martha Brewster, "A Letter to My Daughter Ruby Bliss," in her *Poems on Diverse Subjects* (New London: T. Green, 1757). See also Abigail Adams to Mary Cranch, 9 January 1791, *New Letters of Abigail Adams, 1788-1801*, ed. Stewart Mitchell (Boston: Houghton Mifflin, 1947), p. 68; and Narcissa Whitman to her mother, 2 May 1840, in *Roots of Bitterness: Documents of the Social History of American Women*, ed. Nancy Cott (New York: E. P. Dutton, 1972), p. 231. Julie Roy Jeffrey describes the strong pull of family association on young women moving west in *Frontier Women: The Transmississippi West, 1840-1880* (New York: Hill and Wang, 1979), pp. 3-24.

12. Elizabeth Drinker, Diary, 9 January 1795, HSP; Lucy Tappan Pierce to John Pierce, 15 June 1826, Poor Family Papers, SL; Weltha Stetson to Nancy Shaw, 28 December 1845, Shaw-Webb Family Papers, AAS. See also Fanny Tracy to Polly Rindge, October 1828, Hooker Collection, SL; S. Whiting to Sophia Barnard, 25 January 1837, Barnard Family Papers, LCMD; Sally Wister's journal quoted in Elizabeth Evans, *Weathering the Storm: Women of the American Revolution* (New York: Scribner, 1975), p. 151. Special bonds between mothers and daughters were evident in death as in life. According to Suzanne Lebsock, most grants of separate estate (in Petersburg, Virginia) to other women were from mother to daughter. She also found that women ordinarily favored daughters in their wills. See Lebsock, *The Free Women of Petersburg: Status and Culture in a Southern Town, 1784-1860* (New York: W. W. Norton, 1984), pp. 78, 135.

13. Elizabeth Drinker, Diary, 28 September 1807, HSP. See also Sarah Rhoads on the death of her daughter Mary Rhoads, quoted in Norton, *Liberty's Daughters*, pp. 103-4; Elizabeth Putnam to Samuel Ward, 15 May 1788, Chandler-Ward Family Papers, AAS; and Elizabeth Bowen, Diary, 18 May 1797, EI.

14. Margaret Bayard Smith to Jane Kirkpatrick, 26 October 1838, and Margaret Bayard Smith to Bayard Smith, 25 July 1839, Margaret Bayard Smith Papers, LCMD.

15. Norton, *Liberty's Daughters,* pp. 96-97, 100. See also Terri L. Premo, " 'A Blessing to our Declining Years': Feminine Response to Filial Duty in the New Republic," *International Journal of Aging and Human Development* 20:1 (1985):69-74.

16. "My Mother," 1815, quoted in Ryan, *Cradle of the Middle Class,* p. 31; Elizabeth Phoenix to John Pierce, 1 July 1818, Poor Family Papers, SL; Margaret Bayard Smith to Maria Boyd, Christmas 1835, Margaret Bayard Smith Papers, LCMD. See also Susanna Dillwyn to William Dillwyn, 31 March 1790, Dillwyn Manuscripts, LCP/HSP; Elizabeth Drinker, Diary, 2 August 1798, HSP; Rebecca Shoemaker, Journal, 7 July 1813, Rawle Family Papers, HSP; Elizabeth Graeme Ferguson to Mrs. Campbell, 9 May 1799, in Simon Gratz, ed., "Some Material for a Biography of Elizabeth Ferguson, nee Graeme," *Pennsylvania Magazine of History and Biography* 41 (December 1917):389-90; and, as an indication of the enduring quality of this notion of feminine filial duty, see Mary Israel Ellet, *Memoirs of Mary Israel Ellet, 1780-1870,* ed. Herbert P. Gambrell (Doylestown, Pa.: Bucks County Historical Society, 1939), p. 61.

17. Malenda M. Edwards to Sabrina Bennett, 18 August 1845, quoted in Dublin, ed., *Farm to Factory,* p. 86; Lydia Sigourney, *Letters of Life* (New York: D. Appleton, 1866), pp. 241, 258.

18. Catherine Maria Sedgwick to Theodore Sedgwick, 1 February 1801, Catherine Maria Sedgwick I Papers, MHS; Sarah Logan Fisher, Diary, 25 March and 19 July 1790, HSP. See also Elizabeth Putnam to Dorothy Chandler Ward, 10 February 1789, Chandler-Ward Family Papers, AAS; Grace Growden Galloway, Diary, 5 August 1779, "Diary of Grace Growden Galloway," ed. Raymond C. Werner, *Pennsylvania Magazine of History and Biography* 58 (April 1934):165-66; and Charlotte Chambers, *Memoir of Charlotte Chambers,* ed. Lewis H. Garrard (Philadelphia: by the author, 1856), p. 97.

19. Mary Manning to Elizabeth C. Hawthorne, 7 April 1822, Hawthorne-Manning Collection, EI; Roxana Bolles to Sophia Griswold Barnard, 27 November 1836, Barnard Family Papers, LCMD; Patty Rogers, Diary, n.d. 1785, Rogers Family Diaries, AAS. Responsibilities to both younger and older generations can feel especially burdensome to adult daughters today as demographic changes increase the likelihood of multigenerational families while changes in work patterns extend women's nonfamilial responsibilities. See Audrey Borenstein, *Chimes of Change and Hours: Views of Older Women in Twentieth-Century America* (Cranbury, N.J.: Associated University Presses, 1983), p. 45.

20. Margaret Bayard Smith to Jane Kirkpatrick, 3 August 1834 and 17 July 1835, Margaret Bayard Smith Papers, LCMD.

21. Ibid., 16 April 1835; Margaret Bayard Smith to Anna Thornton, Christmas 1835, William Thornton Papers, LCMD.

22. The overwhelming majority of extant letters and diaries suggest that only material revealing successful mother-daughter ties was retained in family collections; the letters documenting the unhappy relationship between Alice Shippen and her daughter Ann Livingston survive as a rare exception. See Alice Shippen to William Shippen III, 14 August [1801], and Margaret Livingston to Ann Livingston, 24 February 1797, Shippen Family Papers, LCMD.

23. This theme is described in more detail in chapter one, above. From her study on the ethics of caring, Nel Noddings writes that "we behave ethically toward one another . . . because we carry with us the memories of and longing for caring and being cared for." See Noddings, *Caring: A Feminine Approach to Ethics and Moral Education* (Berkeley: University of California Press, 1984), p. 149.

24. Because few women earned substantial incomes of their own, daughters were seldom expected to provide the financial assistance deemed appropriate for sons. Lydia Sigourney proved an exception, however. Maintaining the "privilege of working for my parents" through the sale of her books, Sigourney contributed to her parents' well-being during years of separation from them. It was, she wrote, her "sacred joy." See Sigourney, *Letters of Life*, p. 258.

25. Rebecca Shoemaker to Edward Shoemaker, 26 October 1784, Shoemaker Papers, HSP; Elizabeth Izard to William Shippen III, 16 September 1823, Shippen Family Papers, LCMD; Elizabeth Inman to John Innes Clark, 4 January 1777, James M. Robbins Papers, MHS; Elizabeth Drinker, Diary, 19 November 1793, HSP; Elizabeth Inman to ?, 17 October 1779, James M. Robbins Papers, MHS; Margaret Murray to Dolly Forbes, 21 December 1784, James M. Robbins Papers, MHS. See also Mary McDonald to Alexander and Anna McDonald, 21 February 1813, McDonald-Lawrence Papers, GHS; Elizabeth Putnam to Samuel Ward, 10 February 1789, Chandler-Ward Family Papers, AAS; and Elizabeth Denny Ward to Thomas Ward, 24 February 1836, Ward Family Papers, AAS. The great number of winter dates among these examples suggests that women's concern for their future well-being was heightened during the long, cold months of winter.

26. See Judith Sargent Murray's ["Constantia"] comments on the value of sons in *The Gleaner, a Miscellaneous Production*, 3 vols. (Boston: I. Thomas and E. T. Andrews, 1798), 3:206.

27. Deborah Norris Logan, Diary, 10 August 1825, 9 May 1831, and 14 September 1827, HSP. See Elizabeth Drinker's Diary, 2 December 1802, HSP, where she relates her own mortality to her children's continued existence.

28. Deborah Norris Logan, Diary, 14 October 1822 and 25 May 1828, HSP. See also ibid., 22 February 1835.

29. See ibid., 17 July 1838. Although women of Deborah Logan's generation were denied the right to participate actively in the political process, they could indirectly express themselves through influence on their sons. Linda Kerber discusses this notion of "republican motherhood" in *Women of the Republic*, pp. 12, 269-88.

30. Smith-Rosenberg, "Female World," p. 17.

31. See Betsy Coles to Maria Singleton, 12 March 1825, Singleton Family Papers, LCMD; Deborah Norris Logan, Diary, September 1830, HSP; Abigail Prescott to Mehitable Dawes, March 1805, May-Goddard Papers, SL; and Anna Green Winslow, *The Diary of Anna Green Winslow*, ed. Alice M. Earle (Boston: Houghton Mifflin, 1894), passim.

32. Sally Logan Fisher, Diary, 22 February 1786, HSP; Elizabeth Putnam to Dorothy Chandler Ward, 16 December 1794, Chandler-Ward Family Papers, AAS.

Deborah Logan cared for two orphaned nieces for nearly twenty years. See Logan, *Diary*, April 1815, January 1822, and 13 May 1832, HSP.

33. Sally Logan Fisher, *Diary*, 20 February 1791, HSP; Rachel ? to Nancy Shaw, 15 January 1839, Shaw-Webb Family Papers, AAS; Louisa Adams Park, *Diary*, December 1800, Park Family Papers, AAS. See also the letters of Mary Page to her niece Rebecca Nicholson for an example of an active correspondence between an aging aunt and her niece, in William B. Randolph Papers, LCMD. Note also Sarah Connell Ayer, *Diary of Sarah Connell Ayer, 1805-35* (Portland, Maine: Lefavor-Tower, 1910), pp. 53, 87, 197.

34. According to Carol Gilligan, "in the different voice of women lies the truth of an ethic of care, the tie between relationship and responsibility, and the origins of aggression in the failure of connection." See Gilligan, *In a Different Voice: Psychological Theory and Women's Development* (Cambridge: Harvard University Press, 1984), p. 173.

35. See, for instance, Sarah Hodgdon's 1830 inquiry to her mother as to "whether it is best to go to the babptist or to the methodist," as quoted in Dublin, ed., *Farm to Factory*, p. 45. See also Barbara Welter, "The Feminization of American Religion, 1800-1860," in *Clio's Consciousness Raised: New Perspectives on the History of Women*, ed. Mary Hartman and Lois Banner (New York: Harper and Row, 1976), pp. 137-57; and Mary Ryan, *Cradle of the Middle Class*, pp. 104, 142, passim.

36. Ann R. Page to Mrs. Elizabeth Adams, November 1805, William B. Randolph Papers, LCMD; Mary Few to Rebecca Nicholson, 23 January 1846, Shippen Family Papers, LCMD.

37. Carol Ochs describes the special qualities of maternal insight into questions of morality and spirituality in *Women and Spirituality* (Totowa, N.J.: Rowman and Allanheld, 1983), pp. 28-33, passim.

38. Elizabeth Drinker, *Diary*, 26 June 1794, 6 April 1795, 19 July 1797, 25 September 1798, 1 February 1803, and 9 September 1807, HSP. See also Anne Dade Bolling to George Washington Bolling, 6 June 1840, quoted in Suzanne Lebsock, *The Free Women of Petersburg*, p. 161.

39. See Lucy Tappan Pierce to John Pierce, 8 June 1803, Poor Family Papers, SL; Jane Gray Haxall to Louisa Shippen, 17 September 1825, and Mary Page to Rebecca Nicholson, 2 September 1823, Shippen Family Papers, LCMD; Anna Cunningham to Nancy Shaw, 14 January 1835, Shaw-Webb Family Papers, AAS; and Rebecca Noyes, *Diary*, 29 June 1831, CHS. Adult daughters were well aware that their mothers continued to share many of the same problems they themselves faced. "My dear Mother has just recovered from her confinement with her twentieth Child," wrote Eleanor Parke Lewis in 1802. See Eleanor Parke Lewis to Mary Pinckney, 3 January 1802, Pinckney Family Papers, LCMD.

40. Eleanor Parke Lewis to Mary Pinckney, 9 May 1801, Pinckney Family Papers, LCMD. See also Peggy Livingston to Ann Livingston, n.d., F. F. Chrystie to Rebecca Nicholson, 3 January 1791, and Catherine Few to Rebecca Nicholson, 9 March 1825, Shippen Family Papers, LCMD.

41. See Terri L. Premo, " 'Like a Being Who Does Not Belong': The Old Age

of Deborah Norris Logan," *Pennsylvania Magazine of History and Biography* 107 (January 1983):85-112.

42. Attributes of this new modern family, just coming into focus in the early nineteenth century, are described by Carl N. Degler and include (1) marriages based on mutual affection and respect; (2) child care and household maintenance placed firmly in the hands of women, considered morally superior; (3) increased focus on children as special, unique individuals; and (4) reduced family size. See Carl N. Degler, *At Odds: Women and the Family in America from the Revolution to the Present* (Oxford: Oxford University Press, 1980), pp. 8-9. While the "modern" family is recognized as a nineteenth-century phenomenon, many of its characteristics would have been familiar to the late eighteenth-century women described in this study. Changes in the concept of family are also examined in Philip Greven, *The Protestant Temperament: Patterns of Child-Rearing, Religious Experience, and the Self in Early America* (New York: Knopf, 1977), and in Barry Levy, "The Birth of the 'Modern Family' in Early America: Quaker and Anglican Families in the Delaware Valley, Pennsylvania, 1681-1750," in *Friends and Neighbors: Group Life in America's First Plural Society,* ed. Michael W. Zuckerman (Philadelphia: Temple University Press, 1982), pp. 25-64. See also Linda A. Pollock, *Forgotten Children: Parent-Child Relations from 1500 to 1900* (New York: Cambridge University Press, 1984).

43. The concept of the "empty nest" in contemporary society has itself been challenged. Robert C. Atchley contends that "women generally look forward to having their children launched." See Atchley, *Social Forces and Aging,* 4th ed. (Belmont, Calif.: Wadsworth, 1985), p. 96.

44. Elizabeth Cranch Norton, Diary, 17 October 1808, Norton Papers, MHS. See also Margaret Bayard Smith to Jane Kirkpatrick, 9 February 1839, Margaret Bayard Smith Papers, LCMD; and Mary McDuffie to Marion Singleton, 11 February 1830, Singleton Family Papers, LCMD.

45. Anna Blackwood Howell, Diary, n.d. 1831, AAS; see also entries for 1832 and June 1833.

46. Elizabeth H. Dunbar to Elizabeth Shippen, 21 February 1797 (emphasis added), Shippen Family Papers, LCMD; Anna Cunningham to Nancy Shaw, 14 January 1835, Shaw-Webb Family Papers, AAS.

47. While this sample is certainly not statistically sound, these three diarists (Elizabeth Drinker, Rebecca Shoemaker, and Deborah Norris Logan) reveal detailed data simply unavailable in most other journals of the period. See Elizabeth Drinker, Diary, May 1798, HSP; Rebecca Shoemaker, Journal, 23 October to 22 November 1805, Rawle Family Papers, HSP; and Deborah Norris Logan, Diary, May 1832, HSP. For more complete details, see Terri L. Premo, "Women Growing Old in the New Republic: Personal Responses to Old Age, 1785-1835" (Ph.D. dissertation, University of Cincinnati, 1983), pp. 128-35.

48. All three women were members of the Society of Friends, and their Quaker heritage undoubtedly influenced their attitudes toward family unity and cohesiveness. Nevertheless, from the patterns of family visitation established by these women it is possible to determine to some extent the importance such

middle-class women attached to continued close relationships with their adult children.

49. Elizabeth Drinker, Diary, 29 May 1798, HSP. Drinker had twenty-five grandchildren at the time of her death.

50. See chapter six, below, for further development of the concept of retirement.

51. See Robert V. Wells, "Women's Lives Transformed: Demographic and Family Patterns in America, 1600-1970," in *Women in America: A History*, ed. Carol Ruth Berkin and Mary Beth Norton (Boston: Houghton Mifflin, 1979), pp. 22, 27.

52. Quote from David Hackett Fischer, *Growing Old in America*, 2d ed. (New York: Oxford University Press, 1978), p. 78.

Grandmotherhood in the New Republic

As a young woman about to marry her cousin and friend Samuel Smith in 1800, Margaret Bayard found herself in a precarious position. Although young, she held firm political ideas which usually ran counter to those of her future husband. Well educated for her time and possessing a distinctive talent for writing, she was nonetheless about to enter a union which would encourage her husband's achievements rather than her own. No doubt, too, she sensed the tenuous nature of close relationships, having witnessed the deaths of both her mother and stepmother at an early age. So when she wrote to Samuel Smith during those days of courtship, she often described those elements of her life which seemed permanent. None appeared more stable and more resistant to change than her relationship to her grandmother.

"She possesses my most affectionate and unreserved confidence," Margaret Bayard wrote, recalling time spent with the old woman. "It was my common practice to set at her feet on a little Bench and not only relate the common occurrences of the day, but all the intrests of my heart, and every thing which related to me. . . . My drawing, my writing, my reading, were all of consequence to her, and [she] intrested herself in these pursuits as much as if I was her daughter. . . . My heart feels so intrested in this subject, that I can scarce turn my pen to any other."[1]

Over the years, of course, Margaret Bayard Smith did indeed "turn her pen" to other pursuits. A published writer and well-known commentator on Washington society as well as a wife and mother, she juggled with apparent success a variety of roles and expectations. Yet as a grandmother, she manifested little of that direction and stability she had known and enjoyed as a young woman. The world had changed around her, and in old age she found herself unable to counsel her granddaughter with either the authority or confidence that her own grandmother had exhibited years before. That she relied so heavily on the presence of grandchildren in her late life only added to her obvious dilemma.

For women such as Margaret Bayard Smith whose adult lives spanned a period of enormous, often unsettling change, the reality of that change often surfaced in their relationships with their grandchildren. By the 1830s, grandmothers could no longer feel certain that their values, based on a continuity of roles and traditions, would be appreciated or adopted by a third generation that seemed to embody all that was new and changing. Despite this — or perhaps because of it — grandmothers pinned their hopes on this generation, seeing in them both their past and their future.

A Promise of Continuity

Mothers of adult children in the new republic could not long rest on their laurels. In addition to their continuing interaction with grown off-spring, older women spent their final years actively engaged in yet another round of maternal commitment. Although grandmaternal responsibilities were usually less constant and demanding than those of motherhood, they drew on the special skills and qualities which years of experience granted to aging women. Frequent, often daily contact with young grandchildren offered women a chance to influence the development of a third generation; it also promised a vital (and visible) sense of continuity, enabling women to perceive themselves within a larger, organic vision of life, death, and regeneration. This was most apparent at the birth of a grandchild.[2]

"How anxious shall I be to see the brat," wrote Elizabeth Dunbar in 1791, anticipating the birth of her grandson William Shippen III. "I shall dearly love it," she added. When the "brat" himself became a father in 1818, his own mother repeated similar sentiments. "I am so happy that the dear little soul is here," confided Elizabeth Izard to her son. Well-grounded fears associated with childbirth and infant mortality only increased the elation and relief family members felt at the arrival of a healthy baby.[3]

Grandmothers, reliving the experience of birth and motherhood, quickly recognized familiar qualities in their grandchildren. "You will be as fond of your Grandchildren as ever you was of your own," Abigail Adams wrote to her sister in 1790. "Does not the little fellow feel as if he was really your own?" Indeed, for many grandmothers the distinction between gen-erations blurred, and grandmothers discussed their children and grandchil-dren in interchangeable terms. Although the reality of grandmotherhood imposed certain obvious differences from that of parenthood, many grand-mothers regarded their grandchildren as their own children.[4]

With the arrival of grandchildren, aging women continued their pri-mary role as caretaker, functioning as important sources of nurture and support within the family. During periods of illness or stress, grandmothers frequently took charge of young children, often for months at a time. "I consider it a Providential circumstance that our good Mother has the care of the children, now they are sick," wrote Lucy Tappan Pierce in 1805. "I am sure I should not know what to do for them." When young Nancy Izard's health continued to decline despite the physician's best treatment, her mother wrote anxiously to the child's grandmother: "I confess I should feel more satisfied if she were with her *dear Grand Mama.*" When Nancy Izard did not improve under the doctor's care, she was sent to her grand-mother's home, where she finally began to mend. In these and other cases, grandmothers appeared confident of the quality of care they could bring to their family. Their children shared their confidence. Grandmothers who could combine maternal attentiveness with years of experience were often regarded as the most effective source of pediatric care in the early republic.[5]

Sound minds, grandmothers knew, were as vital as healthy bodies. As opportunities for education expanded following the Revolution, grand-mothers recognized a duty to encourage literacy and schooling among their grandchildren, both male and female. Some instructed grandchildren in their own homes; others living at a distance nonetheless participated in their grandchildren's education. In a letter to her daughter, Mary Parker Norris could not refrain from admonishing each of her three grandsons for their failure to read and study. "If Gustavus means to keep in my favor," she wrote in 1795, "he must be able to read a Chapter in the Bible when we meet." Expectations were set high and at an early age. Abigail Adams's three-year-old granddaughter Susan knew all her "goody Goose stories by Heart," but Adams believed that the youngster would also be reading "if only she had a good school" to attend. Some women financed their grand-children's education. Despite severe family disunity, Margaret Beekman Livingston fought diligently to procure a proper education for her grand-daughter Peggy. Like Peggy Livingston, Frances Mutter appreciated her grand-mother's commitment to education. "[She] says nothing shall be left undone on her part that can possibly tend to our advantage," Mutter wrote to her cousin in 1815. The importance attached to literacy and education during this postwar period can be traced, at least in part, to grandmothers who supported such values.[6]

The eagerness of grandmothers to promote and protect their young grandchildren extended to discipline as well. Love and discipline went hand in hand in guiding a child's development, and grandmothers were seldom reluctant to demand proper behavior. Informing grandmother of bad behavior could be, in fact, "the greatest punishment" inflicted on an errant grandchild, according to Ann Livingston. When another grandmother sent a fan and a thimble to her granddaughter in 1822, she included certain behavioral expectations. "If she does not spit on the floor," wrote Grandmama, "she will find them very pretty indeed." While grandmothers were occasionally cited for "spoiling" their grandchildren, most remained firm in their conviction that behavior could be modified by giving (as well as withdrawing) grandmaternal attention.[7]

Expectations and Obligations: A Mixed Blessing

As grandmothers grew older, relationships with grandchildren changed. Friendships between young children and their grandmothers, often intimate and close, altered as teenage and adult grandchildren assumed new roles of their own. Close ties could remain — and often did — yet the nature of those ties was influenced by prevailing notions of filial duty. Norms motivating adult children to care for aged mothers also applied to grandmothers, leading them to expect care and companionship in old age. For some women, such expectations were met with cheerful, loving compliance; for others more vulnerable to feelings of neglect, the promise of filial duty yielded only frustration and the emptiness of unfulfilled hopes.

Grandmothers expected frequent contact with younger family members. Rebecca Shoemaker found it noteworthy, in fact, if none of her children or grandchildren called on a given day. A number of grandmothers lived with their grandchildren. Margaret Morris, who had raised one granddaughter, spent her final years living with the family of another grandchild. Although grandparents readily acknowledged a child's first duty was to the parents, they believed the child's sense of obligation should extend to all those family members who took part in the child's upbringing. Elizabeth Drinker provides a case in point. In 1800, she gathered her ten grandchildren together, lining them up according to age; her reflections reveal the value she placed on grandchildren as they related to the rest of the family. "May they live to be a comfort to all those that love them," she wrote, adding, "or may they be taken in a state of innocence from the evel to come!" It was better to die an early and innocent death, she seemed to say, than to fail in providing comfort to one's family.[8]

Daughters and granddaughters were, for the most part, interchangeable in providing service and care to ailing grandmothers. Young women who resided with their grandmothers often assumed that sense of special responsibility characterizing mother-daughter relationships. Hannah Emery Abbott, recently married and living apart from her grandmother, felt the frustration of not being able to provide full-time care for the older woman when she became ill. "It has not been in my power to be with her so much as I wished and as she appeared to desire," she sadly admitted to her friend Mary Carter in 1791.[9]

Grandparental care was often long-term, demanding from the caretaker an acceptance of terminal illness and the inevitability of death. Young caretakers often appeared stoical beyond their years. Typical were the comments of Elizabeth Pierce during her grandmother's illness in 1826. "Oh! What a privilege that I have been permitted to be with her so much this winter," wrote Elizabeth Pierce in her journal. Confined to her grandmother's home, she was nonetheless thankful that "kind Providence has shut me up so that I could not leave her much."[10]

The sense of responsibility grandchildren felt toward their grandparents was fostered by parents and grandparents alike. Some grandmothers actively recruited help from their grandchildren. Lucy Pierce's elderly mother proclaimed it would be "cruel" to deprive her of her granddaughter's company and assistance. Such an argument no doubt influenced Lucy in her decision to leave Sarah with her grandmother. For the most part, however, aged parents did not need to resort to such pressure, as parents themselves instilled a sense of duty and responsibility in their offspring.[11]

When grandchildren proved remiss in their behavior, parental reaction could be swift and cutting. "I greatly fear unless you alter your deportment you will be forever detested," Elizabeth Izard warned her son, whose behavior toward his grandmother she could only describe as "unparalleled insolence." Like other mothers, she believed filial duty should be reinforced at each generational level. Such responsibilities, mothers believed, not only eased relationships within individual families but also fostered an appreciation for family stability and order, qualities which seemed occasionally threatened in the turbulent years of the new republic.[12]

Yet even the most persistent reminders of filial duty could fall on deaf ears. Obligations stretching several generations might appear unrealistic to young persons eager to make their own mark in a society that increasingly promoted individuality rather than interdependency. Grandsons were notably negligent. Women growing old discovered that grandsons often failed to provide meaningful companionship, even in cases where grandmothers resided with their grandsons. Jane Mecom appreciated the opportunity to live with her grandson's family, but she admitted that such live-in arrangements had their drawbacks. Anxious for some conversation and perhaps intimacy, Mecom found her grandson taciturn and uncommunicative. He was, she wrote, "agreeable when he talks but that is but little." Deborah Logan, nearly fifty years later, revealed a similar problem in relating to her grandson, despite the fact that he resided with her at Stenton and she was not, like Mecom, dependent on her grandson in his own home. "I seldom see my Grandson except at meals," Logan wrote in 1837. "He is kind and obliging, but neither knows nor cares about what constitutes my Beau-Ideal," she wrote, adding "[he] delights not in company or conversation." Deborah Logan's expectations clearly indicate her need for companionship and, no doubt, intellectual stimulation as well. Both these women acknowledged the gratitude they felt toward their grandsons, but they also revealed something was indeed missing in the relationship.[13]

Ties between grandmother and grandson were often marred by unmet expectations. This could be particularly obvious during times of illness or incapacity when older women came to rely on their grandsons for solace as well as companionship. Alice Shippen's close though demanding relationship with her grandson illustrates the expectations and frustrations of a lonely old woman. Believing, as she reminded her grandson, that "your dear Grandfather left me to your care," Alice Shippen continually hounded her grandson for visits during the last years of her life. Because she raised William Shippen III after his father's death, she expected this favorite grandchild to provide comfort and care in her final days. "Not seeing nor hearing from you so long is too much for me now," she wrote him over and over for a period of many years. She, in fact, could not understand his need for straying from the grandparental home at all. "Where will you go that you will find one who loves you more than your Affectionate Grandmother?" she inquired in 1816 in a tone which had become increasingly demanding over the years. Having earlier cast aside her only daughter, Alice Shippen now depended too heavily on the care and affection of her grandson who, fresh from medical school, seemed anxious to establish his independence. Late in life, Alice Shippen paid a bitter, lonely price for the alienation she had earlier enforced.[14]

The disappointment and conflict experienced by these unhappy grandmothers suggest more than a mere "generation gap" (although elements of this phenomenon were no doubt also at play). The inability of some grandsons to satisfy the emotional needs of their grandmothers—and, as noted earlier, the perception that sons, too, were remiss—attests to the inherently flawed construction of the concept of filial duty. Parents and children agreed theoretically to a bargain regarding parental responsibilities: sacrifices incurred in childrearing should be repaid when parents became old. The burden, however, fell heaviest on women, the primary caregivers at both the beginning and end of life. While sons and grandsons were expected to share filial responsibilities, they often acknowledged such duties by rendering financial support and services; daughters and granddaughters, on the other hand, provided nurturance and companionship. Whereas male contributions were dependent on access to and control of property, female support demanded, above all else, time and energy. Yet, in their old age, women tended to fuse these clearly defined gender roles. On the one hand, they continued to believe that "daughters and only daughters" best served the needs of aging parents; on the other, they demanded from their sons and grandsons the same loving care and companionship which were, by custom and design, deemed "feminine" virtues. As gender roles solidified during the early nineteenth century, the irony of such expectations should have been apparent. Women raised their children to fulfill different functions—indeed, to live in different spheres—but nonetheless they believed that as adults *all* their children would be equally capable and anxious to make good their part of the bargain. That their disappointment was foreordained did not diminish its bitterness.[15]

Conservators in a World of Change

As their grandchildren aged, grandmothers increasingly recognized the generational differences which tended to separate, if not divide, them from their children's offspring. These generational differences, always a factor in relationships between young and old, were clearly exacerbated by changes beyond the world familiar to aging women. Opportunities in a growing nation with an expanding work force lured young people (including even some young women) away from home and the protections that home implied. According to many grandmothers, personal gain rather than civic virtue motivated this new generation of Americans. Social and technological change, so hard for many older women to accept, seemed to be greeted wholeheartedly by young adults eager to jump on the new American bandwagon. Tempted by new possibilities and no longer as rigidly circumscribed by traditional notions of duty, young people embodied new ideas that appeared to threaten the most fundamental sources of stability.[16]

"Youth is thoughtless and Blame Age without Consideration or Pity," complained Deborah Logan in 1838. In her final year of life, often unwell and cranky, Logan increasingly interpreted conflict in generational terms. Over time her sense of self-pity and isolation had intensified, and she had come to believe no one was willing to help her. Her distrust of youth extended from her young household help to youthful friends and occasionally to grandchildren as well. "If the young reflected on how grateful their notice is to their aged friends, I believe they would frequently bestow it," she wrote four months before her death.[17]

Deborah Logan's interpretation of generational disharmony in late life is particularly poignant in light of her determination in earlier years to maintain close ties with young people. "I think a mixture of the old and young makes the most pleasing society," she wrote in 1826, a belief which she actively practiced as well as preached. The following year she again emphasized her commitment to her grandchildren's generation. She had no doubts, she wrote, of the positive effects of friendship between young and old. Benefitting from the "cheerful animation" of youthful friends, she in turn hoped to guide young people in the "practical truths" years of experience had provided. Such truths were best taught through her own "living example," which included a penchant for early rising and a love of literature. Although she sometimes expressed surprise at the attention given her by younger people, she obviously took seriously her role as mentor and model.[18]

In the intervening decade, however, Deborah Logan's dedication to strong intergenerational ties had obviously weakened. To an extent, her attitude might have been influenced by a general disgust with change of all kinds, particularly evident in the political and religious (Quaker) turmoil of the day. It is also possible, however, that she accurately gauged an increased sense of individualism and self-will among her younger acquaintances during the 1830s. When her niece Hepzibah Norris ran away from Stenton and eloped in 1834, for instance, Logan felt powerless against such a strong-willed young woman. Her young household help, whom she complained about so frequently toward the end of her life, walked out on her *in toto* in 1838, leaving her angry and bewildered. Even among her grandchildren she sensed a reluctance to share their time and company. In 1835 she advised young people to "at least *seem* interested" in what old persons had to say, and she suggested some guidelines for conducting conversations with the elderly. Such advice indicates that she preferred an idealized *pro forma* relationship to genuine intercourse and that the honest exchange of ideas between the old and young mattered less than the appeasement of an older ego. It also clearly reveals that by 1835 Deborah Logan no longer believed young persons were interested in her thoughts or ideas.[19]

Deborah Logan's increasing inability to relate to young people might have been symptomatic of the physical and emotional changes which can accompany old age. It also revealed, however, the influence of social change. While the "cult of youth" described by David Hackett Fischer exaggerates the extent of change between age groups in the early nineteenth century, there is no doubt that significant cultural change was underway. Thomas Cole, in his study of old age in the nineteenth century, argues that the theological underpinnings which had provided a "culturally viable ideal of old age" began to erode by the 1830s. Although his research does not specifically address the special concerns of women and aging, it confirms the significance of this period in the history of age relations. Women who grew up and grew old trusting in the ties between generations were challenged by subtle but persistent evidence of change. The growing sense of intergenerational hostility revealed by Deborah Norris Logan suggests the increasing vulnerability and uncertainty that would eventually weaken the confidence and the status of older women over the course of the next hundred years.[20]

Grandmothers/Granddaughters:
A Vision of Themselves

Nonetheless, most women during this early period continued to perceive the world from a distinctly feminine vantage point that blunted the effects of change outside their sphere. As already noted, the consolidation of woman's sphere in the early nineteenth century fortified, rather than diminished, women's status in old age. Basic tenets ascribed to that sphere fostered an ongoing sense of commitment and responsibility which supported aging women in their final years. For women who subscribed to those tenets of domesticity, old age continued to be defined in terms of home, family, and a continuity of values and beliefs. Not the least among these was the conviction that women, young and old, should take special delight in each other.

Grandmothers enjoyed seeing themselves reflected in the voice, appearance, and habits of their granddaughters. "That bad Jane is like a piece of myself," Elizabeth Izard wrote to her son, relishing the special bond she felt toward her eldest granddaughter. Another grandmother, Jane Gray Haxall, expressed both amusement and pride in recounting her granddaughter's propensity to talk "incessantly." "When I rebuke her for it," Haxall wrote, "she says you know Grand Mama[,] Papa says I am exactly like you for talking." In a world which afforded them little opportunity for self-expression, grandmothers found in the shared traits and characteristics of their granddaughters an affirmation of their own identity.[21]

Visits between grandmothers and their granddaughters could have an empowering effect on old women. One ninety-year-old grandmother, for instance, attributed her continued intellectual stamina to the presence of her granddaughter. "These flashes [of intellect], my dear Elvira, are like those of the summer lightning fly," Elvira's grandmother reportedly said. "They are excited by your presence, but when you are gone all will be dark again." The possibility that Mary Carter might visit her ailing grandmother elicited high expectations. "It will make Grandmama 10 years younger to see you," wrote Hannah Emery who, six weeks later, would suggest that such a visit might cure Grandmama's rheumatism. Even Deborah Logan, whose late-life frustrations were often interpreted in generational terms, enjoyed an exceptionally close relationship with her granddaughter Elizabeth Logan, "the most beautiful and the Best of Grandchildren." The special intimacy between Deborah and Elizabeth was apparent in the earliest pages of Logan's diary. "Dear little Elizabeth delighted to see me, and kindly inviting me in her sweet accents to stay all night and sleep with her," Logan wrote after a visit in 1815. In later years, when Logan felt unable to cope with Elizabeth's brother, she took solace in her continuing close ties with "Lisse." "I am always happy when Lisse is with me," she wrote in 1838. While other relationships faltered in the final years of her life, Deborah could count on Elizabeth. She was, Logan wrote, "a cordial in the Cup of Life, to delight and exhilerate my Old Age."[22]

While relationships with granddaughters offered aging women opportunities for intimacy that would be especially valued in late life, grandmothers were not unaware that these young women lived in a world increasingly different from their own. This became especially apparent by the 1830s as the reins of domesticity tightened across woman's sphere. Not all grandmothers were equally comfortable with the heralding of domesticity. For those post-revolutionary women who preferred reading and writing to domestic mastery, the emerging cult of domesticity demanded a reexamination of existing values. Margaret Bayard Smith confronted this dilemma as she attempted to redefine those duties and values she hoped to inculcate in her own granddaughter.

"In the mind alone," Margaret Smith had written in 1830, "is any perfection or happiness to be found. . . ." A decade later, however, she felt compelled to consider the nature of her legacy to her granddaughter in light of unparalleled domestic ascendancy. Would the values associated with her own (relatively) broad education and literary pursuits adequately serve the needs of a young girl growing up in nineteenth-century America? Could she, in good faith, encourage her granddaughter to follow in her own footsteps, to leave domestic duties to others so that she might read and write in privacy? Was it a grandmother's duty to pass on her own values or to adjust those values to a changing society? "In our country and state of society," Margaret Smith reluctantly concluded in 1840, "[domestic duties] make a woman happier than a taste for intellectual pursuits."[23]

Margaret Smith's response to this dilemma illustrates the practical, pragmatic nature of her personality. It was her duty to help prepare her granddaughter for the world as it was, she decided, not as it should be. "I am determined . . . to cultivate in her a taste for those domestic duties, & for the needle," wrote this distinctly nondomestic grandmother. "How I envy . . . other ladies of my acquaintance who take a positive delight in housekeeping!"[24]

Margaret Smith's quandary was not shared by all grandmothers in the new republic. Most would continue to promote the values and judgments that had served them throughout their own long lives. Yet Margaret Bayard

Smith anticipated a major issue which would reemerge with the next generation of nineteenth-century women: to what end are we training our daughters (and granddaughters)? It was a question that would be posed throughout the nineteenth and into the twentieth century, both in private homes and on the campuses of female academies and colleges. Over time, it would become increasingly difficult for grandmothers to claim with any certainty that they, indeed, knew the answer.

Nineteenth-Century Women's Autobiography: Remembering Grandmama

As the nineteenth century progressed, questions regarding women's role within the family and society were raised with increasing fervor. Women themselves were at the forefront (if not alone) in raising issues regarding their legal, political, and moral rights. Whether they joined the work force or reform movements or chose instead to epitomize "true womanhood" through continued domesticity, women acknowledged options and opportunities unknown to their post-revolutionary grandmothers. But as most women learned, few options were open-ended. Frustration and anxiety claimed all but the most resilient of women.

Like many of their post-revolutionary grandmothers, however, women growing old during the middle and late nineteenth century attempted to put their lives in order as the end of life drew near. For some aging women, the task was made easier as opportunities for women's self-expression slowly opened up. Women novelists, although mostly young or middle-aged, set the stage for popular acceptance of female literature. By mid-century, numerous women had begun to record their life histories, some of which would eventually be published. Among those women whose memoirs survive, many were teachers, writers, and reformers whose lives characterized the changing status of women in nineteenth-century America.[25]

Significantly, autobiographies written by aging nineteenth-century women were not self-congratulating accounts of feminist achievement. Even though most autobiographers were women who had achieved a measure of success against high odds, few stressed the point. The life stories recounted were, instead, curious compilations of family histories, childhood memories, and moral reflection, often interspersed with odd bits of poetry and prose. While many recalled years of hard work and sacrifice, few revealed details of close, personal relationships. Yet as these women looked backward to piece together their personal history, many fixed on the old women in their lives — particularly their grandmothers — as important influences. For those aging women, remembering "grandmama" served more than historical or geneological interests. Such recollections afforded the opportunity to locate

viable models of women growing old. How did they remember their grandmothers? What values did they ascribe to these models of aging women?
What, indeed, is the legacy of our post-revolutionary matriarchs?

"My grandmother is among the gentle, yet strong images of my infancy,"
wrote Lydia Sigourney in her late-life autobiography. While no universal
image of grandmother emerges from a sampling of twenty nineteenth-
century autobiographies written by aging women, numerous character traits
consistently, though not surprisingly, reappear. Grandmothers worked hard,
prayed long, and carried their abundant virtue with impressive bearing.
While details varied, grandmama clearly emerges as a woman to be reckoned
with.[26]

Grandmothers were especially remembered for their "saintly virtues."
At a time when feminine virtue was held at a premium, women autobiographers reaffirmed their biological and cultural links to virtuous old age
by rediscovering those very qualities in their own grandmothers. Grandmaternal virtues, however, were not all cut of the same cloth. The Kentucky
educator Julia Ann Tevis stressed traditional images of purity which she
described in visual terms. "I can even now see . . . the tall, queenly form
of my grandmother," she wrote in 1878, depicting the old woman's "dove-
colored dress" and the "snowy whiteness" of her cap, setting off "the most
benevolent of features." Many women recalled their grandmother's strict
ways. Indeed, Catharine Beecher believed that "conscience" was the "pre-
dominating element" in Grandmother Beecher's character. "She was strict
with herself and strict with all around," wrote the well-known writer/
educator in 1874. For other women, virtue seemed synonymous with be-
nevolence and generosity. Anna Matlock Richards, who entitled her own
memoir *Memories of a Grandmother,* recalled vividly the generous nature
of her maternal grandmother. "How freely she gave to the poor! How kind,
how indulgent was this parent to me," wrote this Massachusetts widow at
mid-century.[27]

Each writer, of course, found within memories of their grandmothers
those qualities which best served their own immediate needs. Feminist
writer and lecturer Elizabeth Oakes Smith, confident of her own place in
history, clearly modeled herself on the strong character of her Grandmother
Blanchard. A "stately" woman, her grandmother is depicted as more literate
and better read than any of her contemporaries. "She was able to discuss
theological points like a veritable Anne Hutchinson," wrote Oakes Smith
during the 1880s, after becoming pastor of a nondenominational church.
Catharine Beecher's dispassionate recollection of Grandmother Beecher reveals little that was loving or warm in the old woman's character; she is
presented as a tough and unyielding woman. "Whenever anything went
wrong, or the children misbehaved, Grandma's black eyes peered over her

spectacles like two cold stars," the still-forceful Catharine Beecher remembered while in her early seventies.[28]

These aging autobiographers were often well aware of the importance attached to recollections of grandmother. "She sits in the eye of memory," wrote Anna Richards, as she and others described the ease with which their grandmothers were recalled. Women who grew up without grandmothers felt the loss, even years later. In her mid-sixties, novelist Catherine Sedgwick still regretted that she never knew her grandmothers, believing that her sense of self was blunted by the loss. "This [grandmaternal] relation," she wrote, "extends our being by one generation, and gives us the twilight as well as the dawn."[29]

Not all women's memoirs were published, nor were all written by teachers or professional writers. Many nineteenth-century women considered their private lives inappropriate material for public consumption. Nonetheless, in unpublished memoirs women recalled the past vividly and, occasionally, more openly than is suggested in many well-edited, published autobiographies. The memoir of Eliza Perkins Cabot is an excellent case in point, especially as it relates to her eighty-year recollections of grandmaternal love.

In her old age at the end of the nineteenth century, Eliza Perkins Cabot sat down to dictate her memoirs to her son James Cabot. Like many old people, Cabot's memory for events long past served her well. Recalling in vivid detail the people, conversations, and places of her youth, Cabot rambled and wandered over the terrain of a distant past, ignoring the contemporary world around her. Yet among the friends and relatives who peopled this simple, often prosaic memoir, the images of two old women appear as strikingly different but influential models in the life of the young Eliza Perkins.[30]

Grandmother Perkins emerges from Eliza Cabot's memoirs as a classic eighteenth-century matriarch. Strong, uncompromising, and disciplined, she presented to the young Cabot an image of mature womanhood both powerful and fearful. "They called her 'Madam Perkins,' " Cabot recalled, "and she seemed rather awful to us. Mother always spoke of her, even to the servants, as 'the old lady.' " Nonetheless, Cabot tells us, Grandma Perkins's children "had unbounded respect for her." There is no question that "the old lady" was a hard act to follow. A widow who raised eight children, she also ran her own grocery business. A believer in public service, she founded the Boston Female Asylum. There was little, in fact, that she would not undertake. "She kept a crazy woman in the cellar," wrote Cabot, "and took care of her herself until she was cured."[31]

This vigorous model of feminine aging contrasted considerably with that offered by Eliza Cabot's maternal grandmother. In her recollections of

Grandmother Eliot, Cabot revived with apparent ease feelings of grandparental warmth and love. These memories, in fact, remained entirely in the affective domain. Cabot described *only* feelings and emotions and never considered the older woman's actions or accomplishments. Cabot recalled this grandmother as "indulgent and generous"; she was, said Cabot, "always bent on making you happy." In these recollections, Cabot not only remembered her grandmother's generosity but also attempted to revive the environment that served to set her memories. "It seemed to me we lived in [Grandmother's] kitchen," Cabot wrote, reflecting as well on the shine of the brass and pewter, the delicious food, the massive fireplaces throughout the house, even the "copper-plate" bedhangings over her grandmother's bed. In color and texture, each image evoked warmth and comfort, conveying the most peaceful and joyful metaphors found anywhere in the memoir.[32]

Eighty years separated these memories from their source in turn-of-the-century Boston. Yet, even in her nineties, Eliza Cabot appeared strengthened and invigorated by the recollection of two such distinctive and impressive grandmothers. Madam Perkins, although often cold and aloof, served as a model of age and accomplishment, one that Cabot continued to venerate throughout her life. Grandmother Eliot, on the other hand, was recalled only for her qualities of caring and generosity. Her legacy of loving warmth and security survived intact for nearly a century.[33]

Women like Eliza Cabot, Elizabeth Oakes Smith, and Lydia Sigourney differed markedly in many aspects of their lives, yet in their old age they each turned to memories of their own grandmothers for comfort and direction. Despite the many decades separating them, these aged granddaughters gratefully acknowledged a legacy of strength and integrity. Although grandmothers in the new republic expressed doubts over their ability to influence "thoughtless Youth," the impact of their example would echo for generations to come.

For most women in the fifty years following the Revolution, the role of grandmotherhood promised a continuation of maternal responsibilities and rewards into old age. Maintaining active and vital associations with their young grandchildren, grandmothers performed useful and necessary functions and were reinforced by the expectation that grandchildren would care for and support them in later years. Within a social framework that fostered women's competence and hegemony in the familial setting, grandmotherhood offered the chance to extend and develop the maternal role to its fullest dimensions.

Some aging grandmothers, however, sensed that forces beyond their control threatened to disrupt what they believed to be the natural interdependency of generations. Grandsons, raised within a sphere increasingly separate from their sisters and other women, often failed to provide the comfort and support deemed necessary by aging women. Even young women, while often close to their grandmothers, were growing up in a generation whose values were changing. By the end of the Jacksonian era, a trace of melancholy and hostility toward younger people is discernible in the writings of some grandmothers, indicating that changes outside their own sphere were weakening the fabric within. As the notion of change itself seemed increasingly characterized by youth, grandmothers became fearful that their own values and ideals would be lost on their children's children.

Their fears, however, appear to have been premature. The impact of grandmaternal modeling is apparent in the memorable images of strong and virtuous grandmothers reverberating in the recollections of aged granddaughters. The enduring ties across generations of women, as exemplified in the memoirs of Eliza Perkins Cabot, is evident even today in the memories of aged women, whose ability to recapture and appreciate the past remains as one of the great blessings of age.

NOTES

1. Margaret Bayard to Samuel Smith, 12 September 1797, Margaret Bayard Smith Papers, LCMD. See also Deborah Norris Logan, Diary, October 1815, HSP; and Fanny Nicholson to Rebecca Nicholson, 18 July n.d., Shippen Family Papers, LCMD.

2. John Demos has noted in a study of old age in seventeenth-century New England that "grandparent-grandchild ties were (potentially) close and (relatively) widespread." Grandparenthood, indeed, flourished in early New England, says Demos. Similarly, Laurel Thatcher Ulrich found that the nurturing role of old women extended into old age in seventeenth-century northern New England. "In rural villages any old woman was a 'mother' or 'gammar,' " she writes. While many of the traditional forces holding generations together continued past the Revolution, changes within woman's sphere and larger societal shifts eventually altered the context of these ties. In a contemporary study examining "the vital connection" between grandparents and grandchildren, Arthur Kornhaber and Kenneth L. Woodward argue that grandparents traditionally served in a variety of significant roles, including those of historian, mentor, role model, "wizard," and nurturer. Only in the last generation, they conclude, has this vital connection been broken, thus thwarting the instinct of nature. See Demos, "Old Age in Early New England," in *Turning Points: Historical and Sociological Essays on the Family,* ed. John Demos and Sarane Spence Boocock (Chicago: University of Chicago Press, 1978), p. 260; Ulrich, *Good Wives: Image and Reality in the Lives of Women in Northern New England, 1650-1750* (New York: Oxford University Press, 1980), p. 158; and Kornhaber and Woodward, *Grandparents/Grandchildren: The Vital Connection* (New York: Anchor Press–Doubleday, 1981), pp. 92, 167-77.

3. Elizabeth Dunbar to Elizabeth Shippen, 13 November 1791, and Elizabeth

Shippen Izard to William Shippen, 25 February 1818, Shippen Family Papers, LCMD.

4. Abigail Adams to Mary Cranch, 5 January 1790, *New Letters of Abigail Adams, 1788-1801,* ed. Stewart Mitchell (Boston: Houghton Mifflin, 1947), p. 36. Quaker grandmothers appeared more reticent. See Rebecca Shoemaker to Samuel Shoemaker, 5 April 1785, Shoemaker Papers, HSP; Elizabeth Drinker, Diary, 31 May 1795, 25 September and 8 November 1798, HSP; and Deborah Norris Logan, Diary, 31 December 1826, HSP. See also Margaret Bayard Smith to Jane Kirkpatrick, 19 December 1838, Margaret Bayard Smith Papers, LCMD; Mary Meade to William Randolph, 8 November 1808, William B. Randolph Papers, LCMD; Alice Shippen to William Shippen III, 25 May 1816, Shippen Family Papers, LCMD; Ann Livingston to Margaret Beekman Livingston, n.d. [early 1790s], reel 4, Shippen Family Papers, LCMD; Deborah Norris Logan, Diary, 3 June 1838, HSP; Rebecca Shoemaker, Journal, 30 October 1805, Rawle Family Papers, HSP; Elizabeth Drinker, Diary, 12 June 1802, HSP; and Eliza Pinckney to grandson Daniel Horry, 7 August 1783, Pinckney Family Papers, LCMD.

Mary Beth Norton discussed the significance of child-naming patterns in determining both parental affection and generational continuity in revolutionary America. Her study of child-naming patterns among Jefferson's slaves revealed that Virginia's black families had "a strong sense of lineage" and, in fact, named children after grandparents more often than did white New Englanders. Daniel Scott Smith, in his study of child-naming patterns in Hingham, Massachusetts, concluded that the importance attached to family continuity was evident in the naming of children after their grandparents, a practice which persisted well into the nineteenth century. Indeed, the recurrence of traditional family names is evident throughout the personal writings of old women during this period. Reluctance to show affection to infant grandchildren, when evident, could be linked to high infant mortality rates during this period. For instance, only two-thirds of the girls born in the eighteenth century survived to age twenty; nearly one-fifth failed to reach their first birthday. See Norton, *Liberty's Daughters: The Revolutionary Experience of American Women, 1750-1800* (Boston: Little, Brown, 1980), pp. 85-90; Daniel Scott Smith, "Child-Naming Patterns and Family Structure Change: Hingham, Massachusetts, 1640-1880," Newberry Papers in Family and Community History, 76-5, January 1977; Robert V. Wells, "Women's Lives Transformed: Demographic and Family Patterns in America, 1600-1970," in *Women of America: A History,* ed. Carol Ruth Berkin and Mary Beth Norton (Boston: Houghton Mifflin, 1979), p. 22.

5. Lucy Tappan Pierce to John Pierce, 17 September 1805, Poor Family Papers, SL; Elizabeth Izard to Alice Izard, 31 July 1812, Izard Family Papers, LCMD. See also Louisa Shippen's correspondence with her mother Jane Haxall, Shippen Family Papers, LCMD. Even though Louisa Shippen's husband was a nonpracticing physician, her mother never failed to diagnose and prescribe for her in times of illness.

Kornhaber and Woodward describe the continuing importance of the caretaker-nurturer role played by grandparents in contemporary society in *Grandparents/Grandchildren,* pp. 167-77.

6. Mary Parker Norris to Deborah Logan, 16 December 1795, Norris Family

Letters, HSP; Abigail Adams, 31 October 1799, quoted in June Sprigg, *Domestick Beings* (New York: Alfred A. Knopf, 1984), p. 126; Margaret Livingston to Nancy Shippen Livingston, [2] February 1793, Shippen Family Papers, LCMD; Frances Mutter to William Randolph, 24 February 1815, William B. Randolph Papers, LCMD. See also Alice Izard to Margaret Manigault, 8 August 1813, Izard Family Papers, LCMD; Elizabeth Drinker, Diary, 20 December 1798 and 15 January 1799, HSP; and Elizabeth Izard to Willliam Shippen III, 26 March 1825, Shippen Family Papers, LCMD. Sophia Smith, founder of Smith College, credited her grandmother, Mary Norton Smith, for early inspiration. She is quoted by Daniel White Wells and Reuben Field Wells in *A History of Hatfield, Massachusetts, 1660-1910* (Springfield, Mass.: F. C. H. Gibbons, 1910), pp. 207-8.

7. Ann Livingston to Margaret Beekman Livingston, n.d. [1787], Letterbook, Shippen Family Papers, LCMD; Elizabeth Izard to Louisa Shippen, 13 July 1822, Shippen Family Papers, LCMD. See also Eleanor Parke Lewis to Mary Pinckney, 9 May 1801, Pinckney Family Papers, LCMD; Mary Parker Norris to Deborah Logan, 14 August 1798, Norris Family Letters, HSP; Betsy Coles to Marion Singleton, 12 March 1825, Singleton Family Papers, LCMD; and Deborah Norris Logan, Diary, 20 November 1825, HSP.

Mary Beth Norton has noted that grandmothers were "commonly charged with spoiling their grandchildren." Similarly, grandparental "indulgence" was common in the seventeenth century, according to John Demos. Daniel Scott Smith has argued that "grandparents did not exercise authority over their grandchildren" in early New England. His evidence, however, consists of male-directed forms of power and authority (wealth and property) and does not address the affective power yielded by many grandmothers. See Norton, *Liberty's Daughters,* p. 96; Demos, "Old Age in Early New England," p. 259; and Smith, "Old Age and the 'Great Transformation': A New England Case Study," in *Aging and the Elderly: Humanistic Perspectives in Gerontology,* ed. Stuart F. Spiker, Kathleen M. Woodword, and David D. Van Tassel (Atlanta Highlands, N.J.: Humanities Press, 1978), p. 291.

8. Rebecca Shoemaker, Journal, 30 October 1805, Rawle Family Papers, HSP; Margaret Morris, *Margaret Morris: Her Journal with Biographical Sketch and Notes,* ed. John W. Jackson (Philadelphia: Historical Society of Pennsylvania, 1899), pp. 28-29; Elizabeth Drinker, Diary, 15 March 1800. John Demos's study of seventeenth-century New England probate records reveals that grandchildren early practiced filial duty to their grandparents. See Demos, "Old Age in Early New England, " p. 259.

9. Hannah Emery Abbott to Mary Carter, 30 December 1791, Cutts Family Papers, EI.

10. Elizabeth Pierce, Journal, 24 March 1826, Poor Family Papers, SL.

11. Lucy Tappan Pierce to husband, 4 November 1819, Poor Family Papers, SL. See also Rebecca Shoemaker to daughters, 28 October 1780, Shoemaker Papers, HSP; and Elizabeth Phoenix to Lucy Pierce, August 1818, recorded in Elizabeth Pierce's journal, Poor Family Papers, SL.

12. Elizabeth Izard to William Shippen III, 5 September 1805, Shippen Family

Papers, LCMD. See also Abigail Bradley Hyde to daughter Adeline Hyde, 5 April 1829, Abigail Bradley Hyde Papers, SL.

13. Jane Mecom to Benjamin Franklin, 5 May 1778, "Three Jane Mecom-Franklin Letters," *Pennsylvania Magazine of History and Biography* 72 (July 1948):269; Deborah Norris Logan, Diary, 30 June 1837, HSP. See also Anne Firor Scott's discussion of Jane Mecom's family obligations in *Making the Invisible Woman Visible* (Urbana: University of Illinois Press, 1984), pp. 4-13.

14. Alice Shippen to William Shippen III, 2 August n.d., reel 3, and 25 September 1816, Shippen Family Papers, LCMD.

15. See, as well, discussion on the ambiguous impact of filial duty in chapter two, above.

16. Although widespread industrialization and urbanization were yet to take firm hold in the new nation, growth and expansion spurred the development of markets and systems of exchange. Large labor reserves, supported by increasing immigration and high fertility rates, promoted industrial experimentation and encouraged separation of home and workplace. The temperament of the time also echoed change. As Rowland Berthoff and John M. Murrin have noted, the major turning point of the period was in the emergent *perception* of a changing society rather than the reality of change. See Edward Pessen, *Jacksonian America: Society, Personality and Politics* (Homewood, Ill.: Dorsey Press, 1978), pp. 149-70, passim; John K. Alexander, *Render Them Submissive: Responses to Poverty in Philadelphia, 1760-1800* (Amherst: University of Massachusetts Press, 1980), pp. 160-74; and Berthoff and Murrin, "Feudalism, Communalism, and the Yeoman Freeholder: The American Revolution Considered as a Social Accident," in *Essays on the American Revolution*, ed. Stephen G. Kurtz and James H. Hutson (Chapel Hill: University of North Carolina Press, 1793), pp. 256-88.

17. Deborah Norris Logan, Diary, 22 July and 22 October 1838, HSP.

18. Ibid., 16 August 1826, 15 September 1827, 12 August 1815, 28 December and 5 June 1824.

19. Ibid., 15 May 1835, mid-1834 passim, and early 1838 passim.

20. David Hackett Fischer, *Growing Old in America*, 2d ed. (New York: Oxford University Press, 1978), pp. 115-22; Thomas R. Cole, "Past Meridian: Aging and the Northern Middle Class, 1830-1930" (Ph.D. dissertation, University of Rochester, 1980), pp. 2, 93, 156, 210. According to Cole, "a sense of generational continuity is precisely what many Jacksonian Americans lacked; breaking the connections between generations to establish themselves as democratic individuals, the urban bourgeoisie consequently deprived themselves of the inner resources of intergenerational solidarity needed to reconcile themselves to their own super-session and death" (p. 210). I would argue that women during this period were less active in establishing themselves as "democratic individuals" and that the experience of generational discontinuity was only *beginning* to be realized by some antebellum women.

21. Elizabeth Izard to William Shippen III, 1 July 1823, and Jane Gray Haxall to Louisa Shippen, 17 September 1825, Shippen Family Papers, LCMD. See also Elizabeth Dunbar to Elizabeth Shippen, 29 September 1796, Shippen Family Papers, LCMD; and Elizabeth Pierce, Journal, June 1818, Poor Family Papers, SL.

22. Sarah Ripley to David Bradford, 29 February 1820, Ripley Papers, SL; Hannah Emery to Mary Carter, 24 February and 4 April 1789, Cutts Family Papers, EI; Deborah Norris Logan, Diary, 20 August 1837, n.d. October 1815, 1 January 1838, and 20 August 1837, HSP.

23. Margaret Bayard Smith to Anna Thornton, 26 March 1830, William Thornton Papers, LCMD; Margaret Bayard Smith to Jane Kirkpatrick, 28 September 1840, Margaret Bayard Smith Papers, LCMD. Margaret Bayard Smith contributed numerous articles to leading ladies' magazines during this period and wrote, among others, a two-volume novel, *A Winter in Washington: Or, Memoirs of the Seymour Family* (1824).

24. Margaret Bayard Smith to Jane Kirkpatrick, 28 September 1840, Margaret Bayard Smith Papers, LCMD. Kathryn Kish Sklar discusses the "heightened concern over the quality of domestic life in the 1840s" in *Catharine Beecher: A Study in American Domesticity* (New York: W. W. Norton, 1973), pp. 152, passim.

25. See Patricia Meyers Spacks, *The Female Imagination: A Literary and Psychological Investigation of Writing by Women — Novels, Autobiographies, Letters, Journals that Reveals How the Fact of Womanhood Shapes the Imagination* (New York: Knopf, 1975).

26. Lydia Sigourney, *Letters of Life* (New York: D. Appleton, 1866), pp. 11-12. Lydia Sigourney's relationship with Mrs. Daniel Lathrop, her father's aged employer, suggests the significance of surrogate grandmotherhood. In describing this relationship, Sigourney maintained that "the cream of all my happiness [in youth] was a loving intercourse with venerable age." Ibid., p. 42.

27. Ibid.; Julia Ann Tevis, *Sixty Years in a School-Room: An Autobiography of Mrs. Julia A. Tevis, Principal of Science Hill Female Academy* (Cincinnati: Western Methodist Book Concern, 1878), p. 42; Catharine Beecher, *Educational Reminiscences and Suggestions* (New York: J. B. Ford, 1874), p. 17; Anna Matlock Richards, *Memories of a Grandmother, by a Lady of Massachusetts* (Boston: Gould and Lincoln, 1854), pp. 30-31.

28. Elizabeth Oakes Smith, *Selections from the Autobiography of Elizabeth Oakes Smith*, ed. Mary Alice Wyman (Lewiston, Maine: Lewiston Journal Press, 1924), p. 15; Catharine Beecher, *Educational Reminiscences and Suggestions*, p. 17.

Granddaughterly interest in the lives and values of their grandmothers may relate to the "alternating generational phenomenon" suggested by Alice Rossi regarding the rise and fall of activist feminism. "Perhaps daughters . . . forget what granddaughters wish to remember," she writes. See Rossi, ed., *The Feminist Papers: From Adams to de Beauvoir* (New York: Columbia University Press, 1973), p. 619.

29. Anna Matlock Richards, *Memories of a Grandmother*, pp. 30-31; Catherine Maria Sedgwick, *Life and Letters of Catherine Maria Sedgwick*, ed. Mary C. Dewey (New York: Harper and Bros., 1871), p. 15.

30. The unpublished, forty-page typescript of these recollections is available at the Schlesinger Library. See Eliza Perkins Cabot, Memoirs, Cabot Family Papers, SL; see also T. Premo, "Eliza Perkins Cabot and the Meaning of Reminiscence,"

unpublished paper delivered November 1984 at the Gerontological Society annual meeting, San Antonio, Texas.

31. Eliza Perkins Cabot, Memoirs, pp. 5-6, Cabot Family Papers, SL. Eighteenth-century definitions of "awful" usually translate as "being filled with awe" rather than the twentieth-century connotation of the term which is unreservedly negative.

32. Ibid., pp. 10-11.

33. David Hackett Fischer has suggested that veneration for the aged declined after the Revolution, indicative, he says, of a loss of status for old persons. Fischer describes veneration as a cold, detached response more akin to respect than love. The character of Madam Perkins serves as an apt example of this definition of veneration; Grandmother Eliot, on the other hand, enjoyed intense intimacy with her grandchildren and, like many women, was loved rather than venerated. Veneration, as an indicator of power and status among the aged, appears to have only limited viability when applied to the lives of women growing old. See Fischer, Growing Old, p. 30.

PART TWO

The Self
Turns Inward

In their old age, women in the new republic found meaning and strength in their continuing relations with others and in the connections they forged between generations. The domestic sphere proved a fertile environment for nurturing these bonds and fostering the continuation of productive activity within the confines of that sphere. Unlike aging men, old women sensed little diminution of status or value in this early period. On the contrary, the enhanced domestic purview of woman's sphere responded very closely to many of the needs and special concerns of women facing old age.

At the same time, however, women growing old confronted the unshakable reality of their individuality and aloneness as age advanced. Despite their commitment to a morality of connection and continuity, women in old age grew increasingly aware of their need for a more contemplative focus—one that encompassed a fuller identity with the world while enabling them to face the singular reality of their own supersession. As age advanced, women looked further inward through reading, reminiscence, and reflection to gain direction along that final path they would be walking alone. Circumscribed by factors of age, gender, and historical chance, their focus required continual adjustment as the models and metaphors shaping expectations (explored in chapter four) collided with the lived experience of being old (described in chapter five). As death approached (chapter six), women would ultimately face these two seemingly conflicting forces—connection and secluded introspection—to find identity and peace in their graceful merger at life's end.

Defining the Metaphors
of Old Age

Gathered on the lawn of a sumptuous English country estate, excited spectators sized up the competition and made their bets. The race would be run over a gravel course of twenty yards. As the two contestants neared the starting point, laughter peeled from the crowd. "When the signal was given to set off," wrote novelist Fanny Burney, "the poor creatures, feeble and frightened, ran against each other... [and] both fell on the ground." The spectators, however, had only just whetted their appetites and demanded that the race continue. "Again, therefore, they set off, and hobbled along, nearly even with each other for some time, yet frequently and to the inexpressible diversion of the company, they stumbled and tottered." After a second, more serious injury to a "runner," Burney finally ended the race — and her farce.[1]

Readers of this vignette, tucked deep inside Burney's 1778 novel *Evelina,* were certain to sympathize with the two victimized runners. And no wonder. These two unlikely objects of derision were eighty-year-old women. "The mind naturally accommodates itself, even to the most ridiculous improprieties," conceded an organizer of Burney's fictive race.[2]

Indeed, the sympathetic response of Burney's many British and American readers was guaranteed *because* of the "ridiculous improprieties" so blatant in the tale. While the obvious moral lesson of this satire was directed at the excesses of British society, its underlying premise was what constituted proper behavior toward and by old women. By selecting two such old and "feeble" women as the butt of this cruel joke, Burney reveals just how well she knew her audience.

Burney's American readership (composed largely of women, including the Philadelphia matron Elizabeth Drinker) understood well what was expected of old women. In their piety and passivity, their dignity and their wisdom, old women were to serve as models of decorum in a world of flux. The values associated with old women, so clearly reflected by their antithesis in Burney's satire, were well established prior to the onset of any "cult of domesticity" in early nineteenth-century America and would prevail for several generations to come. What were the normative elements associated with feminine aging? And how did changes in post-revolutionary society alter those cultural expectations?[3]

"Spectators Only": Passivity as a Way of Life

As their hair grayed, their bones ached, and their eyesight diminished, aging women understood the physical reality of growing old. Most learned to cope with each new sign of advancing age, adjusting the tempo of their lives to changing physical capacities. Yet the signs of age also demanded a reevaluation of their relationship to the larger society. With age came new roles and expectations, many of which seemed at odds with other long-established patterns and values.

Long before elements of antebellum society attempted to put women "on a pedestal," deprived of opportunities for productivity and self-esteem, aging women were expected to model their own behavior on a similarly passive vision of femininity. In their interactions with friends and relatives, their daily activities, and even their emotions, old women were to begin the process of withdrawal and retirement through a gradual "loosening" of worldly ties. Such a passive approach, it was believed, diminished the pain and anguish that accompanied old age and mitigated the fear of approaching death.[4]

In their attempts to adopt attitudes deemed more appropriate for their time of life, older women took comfort, no doubt, in their belief that nature was on their side. Women viewed callousness, for instance, as a natural development of growing old. Related to this perception was the notion that advanced years brought with them a "chilling of affections." Young and old women alike shared the expectation that old age signified a lack of sensitivity. When the young invalid Julia Cowles expressed surprise at the "warm" feelings of an aged couple, she manifested sentiments familiar to many. The elderly Hannah Adams admitted that "age and experience have in some measure repressed the warmth of my feelings. . . ."[5]

Women's expectations of callousness and "repressed warmth" in old age imply a lost sense of passion as the years passed. The perception that emotions and feelings diminished with age reinforced the view that women should withdraw from earthly ties. By losing "that quick sense of feeling," as Elizabeth Drinker described it, women expected to grow impervious to the added pains and sorrows of old age. Beyond this increased ability to transcend daily problems, the loss of strong emotions and feelings, as it was perceived, accelerated the gradual process of resignation, the central task of old age.[6]

It was expected that appropriately subdued feelings would be manifest in both word and deed. As women grew old, their world was to be increasingly restricted to the confines of their home, the only proper setting for contemplation and "retirement." Women who desired to range beyond that setting pushed the limits of good sense. Writing to her daughter in 1812, Alice Izard frowned on the peripatetic Mrs. Horry for her continued outside interests, as she was "too far advanced in life." Women in Jacksonian America expressed the same disapproval when elderly women insisted on carrying out an active social life. "She is continually wanting to ride & will not be content at home," wrote Margaret Bayard Smith of her aging neighbor Mrs. Bourdeaux. Despite immense physical debility, Mrs. Bourdeaux apparently craved activity and social interaction, particularly among young persons. Yet the expectations of those around her were solidly aligned against such an active, mobile old age.[7]

Ironically, the passivity and piety considered appropriate for elderly women produced a readily identifiable image of feminine aging, one which younger and middle-aged women could actively emulate. Women's descriptions of esteemed old ladies provide ample evidence of this idealized vision of feminine old age. Martha Washington, as she was briefly but vividly described by Abigail Adams in 1789, possessed brilliant white hair and "beautiful Teeth," together with "a most becoming pleasantness . . . upon her countenance & an unaffected deportment which renders her the object of veneration & Respect." A generation later, the aging Deborah Logan recalled the special qualities of her late friend Sally Rawle who had been, she wrote, among "the old order of Ladies." According to Logan, the sixty-three-year-old Rawle was "Gentle, affectionate, and feminine, unpretending and unobtrusive, perfectly well bred, an excellent wife and mother, but delicate. . . ." The best of aging women were "always cheerful," possessed "lady like manners," and exuded "peace and quietness."[8]

Such descriptions of beloved older women span a half-century, revealing a continuing pattern of traits and characteristics which many women obviously emulated. Invariably cheerful, pleasant, and affectionate, they excelled in passivity and would clearly pose no threat to man or beast. Dignified yet possessing a "becoming" humility, they took pains not to appear affected or pretentious, despite their station in life. They were, as one woman wrote, ultimately "feminine."[9]

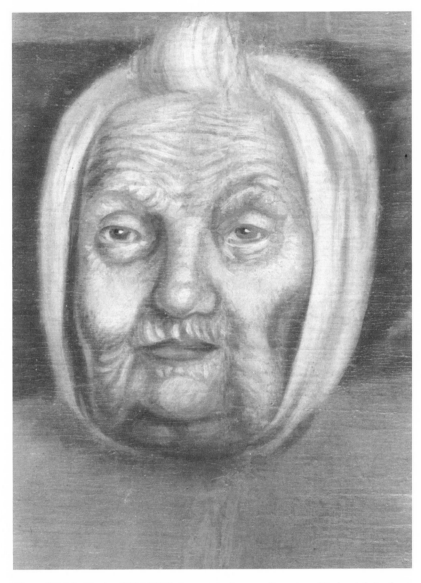

Mary Mirick Davie (1635-1752) in a painting attributed to Nathaniel Smibert,
circa 1750, courtesy of Massachusetts Historical Society. This portrait of a 117-
year-old woman reveals the relaxed, informal perspective that characterized colonial attitudes toward the aged. The artist appears more interested in the phenomenon of extreme old age than in portraying distinctive qualities associated
with feminine aging. Post-revolutionary portraits, in contrast, were notably more
formal, usually depicting the dignity and piety expected of aged women at that
time.

Hannah Adams (1755-1831) by Chester Harding, circa 1827, courtesy of Boston Athenaeum. This portrait in many ways epitomizes the piety deemed appropriate for "women of age."

Age-appropriate behavior was expected in even the most intimate relations. Friendships with men, even when clearly leading to the altar, were
sanctioned only for their platonic nature. Old women understood, too, that
prospective mates could not be younger. Many women frowned on "May-
December marriages" if the bride was older than her husband. Younger
women were under no such exacting policy with regard to the age of a
marital partner. In fact, according to Margaret Bayard Smith, a twenty-five
to thirty-year age gap might be wholly appropriate. Once a woman was past
the age of thirty-five or forty, she argued in 1835, "the reign of fancy &
first rush of strong feelings are passed. . . ." At that point, "a woman may
do very well with a man of 60." Margaret Smith's obvious implication, of
course, is that sexual desires no longer animated women over forty. It was
generally acknowledged that women were motivated by the heart rather
than the libido, and older women were expected to denounce the physical
nature of conjugal bliss. It is little wonder that so few elderly widows chose
to remarry.[10]

Were such stringent behavioral guidelines evident before the Revolution?
Apparently not. In his study of old age in colonial New England, John
Demos discovered "a certain looseness or flexibility in the application of
age norms." Julia Cherry Spruill recognized similar findings in her study
of southern colonial women. Dancing, once enjoyed in the South by young
and old women alike, became "almost exclusively the amusement of the
young" in the years following Independence. By the late eighteenth century,
such restricted activities were already apparent in New England, where older
women maintained a tradition of sobriety. Although she attended a party
in Boston in 1772 where there were games and dancing, an older Bostonian
matron later told her relatives that "the elderly part of the company were
spectators only. . . ." The passive role of spectator was indeed the only
justification for her attendance at all.[11]

By the post-revolutionary era, behavioral expectations imposed on old
women mirrored both the values long associated with old age (veneration
and respect for long lives well lived) and those increasingly identified strictly
with women (piety and passivity). The congruence of these two value
systems is evident in the strength and durability of this fortified image of
feminine aging. With only minor adjustments, this image would endure
for nearly a century.

The Importance of Looking One's Age

Old women paid close attention to their appearance. Most, however,
were not concerned with appearing younger than their years. In fact, quite
the opposite. Women admired other women whose dress and demeanor

enhanced the dignity and respect associated with feminine aging. Those whose appearance suggested otherwise, however, exposed themselves to ridicule in this age-conscious society.

Dark colors were requisite for "women of years." Such women regularly wore close caps, sometimes with ribbons. New fashions were seldom seen on old bodies. Although Abigail Adams sent a fashionable new "drapery dress" to her niece, she declined to wear one herself "as I consider it too youthfull for me." On the other hand, it was deemed inappropriate for young women to dress in dark colors and dated fashions. The young New Englander Hannah Emery quickly realized that her own somber apparel would not pass unnoticed. "I thought I might have been allow'd to dress as was most agreeable to my feelings," she lamented to a friend, "but I was mistaken. . . ." For most women, a self-imposed dress code merely reinforced the separate status accorded to older women.[12]

In some respects, the careful observance of dress codes appropriate to different age groups suggests a form of age segregation counter to the "democratizing" spirit of the time. Although Thomas Jefferson might greet guests in his house slippers, few old women could express such flexibility in their own attire. Older women both before and after the Revolution carefully supported and maintained their own dress code. Apparently comfortable with the notion of "dressing old," such women often revealed a pride in their distinctive style of clothing. This may be due to the smaller percentage of people who were "old," but relative rarity offers only part of the explanation. As long as old age continued to provide women with meaningful activities and sustained purpose, the official trappings of old age could be greeted with apparent favor. Through their dress, old women might display the dignity and discipline deemed appropriate for their age and status.[13]

Looking one's age, of course, implied more than the proper choice of apparel. Older women believed they should serve as models of decorum. As such, their entire demeanor needed to suggest a single, unified vision of feminine aging. Deborah Logan not only attempted to serve as such a model but also undertook to direct other women toward age-appropriate behavior and appearance. In her "Treatise on Old Age for the benefit of my own sex," included in an 1827 diary entry, Logan urged a cheerful yet contemplative appearance for women growing old. It would not do, she argued, for women to reveal the "peevishness" that she admitted was a familiar tendency among old women. Nor should women continually manifest "discontent," despite the difficulties of advanced age. On the other hand, the prudent old woman should be able to distinguish between an appropriately cheerful demeanor and "the levity and affectation of youth, which of all counterfeits is most sure to be detected." Only when the reality of growing old was ignored or distorted through unseemly dress or behavior, Logan argued, were the rewards of old age denied.[14]

This is not to suggest that some old women didn't attempt to hide their age. In describing her "excellent plan for a wrinkled chin," E. H. Dunbar detailed in a 1799 letter an ingenious if awkward disguise. By running a necklace "through a cravat . . . tied on the head after placing it behind the ears," one could (and, by implication, *should*) mask the objectionable chin. Clearly, not all women were comfortable with the physical manifestations of age. Other women sometimes simply failed to "act their age." One Mrs. Thompson "made herself extremely ridiculous by her Folly and levity," reported a similarly aged matron. "She had a Son and daughter grown up with her and yet behaved like a Coquettish girl, tho' owning to 55 (she might have added 4 or 5 to the number) and without a tooth in her head. . . ." Such behaviors, however, were the exception to these well-understood rules.[15]

Age, Wisdom, and Women's Revolutionary Heritage

Expectations for women to grow old quietly and unobtrusively suggest that old age was not to be considered a period of growth and continued development. Such was not entirely the case. As women aged, many expected their wisdom to increase as their minds matured. One aging Quaker found great comfort in the fact that the "mind ripens," even when the physical form "decays." According to her interpretation, the mind's capacity to "support itself" gradually increased over time, allowing her to "understand things better" than before.[16]

"My having gone on so long . . . before you gives me to understand the intricacies of the way," Elizabeth Denny Ward wrote to her son in 1836. She and other old women believed that experience gained over the course of a long lifetime served as the basis for increased wisdom. Experience also enabled the aged to distinguish the significant from the trite, the intrinsically valuable from the superficially desirable. "As the shadows lengthen, we see through a different medium," Abigail Adams wrote to her sister, "and may justly estimate many of our pursuits, as vanity and vexation of spirit." Such beliefs in the growth of wisdom with age were expressed by women publicly as well as privately. Attacking the observation that women were "at their zenith" at age twenty-one, the New Haven pamphleteer "The Female Advocate" announced her full expectation for years of continual growth and improvement. She had long planned, she wrote, that with increasing age she "should be advancing in grace, and augmenting in knowledge, with views penetrating to a future world, and expanding with eternity."[17]

The wisdom and experience that can come with age had, of course, long been acknowledged as basic criteria for leadership among men in many preindustrial societies. Both the memory and accrued wisdom of the elderly were considered necessary for the continued functioning of early societies. Old women seldom gained positions of leadership as rewards for their memory or their judgment, but they nonetheless continued to play a vital role within the familial setting. This enduring utility was due in large part to the store of knowledge and data long collected by older women. Even as America industrialized in the early nineteenth century, old women still understood the value attached to their memories and their perceptions. In fact, as the arcadian past was increasingly idealized in Jacksonian America, a long, last look at the "glory" of former years briefly heralded the lives and memories of the old.[18]

For these women, of course, past "glory" inevitably meant their association with the American Revolution. Such women considered themselves members of a unique and special generation. Their shared revolutionary heritage created a strong bond between the war's survivors, both men and women. Despite the generally noncombative, nonpolitical role women played in the fight for independence, they too experienced a sense of accomplishment and pride in the victory over Britain and the successful establishment of a new republic. As the "daughters of the Revolution" grew old, their sense of pride remained intact while their rarity as revolutionary-war survivors increased. Old women in the new republic often believed their generation experienced and understood the past differently. More important, they were certain their unique experiences enhanced the quality of wisdom they brought with them to old age.[19]

Because she had "grown grey with years, and was witness to what I relate," Abigail Adams believed she was specially qualified to recognize the misguided political rationale of many (often younger) political leaders, who seldom compared favorably to the "patriots" of the past. When war broke out with Great Britain in 1812, she considered "the few remaining patriots" among the only citizens possessing "Native American spirit." Like other aged women, she continued to identify with her fellow patriots throughout her life.[20]

In the expansive diary of Deborah Norris Logan, the enduring influence of the Revolution is again evident. Logan alluded frequently if not daily to persons or events of the past, usually the revolutionary past. As an old woman, she could still vividly remember hearing the Declaration of Independence read while standing by her father's garden wall in Philadelphia. As a member of a leading Quaker family, she had met many of the framers of the Declaration. Later, as the wife of a prominent Pennsylvania politician and active Jeffersonian Republican, she reinforced her sense of participation in the major events of the day. Despite the somewhat indirect nature of her revolutionary experience, she identified fully with the men of the revolutionary generation and viewed them as figures larger than life. In the 1820 poem "Recollections" inscribed to her husband, Deborah Logan eulogized the past while placing herself firmly as a witness, if not a participant, in the great event. "I have marked an empire's birth," she wrote. "I saw the eaglet mount the skies." As the years passed, her focus often was fixed on the people and events that bound her to the past and frequently alienated her from the future.[21]

From their revolutionary heritage, many women inherited new opportunities for expanding their awareness of themselves and the world around them which, in turn, influenced their perceptions about women and aging. Although most women were unable to avail themselves of a truly well-rounded education, many women benefitted from the increased emphasis placed on reading and writing in the new republic. This new devotion to women's literacy not only prepared women for their roles as "republican mothers" but also provided them with valuable tools for self-expression and vicarious participation in a world from which they were largely exiled. In their old age, these literate women relied heavily on these tools to expand their daily world, to participate in active and meaningful intercourse with others, and to leave a permanent record of themselves which could be passed down to later generations. Writing remained, however, an avenue of private rather than public expression. Only a few women with creative talents gained professional recognition or even a modest amount of fame.[22]

Women's literacy, of course, was not strictly a product of the Revolution. Exceptional old women such as the poet Susanna Wright "could not live" without books, according to Benjamin Rush in 1784, the year of Wright's death at age eighty-seven. After the Revolution, increasing numbers of women with varying amounts of talent and intellectual curiosity found pleasure in reading, pleasure which often seemed to increase with age. Elizabeth Drinker, who insisted she was not "remarkably Bookish," systematically recorded her book lists, revealing a wide and impressive range of reading. In her sixties, Drinker acknowledged that she had read more in the past few years than ever before. Susanna Nancarro, an eighty-year-old friend of Deborah Logan, apparently also read more frequently during her last years. Significantly, Logan perceived this late-life literacy as both appropriate and timely. Such reading, she argued, "perhaps contributes more to form a solid mind than great reading in early youth. . . ." Reading continued to serve an important role in the daily lives of women, even in extreme old age. Anna Cunningham's ninety-year-old mother, for instance, increasingly turned to her books as her ability to hear declined. "I believe she reads as understandingly as she ever did," Cunningham wrote in 1835. This devotion to reading expressed by many aging women indicates the degree to which literacy altered the tenor of women's lives as they grew old and increased the opportunities for intellectual growth in old age.[23]

Because Elizabeth Drinker's late-life reading habits are so well documented, an examination of the kinds of books she read and some of her responses to those works may help determine the intellectual framework of women's lives as they grew older. Although Drinker's family wealth and position allowed her to indulge in more reading than enjoyed by most older women of the time, Drinker was not an intellectual and, aside from being a diarist, was not a writer. Her absorption with books stemmed from her need to occupy time during long bouts of illness and from an obvious love of the written word.[24]

"Tis a practice I by no means high approve," Drinker confessed when she considered her indulgence in the reading of "romances," "yet I trust I have not sinned—as I read a little of most things." That she did. At the end of 1802, for instance, the sixty-eight-year-old Drinker recorded the names of sixty-four works she had read during the course of the year, a figure consistent with her average reading list over the previous ten years. During that year, her reading ranged from romantic novels to natural science, instructional books to religious tracts, history to moral tales for young people. This wide range was evident in all her reading during the past decade. While religious and moral tracts were among those most frequently cited, novels remained remarkably consistent items on her reading list. Even books intended for children were among her favorites. "I read those books for young persons with pleasure, 'tho I am old," she wrote in 1800.[25]

Elizabeth Drinker's Quaker background and her eighteenth-century upper-middle-class heritage strongly influenced her views on the roles and duties of women. Her choices of literature may have reinforced those beliefs, for there is little indication that her views were profoundly altered by the books she read about women. Nevertheless, Drinker and her cohorts read many books by and about women, indicating the need to contemplate the status of women in both traditional and new ways. The frequency with which she read William Kendrick's *The Whole Duty of Woman,* a veritable classic by that time, reveals her basic conservatism, which indeed never left her. Yet the willingness of Drinker and many other women of her age and social class to read Mary Wollstonecraft's *Vindication of the Rights of Women* suggests that women's interests began to change by the end of the eighteenth century. Aging women such as Elizabeth Drinker and Abigail Adams were sympathetic to many of Wollstonecraft's views, particularly as they related to women's education. This sympathy affirmed a new self-consciousness among women, young and old, who were able to consider

the possibility of a changing, dynamic woman's role in society rather than
the static position to which they might well have grown accustomed.[26]

While Mary Wollstonecraft introduced many readers to an emergent
British feminism, American writers also offered images of women which
challenged traditional concepts. As the writings of Judith Sargent Murray
were increasingly circulated in the late eighteenth century, an American
feminist ideal began to emerge. Significantly, this ideal was expanded by
1798 to include a new and vigorous model of feminine aging.

In a 1798 compilation of her writings, Judith Sargent Murray ("Constantia") endeavored to prove "female capability" by describing the impressive characteristics and achievements of an elderly Massachusetts woman
whom she apparently considered the epitome of feminine competence. This
"complete husbandwoman," according to Murray, was "a marvel of self-
education, industry, & strength." An avid reader who read "everything she
could procure," she was, as well, a "mistress of agricolation . . . a botanist
and florist." Her knowledge of farming, in fact, was so complete that farmers
throughout the vicinity sought her advice. Her neighbors considered her
general knowledge and judgment exceptional, and they consulted her, said
Murray, on "every perplexing emergency." Her physical achievements were
equally impressive. Murray described her as uncommonly tall, her early
rovings having "expanded" her limbs. Because she exercised regularly, she
was "wonderfully athletic," often exhibiting remarkable strength. The old
woman never indulged in "imaginary complaints," and she served others
as a "valuable nurse." Despite such strength and power, her "tenderness of
disposition [was] not to be exceeded." She was, in sum, a totally self-reliant
and independent woman.[27]

Although Judith Sargent Murray's image of the aged "complete husbandwoman" appears unusual for this or even later periods of American
literature, Murray's choice of an old woman to represent total feminine
independency is noteworthy. Murray turned topsy-turvy the traditional,
male-derived images of sedentary, saintly old women without bodies or
minds of their own. Free of male control, Murray's idealized old woman
gained respect from men and women alike within her community. Asser-
tively physical, intellectually active, and capable of sustaining herself and
others, the aged spinster symbolized to Murray women's potential for
achievement outside marriage and the family. It is difficult to determine if
and how much Murray's vivid description influenced the lives of the women
who read it. Still, Murray's aged woman stands as a valuable turning point
in early feminist literature. The "complete husbandwoman" offered a new
and challenging model for women growing old at the turn of the century.[28]

Despite the impressive new image of feminine aging offered by Murray,
most women relied on more traditional, classical interpretations of growing

old. First and foremost, women read and contemplated the Bible, drawing
from it both solace and inspiration. At times of illness and death and at
other critical points where rational explanations failed, the Bible reiterated
the need for faith and promised reward to the faithful. As women grew
older, they were comforted in the scriptural recognition that age signified
honor in the eye of God. "The hoary head is a crown of glory," according
to the Book of Proverbs. Biblical precepts commanded filial respect and urged
veneration for those who lived long and righteous lives, principles which
set well with women approaching the end of life.

Beyond the obvious comfort that the aged could derive from biblical
exhortations on old age, the Bible counseled all men and women to "walk
with the spirit" and to denounce "the desires of the flesh" (Gal. 5:16). For
those growing old, such counsel reaffirmed the reality of their declining
physical state and the need to concentrate on spiritual matters. Paul, in this
same letter to the Galatians, detailed those qualities that constituted the
"fruit of the spirit: love, joy, peace, patience, kindness, goodness, faithfulness,
gentleness, [and] self-control" (Gal. 5:22-23). These qualities were considered
appropriate moral exercises for the aged. They constituted, as well, an
excellent compendium of feminine virtue as it was defined in the early
nineteenth century. Aging women, indeed, exemplified well-ripened "fruit
of the spirit."[29]

While many elderly women kept the Bible close at hand during this
and later periods, it was not the only well-thumbed source of instruction
for the aged. Numerous eighteenth-century reissues of Cicero's classic essay
On Old Age (*De Senectute*) affirm its place as an important guide for both
men and women growing old. Cicero's central theme is one of hope and
promise: the transference from physical to intellectual strength and wisdom
in old age, accompanied by a loosening of earthly bonds while preparing
(through resignation) for everlasting life in heaven. The elderly, being superior in wisdom and judgment according to Cicero, were counseled to
refrain from the hard physical labor of former years and concentrate instead
on the rewards of intellectual growth.[30]

When he wrote *De Senectute* in 44 B.C., Cicero undoubtedly anticipated
an exclusively male readership. Centuries later, however, Cicero's model
would appeal to post-revolutionary women for a number of reasons. In a
period when women's intellectual opportunities were limited by forces
seemingly beyond their control, women still believed in their own accumulated wisdom and experience. As nurturers and caretakers of their families and friends, women perceived the "natural order" of the world in ways
often unfamiliar to their male counterparts. And, as valuable members of
society who still were denied many of the basic freedoms enjoyed by their
husbands, brothers, and sons, women knew only too well the need for

resignation. Although many women might not have attributed their views on old age directly to Cicero, many appear to have absorbed his message, often reiterating it throughout their later years.[31]

Life's Full Circle: Identifying the Metaphors of Age

Among the many useful elements found in Cicero's advice to the aged, perhaps none had more impact than the metaphors he employed to describe and illuminate the mysteries of old age. Emphasizing the natural qualities of aging, he compared old age to the "autumn of life," popularizing the metaphors of "ripened fruit" and natural decay which have permeated the literature of aging for centuries. By the end of the eighteenth century, such metaphors reverberated throughout women's writings. In youth and old age, women found both explanation and direction in such natural symbols.[32]

In 1757, Martha Brewster, a New England poet and grandmother, presented a classical interpretation of life's stages in her poem "On the Four Ages of Man Resembling the Four Seasons of the Year." Like others before her, she portrayed the inevitability of "man's budding, blooming, ripening, withering State." This organic vision of life, rather neatly divided into recognizable quadrants, differs in many ways from present-day constructs, which offer few such integrated visions of the life cycle. Brewster's "Four Ages of Man" and other models of aging provided not only a host of metaphors giving symbolic meaning to old age but also a framework for visualizing the whole of life.[33]

Women in youth as well as old age drew on seasonal metaphors to explain or anticipate changes in their own lives. Forecasting the "mournful days" of her "winter," twenty-year-old Ann Livingston expected soon to witness the withering of her "exterior splendor . . . like the foliage that crowned this youthful shrub." Rebecca Noyes, in her fiftieth year, began to prepare "for the approach of *Winter* (old age)." Deborah Norris Logan, having turned seventy-six in the fall of 1837, admitted that autumnal metaphors no longer applied. "Surely it is Winter with Me," she wrote, "and though Frosty — yet kindly."[34]

Indeed, Deborah Logan's admission that old age/winter could be "kindly" suggests that within this highly structured metaphorical framework existed a latitude and an ambiguity that mirrored the experience of growing old. Like other women, Logan appeared to draw considerable comfort from these seasonal associations, which she frequently employed in her writing. In her 1830 poem "October," she acknowledged the ambivalent nature of autumn and the aging process itself. Despite the reality that "cold decrepitude is coming fast," she wrote, autumn "counsels Hope — since things that fade on earth / Light, Seasons, Flowers, / All know a second birth." The ease with which such seasonal metaphors coalesced with widely held expectations of old age, death, and rebirth — and yet reflected the ambiguity inherent within the aging process — assured their longstanding usage.[35]

Other familiar metaphors also mirrored a world still bound to the mundane associations of preindustrial rural life. The deaths of aged friends and neighbors were frequently interpreted in terms redolent of harvest time. When an elderly friend died, Harriet Gray Otis appeared comforted by the knowledge that he was "gathered in as the ripened sheaf." He was, after all, "full of years." Other metaphors reflected more closely the domestic activities associated with women's lives. "Poor Betty Burrage," wrote Elizabeth Drinker, "she is untwisting the thread of life very fast." Although both Harriet Otis and Elizabeth Drinker were sophisticated urban women, they continued to utilize metaphors which drew on the rural and "distaff" associations of past generations of women.[36]

Women contemplating their own old age frequently employed a similar, although seemingly less reassuring, metaphorical device in which the onset of old age marked the "decline of life." Hannah Winthrop wrote to her friend Mercy Warren in 1778 that she was no longer "upon the summit" of life, "but alas in the descent [where] clouds intervene." Elizabeth Cranch Norton, at the age of forty-four, anticipated with some foreboding the swiftness with which she would "slide down the declivity of life!" Other frequently used metaphors emphasized the "decay" that advanced with old age, accounting for the physical and sometimes mental decline witnessed by so many aging persons.[37]

Within this perception of life in "decline," certain life changes could be expected at regular intervals. The most notable and critical interval occurred at age sixty-three, known as the "grand climacteric" and familiar to women since the early seventeenth century. While other climacterics were often associated with the "change of life," the grand climacteric supposedly marked the onset of old age. When Elizabeth Ambler Carrington of Virginia reached her grand climacteric in 1823, she expressed the hope that her periods of suffering were "now fast drawing to an end." For others, the onset of the sixty-third year signalled a period of unparalleled decay.[38]

Yet not all aspects of "decline" are to be construed as negative. Viewed in the context of a unified, continuous vision of life, decline and decay were to be expected. Evidence of natural decline was abundant in the agrarian world of post-revolutionary America. To be synchronized with life's full circle, one anticipated both ascendancy and decline. Such metaphors offered reassurance that life's "declivity" promised connection and continuity as the circle closed.

Symbols, of course, also helped separate mind from matter. By employing metaphors of aging, women (and men) could begin the task of disassociating their physical from their metaphysical selves, a necessary if difficult intellectual leap as age and death approached. By interpreting their senescence in the language of natural decline, the aged envisioned a separate and distinct fate for the physical body, one which was shared by everyone and everything in their universe.[39]

The continuing popularity of natural/seasonal metaphors reflected, in many ways, the intellectual climate of the new republic. Those who built its new social and political edifices relied heavily on classical scholarship for guidance and direction. Indeed, Cicero's wisdom would be consulted on a wide variety of topics, most far removed from the concerns of old age. Not all Americans, of course, accepted without question the wisdom of the past. Many men and women of the Enlightenment preferred to relate observations of the natural world to their own personal experiences. Here, too, organic metaphors of life appeared wholly justified, reflecting the reality they knew and witnessed.[40]

What is remarkable about these metaphorical devices, however, is not their validity (still unchallenged by the eighteenth-century reader) but the lack of alternative visions for contemplating old age. Most images of old age were age-old. While philosophers and medical practitioners over the centuries had occasionally reinterpreted symptoms and signs of aging, the aged themselves continued to resort to traditional, natural symbolism to explain their changing lives. The lack of popular texts on the subject, aside from Cicero and the Bible, served to reinforce these traditional views. Even Romantic literature, which was growing in popularity by the early nineteenth century, failed to offer alternative visions. While Romanticists in both Britain and America became increasingly obsessed with the loss of youth and beauty, they continued to utilize images of decay, reinforcing natural metaphors long associated with lost youth. Indeed, until the mid-nineteenth century, these images would continue to dominate personal expressions of old age. By then, increasing literacy combined with an expanding publishing industry promised new possibilities for alternative visions. As other writers have suggested, by the mid-nineteenth century, alternative visions were clearly needed.[41]

Women growing old two hundred years ago understood what was expected of them. In their dress and demeanor, their activities and their relationships, women could approach old age with a clear vision of the future. It would be a quiet future, removed from the day-to-day concerns outside the home. In this idealized tomorrow, peace and cheerfulness would counter any negative visions of growing old. Wrapped in the dignity of age (and in appropriately somber attire), old women could contemplate their final years with the wisdom that comes only with age. They knew, as did their grandmothers before them, that "the sere and yellow leaf" of autumn would soon be blanketed by the "snows of winter," and they took comfort in the fact that new generations would feel the warmth of "a bright and only spring."

Some aspects of this idealized vision differed (at least in degree) from those known to earlier generations of women. Although it is likely that aged colonial women failed to perceive strongly gender-defined guidelines for appropriate aging, women in Jacksonian America understood clearly the relationship between gender and age. Any flexibility in attitudes toward pre-revolutionary women appears to have been largely obliterated in the new nation. Ironically, this may be due in part to the peculiar nature of women's revolutionary heritage. Despite a legacy of increased opportunities for female literacy—a legacy which promised to expand women's vision of themselves and their future—expectations regarding women's roles grew more rigid with time. Few women emulated such radical if rare models of feminine aging as Murray's "complete husbandwoman." Instead, traditional images prevailed, apparently reinforced by literacy and, in time, a reified "woman's sphere."

By the 1830s, developments beyond woman's sphere suggested that women's age-old expectations might be changing in the decades to come. Feminine aging, once merely a personal concern, was rapidly becoming an object of intense medical interest. A growing medical profession promoted its own expectations about aging women that often contradicted other prevailing notions of resignation and contentment. Menopause, according to many physicians, marked the onset of old age. With it supposedly came an assortment of physical and emotional ailments, including melancholy, irritability, depression, and even insanity. Despite the fact that few women openly described any apprehension associated with menopause, physicians contended that it was the final, pivotal turning point in a woman's life.[42]

Larger theological and cultural shifts in American society would soon allay, as well, some of the idealized images long associated with feminine aging. In time, images of rocking chairs and empty nests would better serve the needs of an increasingly gerontophobic society. But as such twentieth-century metaphors failed to depict accurately the lives of women growing old, so too did earlier images fail to portray the complexity of women's lives.

NOTES

1. Fanny Burney [Madame D'Arblay], *Evelina: Or the History of a Young Lady's Entrance into the World,* 3 vols. (London: Thomas Lowndes, 1778), 3:311.

2. Ibid., 3:295.

3. Normative values were transmitted by numerous vehicles, including books, sermons, and published tracts, some of which we will examine. Mainly, however, we will explore those elements evident in the written record of women as they attempted to describe those values they expected in others and, of course, those which guided their own lives.

4. The association of withdrawal, disengagement, and approaching death is more fully explored in chapter six.

5. Elizabeth Drinker, Diary, 6 April 1795 and 23 October 1799, HSP; Julia Cowles, *Diary of Julia Cowles: A Connecticut Record, 1797-1803*, ed. Laura Hadley Moseley (New Haven: Yale University Press, 1931), p. 64; Hannah Adams, *A Memoir of Miss Hannah Adams, Written by Herself* (Boston: Gray and Bowen, 1832), p. 5. See also Abigail Adams to Mary Cranch, 13 March 1798, *New Letters of Abigail Adams, 1788-1801,* ed. Stewart Mitchell (Boston: Houghton Mifflin, 1947), p. 142; Margaret Bayard Smith to Jane Kirkpatrick, 12 June 1835 and 10 February 1840, Margaret Bayard Smith Papers, LCMD; Anna Thornton, Diary, n.d., reel 7, William Thornton Papers, LCMD. Even young women perceived that their very early youth was filled with more "vivid feelings" than later years. See Harriet Otis, Diary, 10 March 1812, Harrison Gray Otis Papers, MHS.

6. Elizabeth Drinker, Diary, 23 October 1799, HSP.

7. Alice Izard to Margaret Manigault, 29 March 1812, Izard Family Papers, LCMD; Margaret Bayard Smith to Jane Kirkpatrick, 17 July 1835, Margaret Bayard Smith Papers, LCMD; Deborah Norris Logan, Diary, 14 August 1815, HSP.

Women often linked the concepts of retirement and domesticity. See, for instance, Ann R. Page to Elizabeth Adams, n.d. [1803], William A. Randolph Papers, LCMD.

8. Abigail Adams to Mary Cranch, 12 July and 28 June 1789, *New Letters,* ed. Mitchell, pp. 15, 13; Deborah Norris Logan, Diary, 15 September 1824, HSP; Sally Richmond to Nancy Shaw, 18 February 1846, Shaw-Webb Family Papers, AAS. See also Elizabeth Smith's diary, 5 December 1822, AAS, for an idealized retrospective description of one's own life, and compare Susan Lear, Journal, 3 June 1788, Miscellaneous Manuscript Collection, LCMD.

9. Deborah Norris Logan, Diary, 15 September 1824, HSP. In late eighteenth-century England, Mary Granville Delaney epitomized all that was proper and respectful in old age. She was described as possessing "venerable cheeks," "native humility," and "the blush of a young girl." See *Mary Hamilton, afterwards Mrs. John Dickenson, at Court and at Home,* ed. Elizabeth Anson and Florence Anson (London: J. Murray, 1925), quotation on p. 172; Frances Burney, *The Diary and Letters of Frances Burney, Mrs. D'Arblay,* 2 vols., ed. Sarah Chauncey Woolsey (Boston: Little, Brown, 1880), quotation on 1:157; and Hannah More, *Memoirs of Hannah More,* ed. W. Roberts (New York: Harper and Bros., 1835), quotation on p. 281.

10. Margaret Bayard Smith to Jane Kirkpatrick, 4 August 1835, Margaret Bayard Smith Papers, LCMD. See also Mary Crowninshield to husband, 18 January 1815, Crowninshield Family Papers, EI; and Elizabeth Drinker, Diary, 28 December 1794, HSP. Julia Cherry Spruill noted that no one in the colonial South "whether

man or woman, was too old to marry." See Spruill, *Women's Life and Work in the Southern Colonies* (New York: W. W. Norton, 1972), p. 160. See also Carroll Smith-Rosenberg, "Beauty, the Beast, and the Militant Woman: A Case Study in Sex Roles and Social Stress in Jacksonian America," in *A Heritage of Her Own: Toward a New Social History of American Women,* ed. Nancy F. Cott and Elizabeth H. Pleck (New York: Simon and Schuster, 1979), pp. 197-221; and Daniel Scott Smith, "Family Limitation, Sexual Control, and Domestic Feminism in Victorian America," ibid., pp. 222-45. A woman's advanced age could provide sanction for platonic relationships with men, relationships which might earlier have been considered inappropriate. See Alice Izard to Margaret Manigault, 8 May 1814, Izard Family Papers, LCMD.

11. Demos, "Old Age in Early New England," in *Turning Points: Historical and Sociological Essays on the Family,* ed. John Demos and Sarane Spence Boocock (Chicago: University of Chicago Press, 1978), p. 250; Spruill, *Women's Life and Work,* p. 107; Anna Green Winslow, Diary, 17 January 1772, in *Lives of American Women: A History with Documents,* ed. Joyce D. Goodfriend and Claudia M. Christie (Boston: Little, Brown, 1981), p. 23. See also Mary Parker Norris to Deborah Logan, 4 January 1797, Norris Family Letters, HSP.

12. Abigail Adams to Mary Cranch, 26 April 1799, *New Letters,* ed. Mitchell, p. 166; Hannah Emery to Mary Carter, 2 July 1789, Cutts Family Papers, EI. See also Rebecca Shoemaker to Samuel Shoemaker, 26 August and 19 September 1784, Shoemaker Papers, HSP; Abigail Adams to Mary Cranch, 13 May 1798 and 11 December 1799, *New Letters,* ed. Mitchell, pp. 173, 220; and Alice Izard to Margaret Manigault, 12 February 1814, Izard Family Papers, LCMD.

13. David Hackett Fischer suggests that women's fashions have always differentiated women according to age, with older women wearing longer, fuller gowns even thousands of years ago. See Fischer, *Growing Old in America,* 2d ed. (New York: Oxford University Press, 1978), pp. 89-90.

14. Deborah Norris Logan, Diary, 15 September 1827, HSP.

15. Elizabeth H. Dunbar to Elizabeth Shippen, 29 November 1799, Shippen Family Papers, LCMD; Deborah Norris Logan, Diary, n.d. 1818, HSP.

16. Deborah Norris Logan, Diary, 6 September 1823, 26 December 1820, and 6 April 1830, HSP.

17. Elizabeth Denny Ward to Thomas Ward III, 24 February 1836, Ward Family Papers, AAS; Abigail Adams to Mary Cranch, 27 March 1781, *New Letters,* ed. Mitchell, p. 147; "The Female Advocate," quoted in Linda K. Kerber, *Women of the Republic: Intellect and Ideology in Revolutionary America* (Chapel Hill: University of North Carolina Press, 1980), p. 198.

18. See Fred Cottrell, "The Technological and Societal Basis of Aging," in *Handbook of Social Gerontology,* ed. Clark Tibbitts (Chicago: University of Chicago Press, 1960); and Leo W. Simmons, *The Role of the Aged in Primitive Society* (New Haven: Yale University Press, 1945).

Goodfriend and Christie have argued that women's memories were highly regarded in early America. "Valued as repositories of knowledge because of their extensive experience," they wrote, "elderly women constituted a precious human resource for preindustrial communities." See *Lives of American Women,* ed. Goodfriend and Christie, p. 317. See also W. Andrew Achenbaum, *Old Age in the New Land* (Baltimore: Johns Hopkins University Press, 1978), pp. 33-35; and Fischer, *Growing Old in America,* pp. 13-14.

The ideal of a purer, ascetic agrarian past symbolized by the yeoman farmer was, of course, a popular component of Jeffersonian ideology. It was not until the emergence of Andrew Jackson as a popular if reactionary political figure, however, that the symbol of the frontier farmer gained national political validity. See John William Ward, *Andrew Jackson: Symbol for an Age* (New York: Oxford University Press, 1955), p. 45; and Marvin Meyers, *The Jacksonian Persuasion* (Stanford: Stanford University Press, 1960), pp. 3-16.

19. See Abigail Adams to Mary Cranch, 12 December 1797, *New Letters,* ed. Mitchell, p. 118; and Mercy Otis Warren to Abigail Adams, n.d. 1778, Letterbook, Mercy Otis Warren Papers, MHS. Judith Sargent Murray ("Constantia") described the ties of women of the revolutionary generation in *The Gleaner, a Miscellaneous Production,* 3 vols. (Boston: I. Thomas and E. T. Andrews, 1798), 3:189-93. See also Mary Beth Norton, *Liberty's Daughters: The Revolutionary Experience of American Women, 1750-1800* (Boston: Little, Brown, 1980), p. 194.

20. Abigail Adams to Mary Cranch, 12 December 1797, *New Letters,* ed. Mitchell, p. 118; Abigail Adams to John Quincy Adams, quoted in Charles W. Akers, *Abigail Adams: An American Woman* (Boston: Little, Brown, 1980), p. 186.

21. See Deborah Norris Logan, Diary, n.d. May 1820, HSP.

22. This study is obviously biased in this direction, as only literate women were able to provide lasting records. Kenneth Lockridge estimates that between 1780 and 1850 women's literacy rates in New England doubled. By 1850, when the census first recorded literacy, women could both read and write on an equal footing with men. See Kenneth Lockridge, *Literacy in Colonial New England: An Enquiry into the Social Context of Literacy in the Early Modern West* (New York: W. W. Norton, 1974), pp. 38-44.

Linda Kerber has argued that "old people, who had been educated before and during the Revolution, accounted for most of the illiterates in 1850, [so] we can assume that major improvements in female education took place between 1790 and 1830 or so." See Kerber, *Women of the Republic,* p. 193. This argument fails to account for the fact that many of the over-sixty population in 1850 would have attended school in the 1790s. By 1850, only a tiny fraction of Americans were living who had been able to attend school before or during the Revolution, hardly enough to account for "most of the illiterates" in the country.

23. Quoted in Pattie Cowell, " 'Womankind Call Reason to Their Aid': Susanna Wright's Verse Epistle on the Status of Women in Eighteenth-Century America," *Signs: Journal of Women in Culture and Society* 6 (Summer 1981):797; Elizabeth Drinker, Diary, 22 May 1795, HSP; Deborah Norris Logan, Diary, 6 February 1828, HSP; Anna Cunningham to Nancy Shaw, 14 January 1835, Shaw-Webb Family Papers, AAS. Anna Thornton periodically listed books she read, ranging from medical tracts and romances to "polynesian researches." See Thornton, Diary, William Thornton Papers, LCMD. See also the comments of Anna

Blackwood Howell, an aging widow who operated fisheries in New Jersey, in Howell, Diary, n.d. 1831 and 28 September 1833, AAS.

Although women employed images conveyed by oral tradition as well as the printed word, the impact of literacy on women's lives is evident in many of their perceptions of old age. Recent studies of literacy include Linda Auwers, "The Social Meaning of Female Literacy: Windsor, Connecticut, 1660-1775," No. 77-4A, Newberry Papers in Family and Community History, Newberry Library, Chicago; and Sally McConnell-Ginet, Ruth Borker, and Nelly Furman, eds., *Women and Language in Literature and Society* (New York: Praeger, 1980).

24. See Elizabeth Drinker, Diary, 22 May 1795, 7 January and 13 September 1796, and 31 December 1802, and compare 22 April 1796, 25 November 1798, 31 December 1799, 9 August 1800, and 31 December 1800, HSP.

25. Ibid., 31 December 1802, 7 January 1796, and 31 December 1800. See Kerber, *Women of the Republic,* pp. 237-39, for an examination of Elizabeth's Drinker's reading habits.

The British writer Hannah More's *Cheap Repository Tracts* were popular items on the reading lists of many women. See also Elizabeth Drinker, Diary, 22 April 1796, 25 November 1798, and 31 December 1799, HSP.

Frances Burney's multivolume novels, which often pointed to the vulnerability of old persons in upper-class British society, were widely read by many women. See, for instance, *Evelina: Or the History of a Young Lady's Entrance into the World; Cecilia: Or Memoirs of an Heiress;* and *Camilla: Or a Picture of Youth.*

26. Women, regardless of age, enjoyed books about and by women. For example, see Eliza Southgate Bowne, *A Girl's Life Eighty Years Ago: Selections from the Letters of Eliza Southgate Bowne* (New York: Charles Scribner's Sons, 1887), p. 62; Deborah Norris Logan, Diary, 28 January and 2 May 1835, HSP; Rebecca Noyes, Diary, 14 January 1812, CHS; and Mary Sumner Benson, *Women in Eighteenth-Century America: A Study of Opinion and Social Usage* (New York: Columbia University Press, 1935), pp. 85-92.

27. Murray, *The Gleaner,* 3:220-22.

28. Ibid., p. 220.

29. See Thomas R. Cole, " 'Putting off the Old': Middle-class Morality, Antebellum Protestantism, and the Origins of Ageism," in *Old Age in a Bureaucratic Society: The Elderly, the Experts, and the State in American History* (Westport, Conn.: Greenwood Press, 1986), pp. 49-65.

30. Cicero, *De Senectute* 23.82 and 6.17. Merrill Peterson tells us that both Adams and Jefferson "pondered" *De Senectute* in their old age. See Peterson, *Adams and Jefferson: A Revolutionary Dialogue* (Oxford: Oxford University Press, 1976), p. 125. Cicero was one among many Greek philosophers contemplating old age. Eratosthenes constructed a theory of aging, dividing the expected life span into three units which corresponded to the Greek calendar.

31. See chapter five, below, on resignation. Elizabeth Drinker acknowledged she was "pleas'd" with having read Cicero. See Drinker, Diary, 20 August 1795, HSP; and Deborah Norris Logan, Diary, 12 December 1823, 4 February and 15 September 1827, HSP.

32. Men as well as women employed seasonal metaphors to describe the physical process of growing old. I suspect, however, that such self-conscious metaphors offered different, gender-specific meanings. While such a study is beyond the scope of this book, it is an area "ripe" for examination.

33. Martha Brewster, "On the Four Ages of Man Resembling the Four Seasons of the Year," in her *Poems on Diverse Subjects* (New London: T. Green, 1757). See also Thomas R. Cole and Mary G. Winkler, "Aging in Western Medicine and Iconography: History and the Ages of Man," *Medical Heritage* 1 (September/October, 1985):335-47.

34. Ann Livingston, Diary, 15 October 1784, Shippen Family Papers, LCMD; Rebecca Noyes, Diary, 18 March 1809, CHS; Deborah Norris Logan, Diary, 21 October 1837, HSP.

35. Deborah Norris Logan, Diary, "October," n.d. 1830, HSP. See also ibid., 18 October 1822, 8 October 1823, and November 1829; and Lucinda Storrs, Diary, 26 February 1833, CHS.

36. Harriet Otis, Diary, 1 February [1812], Harrison Gray Otis Papers, MHS; Elizabeth Drinker, Diary, 15 November 1800, HSP. See also Deborah Norris Logan, Diary, 18 August 1822, HSP; Rebecca Noyes, Diary, n.d. 1805, CHS; Margaret Bayard Smith to ?, 19 December 1839, Margaret Bayard Smith Papers, LCMD; and E. H. Dunbar to Elizabeth Shippen, 6 March 1800, Shippen Family Papers, LCMD.

37. Hannah Winthrop to Mercy Otis Warren, 9 January 1778, Warren-Winthrop Papers, MHS; Elizabeth Cranch Norton, Diary, 21 November 1807, MHS; Deborah Norris Logan, Diary, 12 March 1815, HSP.

38. Elizabeth Jacquelin Ambler Carrington to Nancy ?, 11 March 1823, Letters of Elizabeth Jacquelin Ambler, LCMD. See also Deborah Norris Logan, Diary, 4 May and 19 October 1824, HSP.

39. Anthropologist Mary Douglas argues that "the social body constrains the way the physical body is perceived." In the traditional society of post-revolutionary America, symbolism was needed to explain the loss of physical health and vigor in old age which would, at the same time, support the religious and spiritual values of the time. By the mid-nineteenth century, middle-class values emphasizing progress and control would demand new interpretations and new symbols to explain senescence. See Douglas, *Natural Symbols: Explorations in Cosmology* (London: Barrie and Rockliff–Cresset Press, 1970), p. 65.

Writers today are once again recognizing the intrinsic benefits of an organic view of aging. According to Eugene Bianchi, "Middle and later adulthood present opportunities for combining the physical descent or gradual organic diminution with a spiritual ascent [requiring] a healthy acceptance of physical decline and a search for more satisfactory and humane experiences." See Bianchi, *Aging as a Spiritual Journey* (New York: Crossroads, 1982), p. 7.

40. Drew R. McCoy argues that many eighteenth-century thinkers employed a traditional biological analogy to political systems and human aging alike. "This metaphor," he writes, "suggested a cyclical view of historical development in which change or the process of time was eventually and inevitably associated with decay." See McCoy, *The Elusive Republic: Political Economy in Jeffersonian America* (New York: W. W. Norton, 1980), p. 33. See also Stow Persons, *American Minds: A History of Ideas* (New York: Henry Hold, 1958), pp. 123-36.

41. In describing the "Romantic path to immortality," W. Andrew Achen-

baum has argued that "writers after 1830 stressed that people faced '*peculiar sorrows*' in old age." Romantic sensibility described old age as *the* transitional stage of development between life and death, according to Achenbaum. See Achenbaum, *Old Age in the New Land,* pp. 33-35. Many middle- and upper-class women referred to (and copied) the poetry of Scott, Coleridge, and Shelley in their own writings. See, for instance, Deborah Norris Logan, Diary, 30 June 1824, HSP; and Anna Thornton, Diary, n.d. (front page), William Thornton Papers, LCMD.

42. See Carroll Smith-Rosenberg, "Puberty to Menopause: The Cycle of Femininity in Nineteenth-Century America," *Feminist Studies* 1 (Winter-Spring 1973):65-69. See also William P. Dewees, *A Treatise on the Diseases of Females* (Philadelphia: H. C. Carey and I. Lee, 1826), p. 56; and Joseph Ralph, *A Domestic Guide to Medicine* (New York: Leavitt, 1834), p. 130.

Elizabeth Drinker responded positively to the prospect of postmenopausal life as it affected women's health and well-being. According to Drinker, many women after the time of childbearing "experienced more comfort and satisfaction than at any other period of their lives. . . ." Like other women, however, Elizabeth Drinker did not directly relate menopause to her own life. See Drinker, Diary, 26 February 1797, HSP.

W. Andrew Achenbaum contends that after 1830 "descriptions of the aged's health diverged in tone and emphasis from earlier analysis." See Achenbaum, *Old Age in the New Land,* p. 33. Carol Haber discusses the "medical models of growing old" in nineteenth-century America in *Beyond Sixty-Five: The Dilemma of Old Age in America's Past* (New York: Cambridge University Press, 1983), pp. 47-63.

Living the Metaphors
of Old Age

As individuals grow old, memories of the past and visions of the future often merge to create a distinctive view of "reality." Individual perceptions of such reality differed as much two hundred years ago as they do today. Yet in the post-revolutionary period, a unique interplay of roles and values, models and metaphors added pressures and strains as aging women attempted to come to terms with growing old. While for some women old age offered no surprises, for others the reality of old age appeared more painful or at least more complex than they had ever anticipated.[1]

Lives of Active Engagement

The idealized view of old women as passive and content, removed from the pressures of the outside world, and devoted to the pursuit of inner peace prevailed for some women as they grew old. "In no portion of my life have I been so entirely exempt from care, anxiety, sickness, or troubles of any kind," wrote fifty-six-year-old Margaret Bayard Smith in 1834. Sixty-four-year-old Deborah Logan often expressed contentment and continued dedication to quiet and serenity. "I am enjoying myself in my retirement," she assured herself in 1825. Yet women often found retirement and inactivity less desirable than they had expected. Even Margaret Smith and Deborah Logan wrestled with the conflicts these images imposed.[2]

Despite the secluded introspection prescribed for old age, social activity among women growing old continued to serve as an integral part of their lives. Women may have been warned to relinquish "earthly ties" in order to contemplate heavenly ones, but friendships between women grew strong with age and continued until death. In fact, women's active friendships constituted an important, if unexpected, component of life in old age.[3]

"There is no person in the world who loves Company more than me," wrote the lonely and aging spinster Rebecca Dickinson in 1787, a sentiment echoed by other women in similar positions. Even among aging women who hated to admit how often they entertained, "company" was the rule, not the exception. As one aging woman noted in 1833, a "constant current of company... flows at this time to the house."[4]

While aging women often spent time with daughters and other female relatives, old friends devoted considerable attention to each other as well. "*Winter friends* are worth their weight in gold," Mary McDonald of Georgia reminded her good although absent friend Mrs. Rossiter. Contrary to the expectation that women's affections would become cold and callous with age, many friendships grew warmer over the years. "Time cannot destroy the fascination of her manner," wrote Phoebe Bradford of an old friend. "Her voice is music to the ear. . . ." Hannah Winthrop was well aware that "the engaging tie of sisterly affection" to her old friend Mercy Warren was "strengthened by encreasing years."[5]

Old friendships gained strength not only from the shared history of joys and sorrows but also because of the additional needs of women as they grew older. In 1799, for instance, Elizabeth Drinker described the difficulties experienced by her seventy-eight-year-old friend Susanna Swett. Swett, who lived alone with increasing infirmities, "is fearfull she may fall in the fire, or down the celler stairs . . . and lay there without help," wrote her friend. "She is a little panic struck, and no wonder," Drinker concluded. The urgency of her friend's pleas prompted the aging Drinker to provide a room for Swett in the Drinker home. Detachment and "chilled affections" were not deemed appropriate in such moments of need.[6]

Indeed, it was often difficult to strike that right balance between detachment and responsiveness. Particularly among thoughtful and introspective women, the dissonance apparent between expectations of detachment and habits of caring imposed frustration and anxiety in late life. Although aging women were expected to grow meditative and retiring, their need for social intercourse persistently contradicted their expectations. Women were reluctant to relinquish close emotional ties with others and to assume the detachment and frigidity considered appropriate for their age and sex. Contrary to social expectations, women often found their needs for friendship and attention increasing as they grew older. Continued activity and social interaction remained essential ingredients for happiness and contentment in old age.[7]

Women's work was no easier "retired" than were their friendships. The

perpetual nature of household duties assured continuing domestic employment, with little or no regard to advancing age. This was particularly true
in rural areas where households, while not self-sufficient, depended on a
woman's broad skills as well as plenty of muscle. Molly Cooper, on her
Long Island farm, spent many nights without sleep because she was attending
to chores. Preparing for the Christmas holidays in 1772, she stayed up four
consecutive nights preparing food and making candles. Never reluctant to
complain, she frequently acknowledged she was "tired allmost to death."
Although the availability of prepared foods and household goods increased
in urban areas over the next half-century, most women would continue to
undertake many of the same domestic duties that so exhausted the aging
Molly Cooper.[8]

Retirement from work was a luxury many women simply could not
afford. As they aged, many widows, spinsters, and even married women
remained actively involved in a variety of business enterprises in addition
to their daily household chores. Old women operated fisheries, managed
dairies, served as midwives and ministers, and ran boardinghouses as well
as other businesses. Although retirement from such activities might have
been appealing, economic necessity prevailed. "One would think we have
been so long in business we might Retire," wrote Elizabeth Cuming to her
fellow merchant Elizabeth Inman in 1784. But determined not to quit
business until she and her husband enjoyed "easy Circumstances," Cuming
continued to work.[9]

Financial gain was not the only incentive that motivated old women
to continue working. For women in the ministry, preaching would continue
for as long as their health held out. Although extremely feeble in old age,
Mary Mitchell remained actively engaged in the ministry of the Society of
Friends. Another Quaker preacher, Elizabeth Collins, believed that the extended tours undertaken by Quaker ministers served to "revive" aged preach-
ers. Jarena Lee, a black Methodist preacher in the early nineteenth century,
found the "ardor" for her cause not the least diminished by age. Anna
Catharine Ernst, who did not become a Moravian deaconess until the age
of sixty, was refused permission to retire until 1802, when she was seventy-
six. By this time, both she and her husband had suffered from "feebleness
and lameness" for several years. Ministerial work, while still unavailable
to women within most established, orthodox denominations, provided an
ongoing sense of mission and purpose for a number of women in nontra-
ditional sects. Such women appear unhampered by expectations of passivity
and withdrawal in old age.[10]

The active level at which aging women sometimes continued to work,
despite proscriptions to the contrary, is well illustrated in the diary of the
Maine midwife Martha Moore Ballard. In 1797, at age sixty-three, Ballard

celebrated the seven-hundredth birth she had assisted since June 1778. Because her profession demanded that she be available at any time of the day or night and in any season, Ballard often stayed away from home long hours, sometimes spending the night away from her family. The urgent demand for her services often necessitated walking miles from house to house when a ride was not available. Winter seemed to be her busiest season. In January 1797, for example, Ballard made twelve visits to women in her community, never commenting in her diary on the harshness of Maine winters. Despite falling off horses twice that year and "misplacing" several bones, Ballard continued her work with obvious satisfaction. An active wife, mother, and grandmother as well, Ballard maintained her strenuous pace into old age without any apparent attempt to conform to other, more limiting expectations.[11]

Martha Ballard's energetic example appears to belie most traditional images of sedate elderly women. Her diary gives little indication, however, that her behavior was considered deviant. Active in her local church and an apparent "pillar" of her community, Martha Ballard continued to work out of a sense of duty. She took obvious pride in her accomplishments, whose living reminders could be found throughout the community. As a midwife, of course, Ballard provided services which had long been considered appropriate to her sex and which were only beginning to be challenged by the emerging male "specialist." Because of her rural location and the continuing high birthrate in late eighteenth-century America, Martha Ballard's services were greatly valued. Such high regard did not diminish despite the onset of old age. Although it is difficult to determine how many older women maintained the rigorous daily schedule described by Ballard, it appears Judith Sargent Murray's radical image of the "complete husband-woman" was not merely a figment of her feminist imagination.[12]

Poor old women, of course, were forced to lead active and resourceful lives. The harsh reality of old age and poverty sometimes contrasted sharply with the expectations of middle- and upper-class women. Poverty-stricken old women, according to the idealized image of the day, exuded piety, honesty, and deference. Yet, as women encountered poor neighbors and impoverished former employees who frequently asked for help, they saw that poor old women were not always able to live according to these expectations. In revolutionary New Jersey, for instance, a poor old woman and her dog were openly ridiculed for their strange habits and behavior. "What a nasty piece of stuff she is," wrote young Jemima Condict after witnessing the old woman share her breakfast with her dog. This old woman and many others often begged for their food and lodgings, and they apparently were seldom denied. While wealthy women such as Elizabeth Drinker responded to such pleas, they nonetheless expected proper deference in return. Although Drinker noticed that the old Margaret Russel of Virginia was "rather forward in the beging way," she still gave her breakfast. Being "forward" or "flippant," however, doubtless rendered these old women less worthy of the alms they received.[13]

Aging women who were comfortably situated often organized to help their "less fortunate" sisters. Quaker women were especially dedicated to assisting the poor and homeless, as seen in their support of the Friends' Widows' Asylum which opened in Philadelphia in 1817. Because this institution was designed for the "worthy" poor, many women discovered old friends, down on their luck, residing in the asylum. With friends there they knew and loved, the asylum gained a reality and a harshness that made it frightening for women living safely away from its doors. "To me, a cave or a wigwam would be far preferable," the aging Deborah Logan wrote in 1827. As the first of its kind, the Widows' Asylum dramatically symbolized women's need for care and comfort in old age and served as a particularly vivid reminder that poverty could be right around the corner.[14]

The Widows' Asylum was not the only institutional reminder of poverty in Philadelphia, however. The Alms House and House of Employment was an old if not revered facility designed to care for Philadelphia's poor and helpless. Impoverished old women, unable to care for themselves, frequently spent their last days at this house. Barbara Nevel, a former employee in Deborah Logan's household, died at the house in 1834. Nevel's journey to the Alms House was long and protracted. After leaving the Logans, she lived alone in a rented room for many years. Deborah Logan not only paid her rent but offered to take her in and care for her for the remainder of her life. Nevel's refusal to leave her independent existence was difficult for Logan to understand. Nevertheless, Nevel retained her own room until 1834, when "bereft of all reason," wrote Logan, she went to the Alms House. At that time, she was stripped of her earthly possessions, including the small amount she had set aside for her own burial. "So was my poor old Barbara taken," wrote Logan sorrowfully, "calling on me to help her!" Logan's concern for her old friend appears genuine. Her inability to appreciate Nevel's desire for autonomy in old age, however, reveals the ingrained preference for dependency and deference considered particularly suitable for poor old women.[15]

"Depressed Spirits"

Whether rich or poor, women unable to reconcile the reality of old age with their expectations often experienced periods of depression at the end of life. Planning on an old age of peace and tranquility, many women instead encountered periods of depression that could last months, even years.

Such intense depression contradicted the prevailing notion of "chilled affections" in old age and made it difficult to assume the cheerful demeanor so often prescribed. Some old women, deprived of contentment and ease at the end of life, sensed a new and disturbing awareness of their emotional vulnerability. Although depression seldom took the upper hand in the lives of these women, it challenged their expectations and their inner resources.

Anxiety in old age often resulted from honest and justifiable concern. Despite expectations of tranquility, women often faced their greatest trials in old age. Widowhood and the death of near friends and relatives imposed severe emotional strains on many women. Family problems continued, sometimes becoming more intense as children grew older. "Trials of various kinds seem to be reserved for our gray Hairs," wrote Abigail Adams in 1800, concerned about the state of her daughter's marriage and her son's alcoholism. Elizabeth Drinker frequently complained of a "weight" on her spirits which she also related to family trouble. Other women admitted they were frequently "oppressed" by financial worries. While some of these issues were quickly resolved, others lingered, becoming the focus of women's attention and anxiety. As women grew older, "depressed spirits" manifested themselves in a variety of ways and sometimes imposed a new and troubling perspective.[16]

By the 1830s, noticeable changes in women's emotional state were attributed to "disordered nerves," a condition considered untreatable though prevalent. "Of all inflictions," wrote the unhappy Margaret Bayard Smith in 1839, "most insupportable is disordered nerves." She considered her nerves as "tyrants . . . Invisible, mysterious, ungovernable!" What made matters worse, wrote Smith, was the sense of helplessness and dependency nervous disorders imposed while, at the same time, "awaken[ing] neither sympathy or tenderness." Nervous conditions such as those experienced by Margaret Bayard Smith created havoc within both the emotional and social structure of women's lives.[17]

Widows and spinsters often experienced loneliness and pain as they faced the prospect of growing old alone. For some women, the loneliness became all-consuming and altered the course of their lives. Alice Shippen, who had known long and frequent bouts of depression throughout her adult life, continued to the end to attribute her unhappiness to the rejection she sensed from others. Hannah Winthrop found her losses as a widow so great that she came to consider old age as "the season . . . in which I was called to bear every pain the human heart can feel." Rebecca Dickinson attributed her own periods of intense loneliness to her lack of "Children and friends and a hous[e] and homes," the unhappy result of her spinsterhood. For such women, a sense of misery enveloped their final years as they were unable to counter the depression of loneliness.[18]

Other women, outwardly less miserable, nevertheless sensed their lives becoming more melancholy with age. Because "cheerfulness" remained one of the cardinal virtues of the idealized old woman, aging women knew only too well when it was lacking in their own lives. While priding themselves on their "normally" cheerful state, unhappy women sometimes stressed the temporary nature of their melancholia. Others who had lost their cheerfulness, however, considered themselves "the most wretched being[s] in existence."[19]

"I felt as if I wish'd for some one to weep for me," Elizabeth Denny Ward wrote to her son after the death of his brother, "and only because I could not weep." Other women also desired a "good shower of tears" that never came. Because they expected to be towers of fortitude and goodwill, older women could not always release tension or depression. Such pent-up emotion ensured the continuation of pain and grief for many women. Having long ago internalized the strictest behavioral expectations, such women no longer could control the distinction between image and reality.[20]

Emotional struggles in late life could be exacerbated by many of the prevailing, sometimes conflicting notions about women growing old. While the prospects of cheerfulness and resignation might have eased the approach of old age for some, the reality of unhappiness and unease known at least occasionally to many women in late life caused considerable anxiety. Women's expectations, usually supported by a strong religious foundation that reinforced the image of piety and resignation in old age, denied the understandable fears and apprehension of approaching the end of life.

The confusion and dissonance created by these contrasting images of cheer and gloom doubtless added to the difficulties known to some women as they grew old. Writers, artists, and physicians contributed to this confusion by offering new romantic and clinical frameworks for old age. These often negative images of aging gained popularity with the passage of time. By the 1830s the ambivalent and sometimes contradictory values associated with old age were becoming obvious. While women persistently maintained their commitment to peace, contentment, and ultimately resignation in old age, they experienced periods of melancholy and "nervous disorder" that would have surprised and puzzled their counterparts fifty years earlier. The introspective, often self-conscious nature of women's writings in the middle third of the nineteenth century reflects their growing responsiveness to these changing values.[21]

A Dubious Revolutionary Legacy

Despite the influence of changing nineteenth-century values, women growing old shared a number of traits and characteristics formed during their early years as children of the Revolution. As members of the revolutionary generation, these women, on average, received better educations and maintained broader interests than their pre-revolutionary sisters. Growing old in a period of heightened national enthusiasm, older women of the revolutionary generation served as symbols of past values and traditions. While their sense of shared experiences and accomplishment gave many women a unique insight into their own identity, it could also render them prisoners to the past, bound to a retrospective focus which interfered with their ability to apply themselves to the present or the future. In this respect, the Revolution provided a dubious legacy for the women who had shared in its glory.[22]

As these "daughters of the Revolution" grew old, they looked to a past of both tradition and change. Although their own memories of the past were often tinged by a sense of lost glory, these women were well aware of having witnessed great change in their lifetime. Their heritage of revolution did not, however, help prepare them for further changes in the future. Despite the revolutionary events surrounding their early years, later change came hard. As they aged, women perceived disquieting and perplexing alterations within society and within themselves.[23]

"If we are to count our years by the revolutions we have witnessed," wrote Abigail Adams to her old revolutionary colleague Mercy Otis Warren in 1807, "we might number them among the Ante-diluvians...." Among the nation's best-known revolutionary women in the early nineteenth century, Adams and Warren sensed not only their shared generational bond but also the turbulent temper of the times. Changes had been so rapid, Adams continued, "that the mind... has been outstripped by them, and we are left like statues gaping at what we neither fathom, or comprehend." Adams was not alone in her sense of incomprehension; she expressed a fear of change familiar to many old women. Women anticipated orderly progression and natural renewal within the philosophical and religious frameworks structuring their lives, and the depth and scope of change in postrevolutionary America went beyond what they either knew or wanted.[24]

Aging women found much of nineteenth-century life unsettling, even in cases that did not directly affect them. Political and technological change seemed rampant and not necessarily welcome. The coming of the "odious railroad" was only one in a series of developments that irritated and disturbed Deborah Norris Logan. "The present is full of thorns... which wound my feelings very deeply," she wrote in 1830. "The deterioration of public men and measures, the poor Indians! the foolish and unskillful [political] appointments." During this same period, Margaret Bayard Smith despaired of the growing demands of democracy. "What will be the result of this universal liberty," she lamented. Yet while the changing world perplexed and distressed these women, their awareness of change was in itself an aspect of their revolutionary heritage. More literate and better informed than earlier generations of women, old women in Jacksonian America understood the issues of their day. Their discomfort with the direction of change heightened the ambivalence with which they viewed their role in the world. Relatively unable to effect change themselves, such old women became vulnerable to increased frustration as they grew older.[25]

In an 1839 letter to her sister, Margaret Bayard Smith reflected that times had changed — and so had she. "I at moments could almost doubt my own identity," she wrote. Formerly active and energetic, Smith sensed in her later years an atrophy of both mind and body. Other women revealed a heightened awareness of the change immediately surrounding them. In 1805, Elizabeth Drinker noted with some alarm the decline of formality in the Drinker household. Eating in the kitchen rather than the dining room constituted a notable lowering of standards for Drinker. A new coat of paint or a misplaced pen could easily throw off the aged Deborah Logan. "I hate my things to be meddled with," she wrote in her seventy-sixth year. "I hate change of any kind."[26]

Women's uneasiness with change in old age can be viewed as part of a larger issue concerning the very nature of time itself. As post-revolutionary women grew older, their perception of the passage of time changed considerably. Time ran more rapidly, according to many women, emphasizing the "transitory" nature of human lives. Because their own time was running out, its value was noted with increasing fervor and frequency in the letters and diaries of aging women. "How fast the time passes," wrote Elizabeth Drinker in the last decade of her life. "A Week, to me, seems but as a long day." Many aging women shared Drinker's dilemma.[27]

Although the prevailing image of old age promised resignation, contentment, and the prospect of eternal happiness, women seldom passively accepted "time's swift passing" without comment. As time became the last and most precious element of their earthly existence, its significance grew with each year. Feeling increasingly short of time, women attempted to control it by carefully recording names, dates, and anniversaries in their journals and diaries. In her old age, Elizabeth Drinker began regular annual inventories of her family's health and activities for the preceding year. Women's own birthdays, while seldom celebrated, were nonetheless dutifully recorded in their own writings. By keeping careful records of the personal events touching their lives, older women made a permanent register of their own place in time. In a world perceived as rapidly changing, such records reveal the need not only to set anchor but to secure that anchor permanently against the ravages of time and neglect.[28]

Although aging women often attempted, in true Enlightenment fashion, to control time throughout the half-century following Independence, they appear to have undergone a change in perspective by the late 1830s. Margaret Bayard Smith, in fact, praised the *shortness* of time in a letter to her sister. Knowing that her life span was almost completed, she argued, "is an antidote for every ill that flesh is heir to." Unlike women who contended that there was much to do and too little time, Smith considered her reduced span of time necessary in order to assume "a *passive,* instead of an active state of being. . . ." In many ways, Margaret Smith serves as the archetypical example of the conflict between the enlightened and the domesticated woman as they emerged in the early nineteenth century. She longed to "glide smoothly" through her remaining days, but was hampered by a well-trained mind and active intellect which simply could not relent. Disenchanted with her ability to contribute meaningfully to the larger world and unwilling to dedicate herself to past glory, she chose instead to minimize her hopes for the future and to accept willingly the shortness of time.[29]

For many women in the post-revolutionary era, however, time was not just valued — it was revered. Women uncertain of their position in a changing society often reverted to past events and were sometimes consumed with the glory of former days. Mercy Otis Warren acknowledged to her friend Abigail Adams in 1798 that her "greatest pleasure is the retrospect of life. . . ." Her only future hope, she wrote, was her wish to "discharge the domestic & social duties" within her own sphere. A generation later, sixty-seven-year-old Deborah Norris Logan reiterated Warren's message. "What is the *Present* compared with the *Past?*" she asked. "With the future I have nothing to do. It has no promises to me. . . ." Although Deborah Logan was probably more preoccupied with the past than were most of her peers, many old women shared her retrospective focus.[30]

Women's preoccupation with the past in old age was both a symptom of and a reaction to the sense of discontinuity women experienced at critical times while growing old. Spinsters, widows, and mothers of absent children most frequently expressed this sense of separation between past and present lives. Elizabeth Denny Ward, writing a poem to her children who had recently moved to a neighboring state, revealed little attachment to her daily life or hopes for the future. "May you enjoy the coming days," she wrote, "as I've enjoyed the past." Others made comparisons between former and present lives. In some respects, this perception of separate periods of life served as an attempt to promote resignation and detachment from contemporary society as part of the prescribed preparation for approaching death. Yet it also reveals the apparent need of aging women to affirm their own identity and secure it solidly in history. For such women, the future was inextricably tied to the past. While devotion to the past might have helped maintain their identity, it also tended to magnify their sense of estrangement from the society in which they continued to live.[31]

The degree of concern aging women expressed about time, both past and present, was also a response to the generational experiences shared by these women. Having witnessed a period of enormous political and social change, these revolutionary-era survivors apparently had a particularly strong need for generational identity. Sociologist Matilda White Riley has pointed to the continuing interplay between social change and the process of aging. "Inherent in this interplay," she argues, "is the central problem of timing: the tension and strain produced by the differences between the tempo of mankind and the tempo of society." Women growing old in post-revolutionary America confronted this "central problem of timing" by clinging to their unchangeable identity as witnesses or children of the Revolution. Indeed, some women became "cohort-centric," as Riley would refer to their obsession with their own generation. For these women, values and ideas not only changed but invariably become worse, threatening the "natural" timing of old age.[32]

Generational identification with the Revolution, of course, was shared by men and women alike. Yet the special concerns of aging war veterans were not those of women, whose perspective and memories of the war might differ greatly from their male counterparts. Moreover, women had a particular need to identify with their revolutionary heritage because of their dedication to maintaining a connection with the people and values of the past. Naturally drawn to this past and simultaneously repelled by a future which threatened to dismiss former values (and, perhaps, the keepers of those values), women persevered in their devotion to this imperiled legacy.

The ambiguous nature of women's revolutionary heritage extended beyond the problems of generational identification. While women's literacy was encouraged (within bounds), women intellectuals were not. Despite Cicero and others who promised wisdom and intellectual power in old age, few old women in post-revolutionary America had the opportunity or support for extended intellectual pursuits. Moreover, the anticipation of mental "decline" and the increasing rigidity of the "woman's sphere" tempered any remaining expectations for intellectual endeavors or literary success in old age.[33]

For the three best-known American female historians of the period, however, advanced age appears to have been an asset rather than a liability. Mercy Otis Warren, Hannah Adams, and Deborah Norris Logan all pursued serious intellectual activity in middle age and continued to write and publish well into old age. Warren and Logan began their writing careers rather late in life, when their children no longer demanded time and attention; Hannah Adams turned to professional writing as a necessary source of income. Despite their considerable accomplishments, they did not engage in full-time intellectual careers without acknowledging their other, seemingly more important, domestic duties. Even the spinster Hannah Adams described herself as only a "modest compiler, as befits a true woman." Feminine modesty and understatement remained essential characteristics of an intellectual career during the fifty years following the Revolution.[34]

While all three writers eventually gained recognition for their historical contributions, only Warren and Adams published their major works during their lifetimes. Logan preferred the prospect of posthumous publications. "I dread blame, and I want not praise," she wrote in 1825, when the Historical Society of Pennsylvania asked to publish her collection of manuscript letters. Even in their writings, these women ignored the activities of women in history, apparently extending their own "modesty" to all other feminine accomplishments as well. The wisdom that presumably accompanied old age was apparently insufficient to overcome the stringent demands for modesty and femininity in the era of "true womanhood."[35]

Despite their apparent fear of public acclaim, aging women writers relied heavily on their intellectual skills and took pride in their own accomplishments. As they aged, however, they became increasingly wary about the state of their own minds and their ability to carry on intellectual activity. In her diary, Deborah Logan consistently and poignantly articulated the value she attached to her keen intellect and her fears that its powers were diminishing.[36]

When Deborah Logan began keeping her diary in 1815, she was fifty-four years old. She commented on changes in her mental capacity from day to day, but she associated temporary mental lapses with the mind's normal fluctuations rather than the "decline" of old age. After the death of her husband in 1821, Logan suffered from depression yet still maintained a sense of relief that her mind remained intact. Even after her seventieth birthday, she acknowledged "with deep gratitude that the Mind, the Eye and Hand are not impaired, as yet, by infirmities of age."[37]

By the end of 1831, however, the prospect of reduced mental capacity loomed larger. "I cannot bear to see Decay / Usurp the place where Reason lay," she wrote. By 1836, she considered her memory "treacherous" and found it disagreeable to be "thus deprived of one's intellectual furniture." The following year, still claiming to be "famished as to intellectual food," she became increasingly distressed by her inability to remember events in the recent past. "I seem to be losing my wits," she wrote sadly. Frequently unable to date accurately her diary entries, she described her state as "a kind of mental fog, dense and heavy." Yet early in 1838, a year before her death, she persisted in believing that her mind was "unimpaired." During that last year, she continued to assess her mental capacity, acknowledging unhappily she could no longer rely on her memory. Shortly before her death, she reflected with some amazement how memories of childhood remained fresh and vivid while current events were "easily obliterated" from her mind. Like many old persons, then and now, Logan experienced the perplexing clarity of long-term memory juxtaposed with the frustrating inablity to recall recent actions or events.[38] The overall diminution of mental strength she so carefully charted added considerably to Deborah Logan's anxiety in the months before her death in 1839.[39]

As an aging daughter of the Revolution, Deborah Logan enjoyed the intellectual components of her late life, and she clearly agreed with Cicero that an active intellect was essential for happiness in old age. Yet although she still possessed the confidence to undertake significant literary projects, she remained unable openly to proclaim herself an historian or an intellectual. Her refusal to publish her major works during her lifetime attests to the ambivalence she experienced as a woman growing old during a period of domestic ascendancy. Logan and other women in similar positions repulsed any efforts — including their own literary ambitions — that might jeopardize their good standing within the woman's sphere. Their revolutionary heritage, which had provided them with the tools for intellectual growth and creativity, helped sustain such literary women in their old age but failed to liberate them from the constraints of their own sphere.

Bodily Pain and the "Decay of Nature"

Although not all women in post-revolutionary America shared the intellectual life known to Deborah Logan, Hannah Adams, and Mercy Warren, most women were familiar with the metaphors of natural decay and death permeating the literature and the oral tradition of aging. The metaphors associating old age with the natural process of growth, maturation, and decay provided a useful intellectual framework for men and women anticipating their own final years. For women, however, physical closeness to the reality of life and death could not be separated from either their natural or assigned roles. In earlier years, with the experience of childbirth, women participated in the creation of life. As years passed, they nursed the ill and often prepared the dead for burial, maintaining close ties with life's natural dimensions. Witnessing their own physical decline at life's end, aging women took solace if not delight in the realization that they were working hand in hand with nature.[40]

Nonetheless, portrayals of life's "decline" and "decay" suggest a melancholy association with life's inevitable changes. Indeed, as they emerge within the context of women's writings, they most frequently appear at times when lives were in flux, at transitional points when the future seemed uncertain. Women who began to view their life in "decline" in middle age seem less concerned with the end of life than with the loss of youth. The sense of decline among these postmenopausal women might have been an expression of changing roles and duties. Yet because the sense of looming descent continued as women grew into old age, it is clear that the loss of fertility alone did not constitute this sense of decline. Other physical losses, too, contributed to this view of diminishing life forces. Regardless of their socioeconomic level, most women worked long and demanding hours within their homes. The impending loss of physical strength in old age imposed obvious hardship on women who had little choice but to carry on their daily tasks as they grew older. Physical decline presented a clear and present danger to women in preindustrial America.[41]

The decline associated with old age, in fact, was considered the inevitable, final disease. Because Sarah Fisher's aunt was "declining from old age," other explanations for her weakening physical condition seemed unnecessary. Elizabeth Putnam took comfort from knowing, in her sixty-first year, that her problems resulted from "the decay of nature," while her nephew's disorders could only be attributed to a dissolute life. For many women, the reality of old age revealed a growing awareness of the *"achs & pains"* attributed to "decrepitude." Colds, eye and ear problems, "muscular lameness," and swollen ankles were common complaints. Others described more chronic ailments such as "rheumatic pains" and lumbago, obstructed bowels, paralysis, and palsy. Illness often kept women confined to their homes for months at a time. Considering her own chronic illnesses, Elizabeth Drinker admitted that "when a weakly person comes to be near three score and ten," little improvement could be expected. "If they can keep from a large share of what is called bodily pain," she wrote, "'tis all that some of us ought to look for."[42]

Despite the fact that their anticipated "decay" lowered their expectations of a healthy and active old age, many older women suggested a variety of ways to feel better. Walking and exercise were widely prescribed and practiced as useful methods of regaining strength and vitality. Maria Ward Tracy, in her mid-sixties, revealed in 1828 her dedication to the regimen of walking, despite being housebound. "I walked half a mile a day in the house," she wrote. Although lame, she continued daily to "drag about with my staff, some times 30 40 & 50 rods before breakfast." Many women considered travel an excellent way to dispel illness and restore pep. On her ninetieth birthday Mrs. McAdam of New York reportedly took a "jaunt of pleasure," traveling 160 miles. Despite the familiar advice to "retire" from active life in old age, many women recognized physical activity as a valuable method of prolonging good health and alleviating illness.[43]

Women tried many other ways of dealing with declining health. New medicines often supplemented traditional herbal remedies. When medicine failed to work, other curatives were found. Elizabeth Drinker believed that "cool weather perhaps strengthens old women measurably." In some cases, drastic measures were called for. Elizabeth Farmer of Pennsylvania had been plagued by an "ill natured Tooth." "But I have been revenged on it," she wrote, "for I have got it out and burned it." Women such as Elizabeth Farmer did not submit meekly to the physical hardships of old age.[44]

Physical problems were not always resolved by activity, medicines, or tooth burnings. Many women continued to argue the importance of "proper" mental outlook for good health in old age. "I believe," wrote Mary Few, "that an amiable, cheerful, happy disposition is one of the greatest promoters of health and long life." As illness and debilities persisted, many women considered them to be warnings and reminders of the temporary nature of human life. "At my age," Mary Page wrote to her niece in 1828, "infirmities give us warning that this is not our place of rest." Her sentiments were echoed by Elizabeth Prescott. Writing to her friend Nancy Shaw, Prescott revealed her sense of resignation in the face of continuing illness. By such infirmities, she wrote, God is "reminding us that this is not our home and teaches us our duty to prepare for another and better world." Ultimately, a sense of resignation enabled many women to endure the physical and emotional pain associated with old age.[45]

As idealized in the post-revolutionary era, old women symbolized an image of femininity that stressed passivity, amiability, and resignation, qualities which had been highly valued in eighteenth-century society and which corresponded to the emerging values associated with women's "separate sphere." While some women found utility and direction in these images, others did not. In a domestic world where the values of continuity and connection remained vital throughout life and often demanded active engagement and total commitment, expectations for passivity and resignation could impose considerable frustration and anxiety. Women found that, despite expectations to the contrary, their need for social interaction and involvement persisted and, in some cases, increased as they grew older. Similarly, the passive posture considered appropriate for aging women often contradicted their continuing need for work and activity, both as daily ritual and as a means of livelihood.

Other expectations proved more amenable, especially when couched in terms that seemed appropriate to both old age and the physical world around them. For most women, the metaphors of seasonal change provided viable images of old age and death which conformed to women's lifelong experience. Such metaphors offered women an obvious and verifiable framework in which they could anticipate their own "natural decline" within a cyclical vision of birth, growth, decline, and regeneration. Yet even these images could conflict with the sense of discontinuity some women experienced in late life. Personal losses—particularly the death of a spouse—and the perception of a rapidly changing society created for some women a harsh distinction between expectation and reality. Although most women continued to be nourished and supported by continuity in their lives, those without it suffered hardship and a sense of defeat in old age.

Women's revolutionary heritage proved equally ambiguous. For some women this heritage helped confirm a sense of identity and value as they grew older. Yet for others this link to a revolutionary past tended to fix an identity frozen in time, creating retrospective lives estranged from the contemporary world. Such women, having experienced monumental change in the war for independence, were unwilling to expose themselves to further changes, either personal or systemic. Even women's increased literacy, influenced by their revolutionary heritage, proved an ambivalent legacy. Some women gained both knowledge and pleasure from reading and writing, but women's literary and intellectual achievements were seldom recognized. For aging women whose dreams extended beyond their domestic purview, old age might be frustrating indeed.

By the end of the Jacksonian period, changes outside woman's sphere threatened the pattern of continuity that delineated old age. Some women perceived a growing sense of generational hostility, particularly among young males. Changing views within the medical profession also began to alter women's expectations in old age. The romantic literary mood of the period, emphasizing qualities peculiar to old age and death, disrupted the perception of continuity throughout life, making the position of old people more vulnerable. Women responded to these changes by becoming more self-conscious in their writings. Self-styled "nervousness" and apathy were increasingly discernible in the private writings of some aging women in antebellum America. Yet for most women, the anxiety and alienation stemming from rapid social change in the 1830s failed to destroy completely the conceptual framework of life, old age, and death that had long supported them. Later generations of elderly women faced far greater struggles in a society that increasingly devalued older persons and failed to equalize the position of women.[46]

NOTES

1. W. Andrew Achenbaum describes the divergence between rhetoric and reality in nineteenth-century age relations. See Achenbaum, *Old Age in the New Land* (Baltimore: Johns Hopkins University Press, 1978), pp. 57-86.

2. Margaret Bayard Smith to Jane Kirkpatrick, 26 October 1834, Margaret

Bayard Smith Papers, LCMD; Deborah Norris Logan, Diary, 26 August 1825, HSP. See also Margaret Bayard Smith to Jane Kirkpatrick, 31 August 1834 and 17 July 1835, Margaret Bayard Smith Papers, LCMD; and Deborah Norris Logan, Diary, 16 July 1822, 20 January 1825, 4 May 1834, and 24 August 1838, HSP.

Elizabeth Drinker provides an excellent example of a woman who viewed her "retirement" as both satisfying and successful despite the fact that she lived an active, busy life. See Elizabeth Drinker, Diary, 5 February 1795, 10 February 1800, and 1 January 1802, HSP. The concept of retirement was considered by many women as suitable to the female disposition and appropriate throughout life, not only in old age. See Alice Izard to Margaret Manigault, 7 March 1814, Izard Family Papers, LCMD, where she wrote, "retired life is in general better suited to the female character." The concept of retirement within the religious context is discussed in chapter six, below.

3. As Nancy Tomes noted in her study of visiting patterns among Philadelphia Quakers, "When sickness and old age made visiting difficult, women felt a sense of loss, again suggesting the centrality of this social activity [of visiting] in their lives." See Tomes, "The Quaker Connection: Visiting Patterns among Women in the Philadelphia Society of Friends, 1750-1800," in *Friends and Neighbors: Group Life in America's First Plural Society*, ed. Michael W. Zuckerman (Philadelphia: Temple University Press, 1982), p. 181. Robert Gough has analyzed the social interaction of Philadelphia's elite during this same period. He found that wealthy Philadelphians exercised "a degree of personal choice in their associations." His examination of Elizabeth Drinker's visiting patterns, however, indicated that she tended to restrict her company to fellow Quakers in her later years. See Gough, "Towards a Theory of Class and Social Conflict: A Social History of Wealthy Philadelphians, 1775 and 1800" (Ph.D. dissertation, University of Pennsylvania, 1977), pp. 386-93, quotation on p. 393.

4. Rebecca Dickinson, Diary, 13 August 1787, in *A History of Hatfield, Massachusetts, 1660-1910*, ed. Daniel White Wells and Reuben Field Wells (Springfield, Mass.: F. C. H. Gibbons, 1910), p. 206; Deborah Norris Logan, Diary, 14 September 1833, HSP. See also Rebecca Noyes, Diary, 4 January 1803, CHS.

5. Mary McDonald to Mrs. D. Rossiter, 27 June 1814, McDonald-Lawrence Papers, GHS; Phoebe Bradford, Diary, 8 December 1832, quoted in Carroll Smith-Rosenberg, "Female World of Love and Ritual: Relations between Women in Nineteenth-Century America," *Signs: Journal of Women in Culture and Society* 1 (Autumn 1975):13; Hannah Winthrop to Mercy Otis Warren, n.d. August 1777, Warren-Winthrop Papers, MHS. See also chapter two, above.

6. Elizabeth Drinker, Diary, 21 November 1799, HSP. For other examples of the importance of friendship in old age, see Rebecca Noyes, Diary, 18 June 1808, CHS; Deborah Norris Logan, Diary, 8 May and 10 July 1831, HSP; and Martha Jefferis to Ann Sheppard, 12 January 1845, and Phoebe Middleton to Martha Jefferis, 22 February 1848, quoted in Smith-Rosenberg, "Female World of Love and Ritual," p. 13.

7. See Rebecca Shoemaker, Diary, October 1805, Rawle Family Papers, HSP; Margaret Bayard Smith to Jane Kirkpatrick, 24 November 1839, Margaret Bayard Smith Papers, LCMD; and Ann R. Page to Elizabeth Adams, n.d. 1803, William

B. Randolph Papers, LCMD. Elizabeth Drinker stated that she liked being in her own home "better than any where else," but she admitted that such feelings were a "favour." See Elizabeth Drinker, Diary, 7 July 1799, HSP.

Deborah Logan's experience serves as a good example of this frustration. Determined to break her "earthly ties," she nonetheless loved the company of others. "I seem badly to want some communion with People in actual life," she wrote in 1837, "who breathe, and walk, and speak. . . ." Yet she understood the dual nature of her predicament. "I live in two worlds," she wrote, "and the ideal one is by far the happiest." Nonetheless, her active social life continued as an essential element within the daily context of her life. See Deborah Norris Logan, Diary, 31 December 1824, 8 May 1837, and 9 September 1829, HSP; see also ibid., 27 October 1833, 17 August 1837, and 10 July 1838.

Logan's dilemma vividly suggests the turmoil caused by conflicts between concepts and perceptions of reality, or what is described as "cognitive dissonance." See Leon Festinger, *A Theory of Cognitive Dissonance* (Stanford: Stanford University Press, 1962).

8. Molly Cooper, Diary, 21 through 24 December 1772 and 7 March 1769, *The Diary of Molly Cooper,* ed. Field Horne (Oyster Bay, N.Y.: Oyster Bay Historical Society, 1981), pp. 46, 9.

9. Elizabeth Cuming to Elizabeth Inman, 5 May 1784, James M. Robbins Papers, MHS. Such women as Anna Blackwood Howell, Hannah Adams, and Elizabeth Inman worked into late life.

10. See Mary Callender Mitchell, *A Short Account of the Early Part of the Life of Mary Mitchell* (New Bedford, Mass.: Abraham Shearman, 1812); Elizabeth (Ballinger) Mason Collins, *Memoirs of Elizabeth Collins of Upper Evesham, N.J.* (Philadelphia: N. Kite, 1833), p. 70; Jarena Lee, *The Life and Religious Experience of Jarena Lee, a Coloured Lady* (Philadelphia: for the author, 1836), p. 22; and Anna Catharine Ernst, quoted in Adelaide L. Fries, *Road to Salem* (Chapel Hill: University of North Carolina Press, 1944), pp. 300-301.

11. Martha Moore Ballard, Diary, 1797 passim, in *Lives of American Women: A History with Documents,* ed. Joyce D. Goodfriend and Claudia M. Christie (Boston: Little, Brown, 1981), pp. 319-28.

12. Judith Sargent Murray, *The Gleaner, a Miscellaneous Production,* 3 vols. (Boston: I. Thomas and E. T. Andrews, 1798), 3:220-22. Midwives presided over most births throughout this period, despite the fact that physicians were frequently consulted by upper-class, urban women. The solid position of midwives within the preindustrial economy, however, was eroded with the advent of male professionalism. See Mary Beth Norton, *Liberty's Daughters: The Revolutionary Experience of American Women, 1750-1800* (Chapel Hill: University of North Carolina Press, 1980), pp. 79-80, 139-40. By the early nineteenth century, male physicians "virtually monopolized the practice of midwifery in the Eastern seaboard." See Gerda Lerner, *The Majority Finds Its Past: Placing Women in History* (Oxford: Oxford University Press, 1979), p. 22.

13. Jemima Condict Harrison, Diary, n.d. 1775, quoted in Elizabeth Evans, *Weathering the Storm: Women of the American Revolution* (New York: Scribner, 1975), pp. 41-42; Elizabeth Drinker, Diary, 7 August 1797 and 2 to 6 November

1799, HSP. See also Deborah Norris Logan, Diary, 30 September and 1 October 1834, HSP.

Accounts of poor but virtuous old women abound in the diaries and letters of post-revolutionary women. Sarah Logan Fisher, in 1794, visited an "idyllic cottage" where a poor old woman and her family resided. Not only was the family "happy and chearfull," but the small piece of land on which they lived provided for their livelihood "without the cares & perplexities that too often attend Riches, or being exposed to the various temptations that the possession of them frequently gives. . . ." Sarah Logan Fisher, Diary, 16 July 1794, HSP. In their idealized state, poor old women shared some of the same characteristics ascribed to the best of old women in general. Beyond these, however, they exhibited an honesty, a cleanliness, and an industriousness considered peculiar to their social rank. Such poor old women were thought to be more truthful and hardworking in part because they accrued moral advantage from the very fact of their poverty. Not burdened by the weight of social privilege or wealth, old women in poverty symbolized an idyllic, often rustic purity popular among romanticists and insecure members of the upper class. The integrity, honor, and strength of these poor old women made them, it was felt, deserving of the attention and the alms of the neighboring gentry. While some women clearly attempted to draw inspiration from these models of moral poverty, their visions were undoubtedly obscured by their need to rationalize the pain and hunger such women experienced. See Ann Livingston, Diary, 1 September 1784, Shippen Family Papers, LCMD; Deborah Norris Logan, Diary, 18 March 1838, HSP; Elizabeth Drinker, Diary, 16 October 1794, HSP; and Margaret Bayard Smith to Samuel Smith, 6 October 1797, Margaret Bayard Smith Papers, LCMD. The "riches bring cares" argument appeared as early as 1760 and continued throughout the early national period. After the 1780s, this theme was frequently propounded in essays and sermons. According to this logic, the contented and virtuous poor would receive their ultimate reward in heaven. The proponents of this argument, however, expected it would also convince the poor to remain in their place. See John K. Alexander, *Render Them Submissive: Responses to Poverty in Philadelphia, 1760-1800* (Amherst: University of Massachusetts Press, 1980), pp. 48-60.

14. Deborah Norris Logan, Diary, 26 September 1827, HSP. Molly Ross, an aged resident of the asylum, appeared satisfied with her home there despite the pain of witnessing illness and death regularly among fellow residents. See Carole Haber, "The Old Folks at Home: The Development of Institutionalized Care for the Aged in Nineteenth Century Philadelphia," *Pennsylvania Magazine of History and Biography* 101 (April 1977):241-57.

Through the women's monthly meeting of the Society of Friends, Quaker women achieved considerable organizational skill in many areas of administration. Women's meetings were especially concerned with the well-being of poor people and people in crisis. According to Mary Maples Dunn, "Widows in particular found themselves comforted and controlled by the meeting." See Dunn, "Women of Light," in *Women of America: A History,* ed. Carol Ruth Berkin and Mary Beth Norton (Boston: Houghton Mifflin, 1979), p. 125.

15. Deborah Norris Logan, Diary, 22 December 1827 and 11 June 1834, HSP;

see also ibid., 29 March 1830, 20 May and mid-June 1831, 31 October 1832, and 12 August 1834. Philadelphia's indigent women were also housed in the Christ Church Hospital.

16. Abigail Adams to Mary Cranch, 26 May 1800, *New Letters of Abigail Adams, 1788-1801,* ed. Stewart Mitchell (Boston: Houghton Mifflin, 1947), p. 253; Elizabeth Drinker, Diary, 21 July 1799, 19 May and 14 November 1800, HSP. See also Anna Blackwood Howell, Diary, n.d. 1835, AAS.

17. Margaret Bayard Smith to Jane Kirkpatrick, 9 February, 2 September, and 24 November 1839, Margaret Bayard Smith Papers, LCMD. See also ibid., 25 August 1826 and 13 October 1832; and Barbara Welter, *Dimity Convictions: The American Woman in the Nineteenth Century* (Athens: Ohio University Press, 1976), pp. 56-70.

18. Alice Shippen to William Shippen III, 2 August n.d., Shippen Family Papers, LCMD; Hannah Winthrop to Mercy Otis Warren, 28 April 1780, Winthrop-Warren Papers, MHS; Rebecca Dickinson, Diary, 12 August and 2 September 1787, pp. 206-7. See also Lucinda Storrs, Diary, [12] March 1833, CHS.

19. Roxana Bolles to Sophia Griswold Barnard, 24 November 1836, Barnard Family Papers, LCMD. See also Elizabeth Drinker, Diary, 21 July 1799, HSP; and Abigail Adams to Mary Cranch, 26 May 1800, *New Letters,* ed. Mitchell, p. 253.

Deborah Logan's comments about her "depressed spirits" appear frequently but are not dominant in the majority of her entries. In the year 1824, for example, Logan averaged six days per month of expressed unhappiness or melancholy. She usually tried to counter such "negative" days with renewed commitments to cheerfulness and resignation. See Deborah Norris Logan, Diary, 1824 passim, HSP; see also ibid., 9 October 1823, 22 March 1835, and 6 January 1837.

20. Elizabeth Denny Ward to Andrew Ward, 1 March 1817, Ward Family Papers, AAS; Deborah Norris Logan, Diary, 2 August 1826, HSP.

Although older women frequently experienced shifts in mood and behavior as they grew older, old age itself was not responsible for those changes. As sociologist Zena Smith Blau has noted, significant role changes in late life are far more influential in creating alterations of mood and behavior than the physical factors associated with aging. According to Blau, "the role changes that signify permanent detachment from society's two principal institutional systems — the nuclear family and the occupational system — are far more important. . . ." For most women in post-revolutionary America, the nuclear family and the occupational system were one and the same. For those women who continued to remain actively involved in their familial and domestic lives, role change was minimized. Even the emotional pain of widowhood, the most frequent cause of depression for these women, was usually offset by continuing obligations to family and domestic life. See Blau, *Old Age in a Changing Society* (New York: New Viewpoints, 1973), pp. 35-36.

21. Changes during the early nineteenth century affected many areas of women's lives and created values and options previously unknown. For older women, such changes were often irritating and distressing. Carl Degler describes some of these new variables in his *At Odds: Women and the Family in America from the Revolution to the Present* (Oxford: Oxford University Press, 1980), pp. 144-77.

22. Morton Keller has described "historical generations" as "groups of contemporaries whose 'historical co-existence' is determined by the major events of their time." See Keller, "Reflections on Politics and Generations in America," in *Generations,* ed. Stephen R. Graubard (New York: W. W. Norton, 1979), p. 123. Those witnessing the Revolution formed a particularly close "historical generation."

23. Generational differences, of course, cross cultures and time. Zena Smith Blau has argued that younger generations often have ideas and behavior which to the old are "different and alien." "They increasingly feel themselves to be, in Margaret Mead's graphic term, 'immigrants in time.'" See Blau, *Old Age in a Changing Society,* p. 112.

24. Abigail Adams to Mercy Otis Warren, 9 March 1807, in Mercy Otis Warren, "Warren-Adams Letters," *MHS Collections* 73 (1925):353. See also Deborah Norris Logan, Diary, 20 July 1825, HSP. The extent of political, economic, and social change during this period has been examined by many historians within the context of "modernization." See, for example, Richard D. Brown, "Modernization and the Modern Personality in Early America, 1660-1865: A Sketch of a Synthesis," *Journal of Interdisciplinary History* 2 (Winter 1982):201-28; Herman R. Lantz et al., "Pre-Industrial Patterns in the Colonial Family in America: A Content Analysis of Colonial Magazines," *American Sociological Review* 33 (June 1968):413-26; and E. A. Wrigley, "The Process of Modernization and the Industrial Revolution in England," *Journal of Interdisciplinary History* 3 (Autumn 1972):225-29.

25. Deborah Norris Logan, Diary, 19 November and 28 May 1830, HSP; Margaret Bayard Smith to Jane Kirkpatrick, 16 December 1834, Margaret Bayard Smith Papers, LCMD. See Mary Palmer Tyler, *Grandmother Tyler's Book: The Recollections of Mary Palmer Tyler (Mrs. Royall Tyler),* ed. Frederick Tupper and Helen Tyler Brown (New York: G. P. Putnam's Sons, 1925), pp. 118-19. Eighteenth-century revolutionary statesmen, as well, were troubled by potential social change. According to Drew R. McCoy "unsettling social and economic change" distressed many of the new nation's male leaders. See McCoy, *Elusive Republic: Political Economy in Jeffersonian America* (New York: W. W. Norton, 1980), p. 16.

26. Margaret Bayard Smith to Jane Kirkpatrick, 19 December 1839, Margaret Bayard Smith Papers, LCMD; Elizabeth Drinker, Diary, 10 November 1805, HSP; Deborah Norris Logan, Diary, 26 April 1837, HSP. See also Margaret Bayard Smith to Jane Kirkpatrick, 27 January 1839; Elizabeth Drinker, Diary, 1 November 1796 and 23 March 1805, HSP; and Deborah Norris Logan, Diary, 23 August 1829 and 19 November 1830, HSP.

27. Elizabeth Drinker, Diary, 9 May 1799 and 18 November 1802, HSP. See also Sarah Washington to Rebecca Nicholson, 8 December 1828, Shippen Family Papers, LCMD; Anna Blackwood Howell, Diary, n.d. [1831], AAS; and Elizabeth Pierce, Journal, 12 July 1827, Poor Family Papers, SL. See also Robert Kastenbaum, "On the Meaning of Time in Later Life," *Journal of Genetic Psychology* 109 (September 1966):9-25.

28. See Elizabeth Drinker, Diary, 31 December 1793 and each December 31 thereafter, HSP; Deborah Norris Logan, Diary, 4 July 1826, 14 November 1827,

and 14 January 1833, HSP; Rebecca Noyes, Diary, 23 February 1812, CHS; Susan Assheton, "Susan Assheton's Book," ed. Joseph M. Beatty, Jr., *Pennsylvania Magazine of History and Biography* 55:2 (1931):180-86.

29. See Margaret Bayard Smith to Jane Kirkpatrick, 11 July 1834 and 24 August 1840, Margaret Bayard Smith Papers, LCMD.

The changing perspective suggested by Margaret Smith's comment was reiterated in the writings of Lydia Sigourney and Lydia Maria Child. The consolation of old age, wrote Child in 1865, was that it would soon be over. See Child, *Looking towards Sunset* (Boston: Ticknor and Fields, 1865), especially pp. 42-43. See also Sigourney, *Letters to Mothers* (Hartford, Conn.: Hudson and Skinner, 1838), and *Past Meridian* (New York: D. Appleton, 1854). These writers, according to Thomas Cole, were consistent with many "aging advisors [who] often portrayed the 'passive virtues' of powerless old age." See Cole, "Past Meridian: Aging and the Northern Middle Class, 1830-1930" (Ph.D. dissertation, University of Rochester, 1980), p. 318.

30. At the time of this comment, Mercy Otis Warren had yet to publish her *History of the Rise, Progress, and Termination of the American Revolution,* which apparently had not been accorded a place within her "future hopes." Mercy Warren to Abigail Adams, 9 April 1798, Letterbook, Mercy Otis Warren Papers, MHS; Deborah Norris Logan, Diary, 23 May 1829, HSP. See also Elizabeth Drinker, Diary, 20 July 1798, HSP; Deborah Norris Logan, Diary, 23 March 1821, 3 January 1825, 26 January 1829, n.d. January 1834, and 15 June 1836, HSP; and Deborah Norris Logan to Sarah Walker, 8 February 1834, Maria Dickinson Logan Family Papers, HSP.

Deborah Logan was widely known as a "living reminder" of former days. The South Carolina author and editor Caroline Gilman, after visiting Logan in 1836, described her as "one of the few individuals who now remain as noble specimens of our forefathers. . . ." See Caroline Gilman, *The Southern Rose* (Charleston, S.C.), 25 June 1836.

31. Elizabeth Denny Ward, poem, January 1828, Ward Family Papers, AAS. Hannah Adams was considered "not part of this world" by her friend Hannah Lee. See Hannah Adams, *A Memoir of Miss Hannah Adams, Written by Herself* (Boston: Gray and Bowen, 1832), p. 48. Also see Deborah Norris Logan, Diary, 30 August 1816, 6 December 1824, 20 October 1825, 4 July 1826, 14 January and 4 February 1827, 13 January 1830, 17 April and 11 May 1831, 1 March 1832, 14 January 1833, and 22 October 1838, HSP.

32. Matilda White Riley, "Aging, Social Change, and the Power of Ideas," in *Generations,* ed. Graubard, pp. 39-52, quotations on pp. 39 and 41. Mary Beth Norton noted differences between women of the revolutionary generation and their children. See Norton, *Liberty's Daughters,* p. 193. See also Daniel Scott Smith, "Family Limitation, Sexual Control, and Domestic Feminism in Victorian America," in *Clio's Consciousness Raised: New Perspectives on the History of Women,* ed. Mary Hartman and Lois Banner (New York: Harper and Row, 1976), pp. 132-33, for another interpretation of these generational differences.

33. As Linda Kerber has noted, "So long as the literature of domesticity persisted, it would always embody an anti-intellectual connotation, a skepticism

about the capacities of women's minds." See Kerber, *Women of the Republic: Intellect and Ideology in Revolutionary America* (Chapel Hill: University of North Carolina Press, 1980), p. 231.

34. Hannah Adams, quoted in Susan Phinney Conrad, *Perish the Thought: Intellectual Women in Romantic America, 1830-1860* (New York: Oxford University Press, 1976), p. 95. See Mercy Otis Warren to Abigail Adams, 9 April 1798, Letterbook, Mercy Otis Warren Papers, MHS; and Margaret Bayard Smith to Samuel Smith, 4 October 1796, Margaret Bayard Smith Papers, LCMD.

Although Mercy Otis Warren's political satires were published during the Revolution, her greatest work, the three-volume history of the Revolution, was not published until 1805, when she was seventy-seven. Hannah Adams was only thirty when her *Dictionary of Religions* achieved considerable success. She continued to publish works on religious history until 1826 at the age of seventy-one. Her scholarship continued until near the time of her death in 1831. Deborah Norris Logan began serious scholarship in 1814, when she first started to copy and annotate the *Penn-Logan Correspondence* for which she is best known. She was fifty-three at the time. Her other major work, aside from her diary, was the biography of her husband, completed when she was sixty-one. She continued writing articles and poetry into her seventies.

35. Deborah Norris Logan, Diary, 6 August 1825, HSP; Conrad, *Perish the Thought,* pp. 26-27. Conrad argues that women writers did not begin to acknowledge the contributions of other women in their writings until the 1830s. See also Deborah Norris Logan, Diary, 12 September 1825 and 17 December 1827, HSP; and Deborah Norris Logan to Sarah Walker, 6 January 1826, Maria Dickinson Logan Family Papers, HSP. In this letter, Deborah Logan denied that the Historical Society of Pennsylvania would extend membership to her. "They do not want women," she wrote, "and thee ... knows my sentiment on the retirement and modesty which I think we ought never to lose sight of." As it happened, however, Deborah Logan was indeed the first woman to be given honorary membership in the society. See also Mercy Otis Warren to husband, n.d. 1775, Mercy Otis Warren Papers, MHS.

36. A brief biographical description of Deborah Logan by Frederick B. Tolles can be found in Edward T. James, ed., *Notable American Women, 1607-1950: A Biographical Dictionary* (Cambridge: Harvard University Press, 1971), pp. 418-19. See also Sarah Butler Wister and Agnes Irwin, *Worthy Women of Our First Century* (Philadelphia: J. B. Lippincott, 1877), pp. 279-328; and Terri L. Premo, " 'Like a Being Who Does Not Belong': The Old Age of Deborah Norris Logan," *Pennsylvania Magazine of History and Biography* 107 (January 1983):85-112.

37. Deborah Norris Logan, Diary, 4 November 1831, HSP: see also ibid., 27 April 1815, 12 July 1823, 17 September 1825, and 13 November 1831.

38. Ibid., 31 December 1831, 25 July 1836, 30 January and 30 August 1837, and 11 December 1838. The decline of Logan's short-term memory is consistent with contemporary geriatric findings. See Atchley, *The Social Forces in Later Life,* 3d ed. (Belmont, Calif.: Wadsworth, 1980), p. 56.

39. Margaret Bayard Smith experienced similar frustration when she sensed her mental powers declining in old age. Though formerly a successful writer,

Smith despaired in 1839 that she could not "originate, . . . the capacity is gone . . . the mind torpid." See Margaret Bayard Smith to Jane Kirkpatrick, 27 January 1839, Margaret Bayard Smith Papers, LCMD. She made similar comments throughout the last decade of her life. See ibid., 6 March 1838 and 19 December 1839, and Margaret Bayard Smith to Maria Boyd, 11 March 1835, Margaret Bayard Smith Papers, LCMD. See also Mercy Otis Warren to Rebecca Otis, n.d. 1774, and Mercy Otis Warren to ?, n.d., Letterbook, Mercy Otis Warren Papers, MHS.

40. See Carol Ochs, *Women and Spirituality* (Totowa, N.J.: Rowman and Allanheld, 1983), pp. 84-85, on women's potential for spiritual growth and immortality through their association with nature and the natural.

41. Women's anxiety about menopause, if it existed, did not appear in their personal writings. See Carroll Smith-Rosenberg, "Puberty to Menopause: The Cycle of Femininity in Nineteenth-Century America," *Feminist Studies* 1 (Winter-Spring 1973):58-72.

42. Sarah Logan Fisher, Diary, 12 February 1788, HSP; Elizabeth Putnam to Samuel Ward, 9 January 1794, Chandler-Ward Family Papers, AAS; Elizabeth Drinker, Diary, 20 October 1805, HSP. See also Sarah Logan Fisher, Diary, n.d. May 1777, HSP; Deborah Norris Logan, Diary, 5 March 1823, HSP; Anna Cunningham to Nancy Shaw, 30 July 1841, Shaw-Webb Family Papers, AAS; Mary Page to Rebecca Nicholson, 30 May 1828, Shippen Family Papers, LCMD; Elizabeth Drinker, Diary, 28 January 1800, HSP; Rebecca Dickinson, Diary, n.d., p. 207; and Rebecca Noyes, Diary, 21 May 1830, CHS.

The degree to which illness touched the lives of older women is evident in the daily entries of Deborah Logan's diary. During the year 1823, for example, Logan averaged 8.3 notices of illness or death per month occurring in either her own family or her larger circle of friends. During a particularly unhealthy August that year, she noted twenty-three instances of sickness or death in addition to her own three-week illness. Disabilities ranged from toothaches to gout, wrenched backs to consumption. As the widow of a physician and knowledgeable in her own right, Logan administered medicine to neighbors during the summer months. Like other older women, she was familiar with herbal remedies but consented, with some reluctance, to the hapless practice of bloodletting. Her frequent interaction with illness and death often weighed heavily on her, yet she and other women bore the burden as an expected and very real part of their daily existence. See Deborah Norris Logan, Diary, 1823 passim, HSP.

43. Maria Ward Tracy to Mr. and Mrs. Thomas Ward, 11 July 1828, Ward Family Papers, AAS; Mary Few to Rebecca Nicholson, 23 July 1824, Shippen Family Papers, LCMD. See also Elizabeth Farmer to Hugh Farmer, 26 June 1788, Elizabeth Farmer Letterbook, HSP; and Deborah Norris Logan, Diary, 25 December 1837, HSP. Continued physical activity, of course, was increasingly difficult for many women as they grew older, despite their desires to remain active. See Deborah Norris Logan, Diary, 22 May 1823 and 9 February 1833, HSP.

44. Elizabeth Drinker, Diary, 11 September 1806, HSP; Elizabeth Farmer to Jack Halroyd, 17 Feburary 1775, Elizabeth Farmer Letterbook, HSP. See also Rebecca Noyes, Diary, June 1813, CHS.

45. Mary Few to Rebecca Nicholson, 23 July 1824, and Mary Page to Rebecca

Nicholson, 30 May 1828, Shippen Family Papers, LCMD; Elizabeth Ellis Prescott to Nancy Shaw, 21 June 1825, Shaw-Webb Family Papers, AAS. See also Susanna Dillwyn to her father, 9 October 1792, Dillwyn Manuscripts, LCP/HSP; Deborah Norris Logan, Diary, 11 April 1835, HSP; and Lucinda Storrs, Diary, 15 March 1834, CHS.

46. See Achenbaum, *Old Age in the New Land,* p. 160; David Hackett Fischer, *Growing Old in America,* 2d ed. (New York: Oxford University Press), pp. 145-56; and Cole, "Past Meridian," p. 201.

The Feminine
Search for Meaning

I suppose one might think of old age itself as dying, for it too demands the giving up of one attachment to life for another. Toward what end? If one could think of it as a journey toward a real destina- tion . . . everything might take on meaning again.
— May Sarton, *The House by the Sea,* 1977

The approach of death at any age, in any time, imposes strident, often unrelenting demands on our energies, our psyche, and our innermost re- sources.[1] Whether witnessing the death of a loved one or learning our own death is imminent, we find ourselves confronted by our finitude, by the knowledge that we are not in complete control of our destiny, and by the reality that our sense of future, as it has always existed, will end. Of course, how we react to those certainties varies greatly both within individuals and among different societies and cultures. Yet the tendency for twentieth- century Americans to postpone or, more likely, forego contemplation and spiritual preparation in the face of death sets us apart from many cultures and even from our own past. Our disassociation with death and the dying, both physically and psychically, may indeed reduce our immediate anguish and fear. Yet we have paid a heavy price for our immunity. As death advances, we retreat to safety, without experiencing the pain of self- examination, the discovery of meaning, or the hope of transcendence beyond death. Ours is a culture where death does not fit and where its lessons go unheard and unappreciated.[2]

Old age adds a unique and critical dimension to this propensity for denial and retreat. Unlike their younger counterparts, the aged realize the incontrovertible nearness of death. Death may be no more real than before, but its certainty is no longer easily denied. Retrospection and life review, so often engaged in by the aged, have yielded an enduring, often compelling personal literature on old age and death. On the other hand, old age is not synonymous with death. Despite enormous medical advances, we still know death can come at any age and indeed may come to everyone all at once in a day of nuclear devastation. Even the mysteries of death cannot be claimed by the aged alone. As we grow old, our insights into the major ethical and moral issues of our time, our ability to confront and accept death, and our capacity for transcendence and renewal are not *necessarily* enhanced because we have lived long lives. What, then, is the relationship between old age, death, and the search for meaning at the end of life? And, most important for our study, how has the feminine experience modified or affected that relationship? By listening to the voices of old women facing death two hundred years ago, we can begin to address these difficult questions, informed of our past, perhaps more sensitive to our future.

Old women two hundred years ago approached death from a perspective radically alien to that commonly known today. Women of the past aggressively anticipated the end of life, often many years before their actual demise. Supported by a gender system which encouraged women's commitment to connection, to the cycles of nature, and a belief in their own innate spiritual strength, old women approached death as both a mystery and a challenge. This challenge, however, was fraught with complications. Anxious to heed the tenets of traditional Protestant theology, they reluctantly acknowledged the concomitant need to deny those intimate connections which gave meaning to their lives. Some women ultimately recognized spiritual growth and human commitment as one and the same; others met death fearing failure and defeat, unable to integrate spirit and heart at the end of life. Yet the vigor and grace with which they actively pursued meaning in death testifies both to women's intrinsic strength and to the value of a cultural system where death was considered an integral part of the human experience.[3]

Protestant Theology, the "Spiritual Journey," and Feminine Experience

Many factors influenced a woman's expectations and anxieties concerning death in this early period. Her health and age, her familial and economic circumstances, her familiarity with the deaths of others, and even her level of literacy contributed to her own particular perspective on death. Yet it was a strong religious foundation that women primarily relied on as age — and ultimately death — advanced. This foundation can be traced to the earliest days of colonial society when both Puritans and Quakers emphasized meaning through death. Within this religious construct, reflection and preparation were considered important at all stages of life but essential during old age when death might be near. While God intervened with life at his will, he was believed to be closer to those who had lived long lives. Puritans, in fact, interpreted old age as an indication of God's favor. Reinforced by biblical sanctions extolling piety and righteousness in old age, Protestant theology promoted images of retirement and moral purity for the aged that would serve as examples to younger Christians for many generations.[4]

By the end of the eighteenth and early nineteenth centuries, however, certain theological shifts began to alter both the images and expectations of death. Fear of damnation, the central tenet of Puritan theology, was giving way to an emphasis on hope and redemption. Indeed, the certainty of a heavenly reward for having lived the good life motivated all but the most dour Christians in the post-revolutionary era. As the call for salvation and the promise of life after death ran through meetinghouse and campground with evangelical fury, young and old alike experienced a profound sense of hope and renewal. Women, as we shall see, were particularly receptive to this promise.

Critical to the Protestant theology of death was the metaphor of life as a "spiritual journey," a voyage which promised redemption at its end, but only after the spiritual progress requisite for salvation was achieved, step by step. The image of the spiritual journey fortified many aging Christians who identified the end of a long journey with the completion of their own long lives. It provided a clear sense of direction and hope, outlining a path set firmly in both history and the Bible.[5]

Yet the metaphor of the spiritual journey, as philosopher Carol Ochs has observed, is not necessarily synchronous with feminine experience. Contrary to the concept of linear progression implicit in the spiritual journey, women's experience has traditionally been perceived as cyclical. Emphasizing the natural cycles of birth and growth (particularly evident in the maternal role), Ochs contends that spirituality is found at various points throughout life, not merely at its end. According to this view, the concept of the spiritual journey risks diminishing the values and insights evident throughout women's lives and emphasizes the goals rather than the processes of life itself.[6]

For women growing old two hundred years ago, the conflict inherent in this image is no less obvious. Supported and strengthened throughout their lives by a morality of connection and interdependency, women in old age were expected to "improve" on this earlier model by withdrawing from earthly connections to undertake this final journey alone. Their task was thus doubled: first, to sever those ties which nourished them throughout life; and second, to continue alone on this final journey toward salvation. As we shall see, it was a task requiring more than some women were willing or able to undertake.

Survival: A Painful, Joyous Mystery

"Long life!" wrote Margaret Bayard Smith to her sister, "Why is it considered a blessing, when it necessarily makes us the survivor...?" Women surviving into old age often pondered the meaning of their own continued existence. At a time when less than five percent of the population could be considered old, those within that age group were forced to confront the reality of their minority status, a status reinforced with each passing year. Aging women were often plagued with the notion that they were unworthy of continued life, that their contributions were insignificant compared with those of now-deceased friends and relatives. What could be the purpose of their continued existence, they asked, when others more deserving were taken away?[7]

Women's self-doubt regarding their own survival, of course, echoes classic symptoms of the guilt of survivorship. It is a phenomenon as familiar among surviving generations in postwar Japan, as Robert Lifton has movingly described, as it was for aging women in the new republic. For these and other survivors who interpreted their lives within a structured and orderly framework, continued existence often demanded a requestioning of the foundations of that framework. Such skepticism itself, of course, could be the source of increased guilt.[8]

For women, the problems of survivorship were compounded by the nature of the feminine experience during this early period. To survive meant, by definition, to outlive friends and kin. As we have already seen, the loss of loved ones could strike women especially hard as their reliance on others grew with each passing year. Because women's sense of well-being had long been defined through connection, life alone seemed less sweet. "Were I to lose . . . my dearest connections," wrote Abigail Adams, "I should have no further relish for life." Survival without loved ones loomed as an empty prospect.[9]

Widows, of course, understood survival at its most intimate level. For many women, the comfort of deeply religious faith became the critical, often decisive, factor enabling them to survive the emotional trauma of widowhood. After the death of a spouse, women often turned to the Bible, which reminded them that God was the "widow's friend"—an ally, even a husband, to widows. Sometimes citing the biblical source for that precept (Ps. 68:5), friends and relatives would entreat the widow to rely on divine guidance. For some women, this message was both calming and reassuring.

Margaret Bayard Smith (1778-1844) by Charles Bird King, circa 1829, courtesy of Redwood Library, Newport, R.I. As Margaret Smith approached old age, she found her resources and her expectations challenged by a changing society.

"I have been graciously supported and enabled to exercise that fortitude which I [k]new not before, that I possessed," wrote the widow Mary Andrews in 1823, "and a humble resignation to the will of *God* has kept my spirits from flowing into that channel of gloomy despondency. . . ." Women surviving their husbands could find strength, as Mary Andrews demonstrates, by redirecting their love and energy and by acknowledging the reality of their own limitations.[10]

Surviving one's spouse, of course, was always a possibility that could be anticipated in old age. More enigmatic, and sometimes more unsettling, was the reality of continued existence when younger men and women died before them. It was not unusual to speculate, as one woman did, "why my aged and emaciated [body] should be revived" while younger friends died. At such times, women attempted to accept such pain and mystery as an indication of God's inscrutable will. Charlotte Chambers Riske, a middle-aged Ohioan, pondered her own survival in 1821 after the death of a granddaughter. She finally concluded simply that "it is the will of God."[11]

Yet other women expressed a sense of foreboding about their own ability to submit to God's will. After the death of her daughter Abigail Adams Smith in 1813, Abigail Adams wrote of her grief and sorrow to her son John Quincy. "Religion [may] teach submission and silence, even under the anguish of the Heart," she observed, "but it cannot cure it." In 1838, Margaret Bayard Smith described this same sense of lost faith. She would prefer to submit to God's will, she wrote, "but darkness & doubt chill my very soul." Elizabeth Drinker, Mercy Otis Warren, and Deborah Logan expressed similar doubt about their own faith after the deaths of adult children. While these women continued to believe that resignation was critical in the face of death, their acceptance of death demanded some perceivable logic and order within a larger vision of regeneration. When God's will appeared to thwart that vision, faith was not easily restored.[12]

Undoubtedly, the mystery of continued survival was shared by aging men and women alike. Yet the forcefulness of women's reaction to untimely death can perhaps be best understood within the perspective of women's cyclical vision of life, death, and rebirth. The cycle of life could only continue if the aged, not the young, were the first to die. Although death could strike at any age, as everyone knew, it struck harder when it occurred out of sequence. While old women continued to remind themselves of the old adage "the young may die, the old must," they found it difficult to comprehend or accept the death of young persons.

Despite these instances of anxiety and doubt when death came unexpectedly, survivors believed they learned valuable lessons by witnessing the deaths of others. Women eagerly sought the lessons death might provide. Friends, relatives, and neighbors spent long vigils at the sickbed, anxious to witness (with "painful, terefying satisfaction") what they hoped would be an edifying departure from life. After the death of a loved one, women described in letters the final scene at great length, omitting no details which might afford insight. Through such accounts, women hoped to share the lessons of death with those unable to witness the last days themselves.[13]

As caretakers of the sick and dying, women gained insights into the nature of death unknown to those sheltered from the nursing of the sick and the cleansing and dressing of the dead. As Carol Ochs reminds us, women's active involvement in the care of the dead and dying was far from abstract. It demanded an awareness and an acceptance of the boundaries inherent in human experience. It was, as well, another aspect of a feminine culture that reinforced the separation of spheres and contributed to women's distinctive moral perspective.[14]

On the basis of their observations at the deathbed, women interpreted life's final passage as one of hope, even joy, often betraying an eagerness for evidence that would confirm their own desires for spiritual triumph at the end of life. They were seldom disappointed. Women frequently reported, for instance, the survival of "conscience" long after physical and intellectual faculties had diminished. This suggested, in no uncertrain terms, that moral integrity rather than physical vigor or worldly success facilitated one's smooth transition from the mundane to the sublime.[15]

"I never saw a corpse, a coffin and a grave before with only feelings of pleasure," Elizabeth Pierce wrote in 1826 after the death of her grandmother. Neither had she ever seen "so beautiful a corpse as was Grandma's. . . . I spent the greatest part of my time contemplating it, with unmingled pleasure. The expression immediately after death was child-like, even infantile. . . . As Uncle Phoenix said — 'Mourn for Grandma? We might as well mourn for the angels!' "[16]

Indications of such "triumphant" deaths abounded. Women revelled in describing the "happy soul" of the newly departed. Sarah Logan Fisher's dying aunt evinced such "serene Chearfulness" during her last illness that Fisher proclaimed herself "in love with Old Age." Viewing religion and old age as synonymous, she added, "Indeed nothing makes Religion appear so lovely as chearfulness and Resignation." In 1807, Catherine Akerly Mitchell proudly recorded her mother's stoicism during illness. According to the letters of this Washington, D.C., socialite, her mother looked forward to death "with a smile." Surviving women sometimes described their periods of mourning as "the happiest week of my life." Elizabeth Byles reported herself "in rapture" following the death of her father and expressed longing for her own death.[17]

Such sentiments appear ludicrous, perhaps even grotesque, to twentieth-century sensibilities. Nonetheless, they reveal a strong determination on the part of women to derive meaning and hope from life's most critical, most enigmatic, most horrifying hour. To witness a serene and cheerful death was to reconfirm the preeminence of the spiritual self. To encounter directly such triumphs of the spirit was to allay any doubts that the values and beliefs women held dear were indeed those that would ultimately prevail and conquer.

Optimism in the face of death reflected more than justification of one's values. Women fully expected that such faith would ensure their continued spiritual existence beyond life on earth. They expressed infinite confidence in the promise of heaven and believed eternal joy awaited them beyond this "vale of tears." This spark of hope often increased with advancing years. "Never did the goodness of God appear more and brighter," exclaimed the Massachusetts spinster Rebecca Dickinson in her sixty-fifth year. The belief in life everlasting obviously had a profound effect on one's general perspective. "What is fourscore years?" Mercy Otis Warren rhetorically asked when contemplating eternity while in her eighties. Women believed their heavenly reward would include a long-awaited reunion with departed friends and relatives. Margaret Bayard Smith reminded her sister that she could anticipate "a blessed reunion in Heaven" with her dying brother. Her sister's heart, she wrote, should be "softened rather than saddened" because of impending death. In life's final hours, God's promise was one of cheer, hope, and redemption.[18]

Transcendence and immortality, as we perceive it today, can be expressed in many forms. Biological reproduction and the creation of art or literature, for example, confirm that our lives will continue to influence some small part of the world long after we have left it. Yet the notion of transcendence into heaven, as commonly understood two hundred years ago, strikes many today as both irrational and highly fanciful, a device employed by history's underdogs to compensate for lives void of meaning and hope. There is little sense among the women writers studied here, however, that they saw themselves as underdogs or that they required illusion or fantasy to escape their present lives. On the contrary, their notion of transcendence appears quite logical within the framework of morality and interdependency structuring their lives. Heaven implied the continuation of connections to friends and loved ones, the survival of a spirit nourished throughout a long life on earth, and the endurance of a distinctive self long after physical deterioration had taken its toll. Those who responded to the promise of heaven were not necessarily abandoning reality or denying their earthly values. Heaven, instead, served as an extension of the reality women knew — that of connection, continuity, and an enduring moral self.[19]

Preparing to Meet Life's End

"Of late years," Margaret Bayard Smith confided to her sister in 1834, "... I constantly feel as if I stood on the very verge of another world." So vivid was her perception of death's nearness, she wondered how anyone could "indulge hopes beyond the present moment." As survivors and witnesses to death over the course of a long lifetime, women quite naturally turned their attention increasingly inward as they contemplated their own likely demise. Life indeed seemed so precarious that thoughts of death became constant companions for some women. The Connecticut spinster Rebecca Noyes began to anticipate her own death in 1803 at the age of forty-four, twenty-eight years before her actual demise. Elizabeth Denny Ward, a Massachusetts widow, acknowledged she was "reminded day by day of my near dissolution." Aging women such as Elizabeth Drinker and Deborah Norris Logan often contemplated their impending death, despite their continued longevity. By concentrating so heavily on their own mortality, women forced themselves to prepare for life's end.[20]

Among the most remarkably "prepared" women of the early nineteenth century was Mary Moody Emerson, a member of the revolutionary generation and aunt to Ralph Waldo Emerson. According to her nephew, Mary Emerson became obsessed with death as she grew older. "For years," Emerson wrote, "she made her bed in the form of a coffin." To embrace death fully, she wore her shroud both day and night; Emerson believed, in fact, that his aunt wore out many shrouds. Although few women prepared for death with as much vigor and imagination as Mary Moody Emerson, her example illustrates the extent to which some women tried to merge death with life. By heartily accepting the trappings of death, women such as Mary Emerson attempted to control, as much as possible, their passage into the next world. Far from passive, such women aggressively approached death as their final and greatest challenge.[21]

The preoccupation with death expressed by many women diarists and correspondents in the late eighteenth and early nineteenth centuries did not, as might be expected, reflect an unusually high deathrate. Maris Vinovskis, in his study of death in early America, noted considerable "misperceptions of the extent of mortality in New England society." Diarists frequently exaggerated the likelihood of imminent death. Vinovskis attributed these misperceptions to the unusual life experiences of the diarists and the inordinate emphasis placed on death in early New England. In her study of seventy-one American women diarists of the eighteenth and early nineteenth centuries, Kathryn Kish Sklar estimated their average age at death was 56.4 years. Despite their forebodings, these women diarists lived beyond the average life span of most women.[22]

There is much within the feminine experience, however, to explain this extraordinary interest in death that extends beyond individual life histories and a Protestant heritage rooted in death and redemption. For women, death both threatened and beckoned in ways uniquely influenced by issues of biological and gender identification and feminine interpretations of morality. Death during childbirth was a clear and undeniable possibility (one which remained throughout the nineteenth century). Early in their lives, women confronted this possibility of imminent death. Older women's obvious triumph over it did not diminish women's sense of closeness to death. It continued to hover around their sisters, daughters, and grand-daughters as they, too, faced the prospect of death with the giving of life. Even among those women whose immediate circle of friends and relatives survived childbirth, the ever-present *possibility* of death created for women a lifelong association with its specter.

As women aged, their early victories over death during childbirth did not preclude further contemplation over the prospect of life's ending. Quite the contrary, it served to engage women actively in questions of meaning and self-understanding as the years advanced. Women who had not given birth shared as well in this feminine perspective, having cared for and nursed their mothers, sisters, and nieces during both pregnancy and child-birth. Theirs was not a macabre fascination with the rituals of death; nor was it a self-serving, sentimentalized despondency intended to conjure sym-pathy from others. Women's perceptions of their nearness to death, instead, reflected the reality of the lives they knew. Having cared for the dying and having faced death directly themselves, aging women embraced, rather than avoided, the implications of death's nearness.

As she tossed the last of her personal papers into the flames, Rebecca Shoemaker surprised herself with the "calm pleasant sensation" she expe-rienced in destroying those papers she did not wish to be seen after her death. Like other women, she attempted to bring order to her temporal as well as her spiritual world in preparing for the end of life. Anticipating their demise, women settled accounts and organized their personal papers. Eleven years before her death, Deborah Logan straightened her desk and tied her notes and letters, expecting "the final close of life" to be near at hand. Such close attention to detail well before their actual deaths indicates the clarity and precision with which women approached the end of life and their ability to regulate those things still under their control.[23]

Preparation for death, of course, consisted of more than merely tidying up one's personal effects. It was, in its broadest sense, a lifelong process, one that demanded thoughtfulness and contemplation from the onset of adulthood. To be prepared fully for death meant that one had faced squarely her own limitations and had put her faith in a higher authority, serenely confident that life beyond death would more than compensate for the loss of earthly ties. It was, needless to say, a difficult task, but one which most women, to varying degrees, undertook.

Women regarded preparation for death as a basic tenet of Protestant belief. The evangelical Episcopalian Elizabeth Smith spent the last thirty years of her long life in frequent contemplation, each year examining herself "more strictly" than the year before. Alice Izard of South Carolina, although apparently less devout than Elizabeth Smith, nonetheless prayed for a "cheerful readiness" for death many years before her own demise. Protestant theology, reinforced by feminine experience, continued to provide for some women a viable framework for anticipating the end of life.[24]

To varying degrees, all denominations provided guidance and direction in helping members prepare for life's final hour, offering useful instruction for self-examination and self-understanding. Members of the Society of Friends, by the very nature of their commitment to independent spiritual growth (closely monitored by the community of Friends), excelled in this task. Quakers, perhaps more than others, perceived the relationship between self-enlightenment and preparation for the end of life. Drawing from a theology that emphasized the individual search for "light" in the midst of darkness, Friends were constantly urged to look inward and, in doing so, to become "wise and solid" of themselves, as one Quaker women described it. Such demands required considerable intellectual vigor and courage, expected of both men and women alike. In their attempts to become "wise and solid," Quakers concentrated on the core, not the periphery, of life's meaning.[25]

"I fear," wrote the aging Quaker Mary Mitchell, "[that] I have not been deep enough in my mind, to be preserved in that clearness which I desire." Indeed, such continual self-scrutiny could create its own anxiety. Yet Mary Mitchell and other Friends would continue to prepare themselves for that "clearness" that would indicate both perfect love and total acceptance of divine will. This model for life and death served generations of Quaker women and no doubt influenced those non-Friends who bore witness to Quaker preparation for death.[26]

Regardless of denomination, preparing for death required the completion of two widely recognized tasks: resignation to the will of God and withdrawal from earthly ties. Until these two objectives were accomplished, peace and contentment at the end of life—and the promise of heavenly reward—would not be forthcoming. Although few women ever acknowledged (at least in their written documents) feeling *fully* prepared for life's end, witnesses to death often believed that the struggle had been won and that the deceased, with a smile on her dying lips, was indeed ready to leave this world. The serenity reported at the deathbed, however, cannot belie the enormity of the task or the wide-ranging emotions the task could evoke. Preparation for death was indeed a double-edged sword: providing structure, direction, and hope at the end of life while imposing strict, often "unnatural" demands on women whose lifelong values might have been threatened by the strictures of withdrawal. Yet for those women able to accept the completion of life, "letting go" at life's end was a reward, not a punishment.

Resignation, of course, was both an attitude and an acquired skill long known to women in ways not directly related to the expectation of death. Living in a society which severely limited women's access to the public arena, women learned at an early age the necessity of accepting the will of a higher (male) authority. They perceived this authority as necessary within a larger scheme of life, death, and regeneration in which (women knew) they played a pivotal role. While not all women accepted their lot gracefully or willingly, most women during this early period adapted successfully within their sphere and were resigned to the reality of its limitations. Much of this same sense of resignation would be employed throughout life as women encountered obstacles and boundaries that could be neither ignored nor overpowered. Death, of course, was the last and greatest boundary.[27]

As many women knew, resignation in the face of death could ease the burdens of a long life. Seventy-year-old Elizabeth Collins defined in rhyme its salutary benefits in an 1825 diary entry written after recounting many recent deaths in her family:

> What cannot resignation do?
> It wonders can perform.
> That powerful charm, thy will be done!
> Can lay the loudest storm.

Throughout their lives, women such as Elizabeth Collins acknowledged those points over which they had no control. During the course of the nineteenth century, this attitude would shift as the notion of control (a fundamental aspect of middle-class values) gained ascendancy, allowing for increased autonomy but also minimizing the capacity to accept limitations and, ultimately, to prepare for death. Such was not the case, however, for most aging women in this early period. "Happy are those that are prepair'd to meet the great change," wrote Rebecca Noyes in 1807, expressing a sentiment well known to women of the time.[28]

While resignation at the end of life was not always easy to achieve, it involved an individual act of will compatible with a life of spiritual concentration. Less compatible with lived experience, however, was the process of withdrawal from the people and things of this world. In theory, withdrawal from earthly ties (often referred to as "retirement" or "disengagement") encouraged a natural and logical progression from life to death. Such a retreat was intended to reduce the sense of loss associated with death. Withdrawn from their attachments to friends and family, those anticipating life's end could meet death in perfect piety, concentrating only on the immediate task of preparing their souls for heaven. As a necessary step in the preparation for death, withdrawal could facilitate a smooth transition at the end of life.[29]

"Old age warns me that my proper station is now my home," Mary Page wrote in 1828. Margaret Bayard Smith, seven years later, expressed similar sentiments. "The more I stay at home," she wrote her sister, "the more I want to stay at home...." Most women agreed that disengagement at the end of life was both appropriate and necessary. For old women, the reality of imminent death made withdrawal a more urgent and pressing concern that forced them to attempt to separate themselves psychologically from the close and enduring ties of a lifetime. Such disengagement was intended to protect both the dying and the bereaved from the pain and loss imposed by death.[30]

"This Life's a dream, an empty Show," wrote Abigail Adams to her sister. In a similar vein, seventy-four-year-old Ruth Henshaw Bascom recalled the biblical message, "all seems as a dream—a tale that is told." For such women growing old, the denial of life's reality served to facilitate the process of withdrawal. Others perceived withdrawal as a "gradual weaning" from life. Such descriptions reveal the need for a transitional state between life and death, a "dreamy void" separating the pain associated with old age from the joy of spiritual rebirth at the end of life.[31]

Ultimately, however, life's "dreamy void" could not obscure the need to confront the reality of relinquishing earthly ties. It was one thing to acknowledge the "certainty of Death and its awefullness" and quite another to break the connections of a long and fruitful life. While considering the "comfort, Joy, and consolation" resignation could bring, Elizabeth Drinker admitted that withdrawal was "hard, very hard, in many cases to effect...." Yet Elizabeth Drinker and many other women seemed determined to attain the peace and comfort they believed could come only through a withdrawal from earthly ties and resignation to the divine will.[32]

Some women tackled the problem head on. Among the items in Hannah Adams's list of "serious Resolutions" written toward the end of her life was the promise to "pray and guard against loving my friends with that ardent attachment... which is incompatible with supreme love to, and trust in, God alone." Others tried to distance themselves from other forms of "ardent attachment." Writing to her grandchildren, Elizabeth Denny Ward warned it was time for her to break away from the ties that "sweeten life." "I desire to hold it loose," she wrote. To prepare herself for death, she planned to be ready "to leave all, children and grandchildren and great grandchildren." "Live lo[o]se to those dear objects of our tenderness & care," advised Sarah Logan Fisher. By holding loved ones at arm's length, women anticipating death hoped to ease the pain of their greatest burden—separation from friends and family members.[33]

"I do wonder at myself that I should be so earthly-minded," confessed Rebecca Dickinson, still years away from her own death. By its very nature, the demand for withdrawal imposed years of struggle and hardship on many women. Most women found it difficult to separate themselves from long associations with special people and places. As they grew older, they increasingly felt ashamed to admit their need for "some kind comforter" in their final years and feared the implications this lack of faith suggested. Even when their faith was strong, some aging women experienced trouble letting go of life simply because they loved it. While in her eighties, Susanna Boylston Adams continued to express her zest for life. "I *really believe* if I was now sick," she reportedly said in 1793, "I should want to be well again." This preference for life puzzled women who had long anticipated a growing fondness for death. Despite her desire to embrace death, Mary McDonald of Georgia admitted, "I find the grave a gloomy prison, which I often times dread to enter." While women such as Mary Moody Emerson approached death with open arms, other women continued to struggle with the fact that they loved life and feared death.[34]

Women could not always meet the challenge imposed by such high expectations surrounding death. The inability to feel fully prepared to embrace death sometimes brought a sense of spiritual failure and personal defeat to the lives of aging women. "I wish I was more resind to the will of heaven than I can say I am," Elizabeth Putnam sadly told her nephew in 1788. Margaret Bayard Smith, who had long anticipated "gliding Smoothly" to the end of life, desperately tried to find "tranquillity and quietude" in her last years. She faulted herself for being unable to achieve this overdue peace. "I am far more discontented with myself, than with my circumstances," she noted in 1839. "I fall so far short of what I ought to be." While women frequently expressed an understanding of what they "ought to be," they seldom acknowledged that they had achieved this final, important goal.[35]

During the last quarter-century of Deborah Logan's life, the struggle for resignation and withdrawal as recorded in her diary became an overriding issue, growing critical as she became older. Because she so earnestly desired to fulfill all the expectations imposed on her as an aging, upper-middle-class Quaker woman, Logan might have experienced greater trials than other women did. However, since the rising expectations of moral womanhood increasingly extended throughout woman's sphere, Logan's long, uphill battle for resignation was probably familiar to many women.

"[I have] yet hardly advanced one step in what I ought to be," admitted Deborah Logan on her fifty-fourth birthday in 1815. Aging signified moral and spiritual growth to Logan, and she anxiously charted her own path of spiritual enlightenment and moral improvement over the next twenty-four years. Since this path appeared neither smooth nor straight, she often expressed a sense of apprehension and a dread of failure as she contemplated the remainder of her life.[36]

Deborah Logan's anticipation of her own death gained momentum after the illness and death of her husband in 1821. Initially, she allayed her immense sense of grief and loss by concentrating on her own spiritual and moral development in preparation for death. For the rest of her life, she anxiously awaited the time when she would join her husband in the family plot at Stenton, a place she regularly visited for rest and reflection. Resigning herself to George Logan's death, as she saw it, strengthened her ability to resign from "the world" as well.[37]

During these years of preparing for the end of life, Deborah Logan frequently alluded to her spiritual "lamp," which she hoped to find "trimmed and burning." Such a lamp would illuminate the final passage on her voyage through life and would lead her safely to a heavenly reward. As a symbol of the intellectual vitality necessary for achieving the moral tasks of old age, her burning lamp offered a strong and positive image of maturity and readiness for death.[38]

As she grew older, however, Logan often sensed that her lamp was burning only dimly. Afflicted with various aches and pains she attributed to "decay," she frequently expressed the wish for a "release" from the physical ties of an earthly existence. "If prepared for the change a Release would be very wellcome," she wrote in 1824, adding ruefully, "But I am not prepared." Although she expected that death was not far off, Logan insisted that she was "not fit to die." She began to suspect, in fact, that she would never be "wise and solid of myself," regardless of how old she became.[39]

As Deborah Logan approached her seventieth birthday, her anxiety expressed itself in new ways. She described "a kind of nervous excitement" when thwarted in her attempts to cultivate "the right feelings." Expecting to enjoy calmness and serenity in contemplation, she was instead overwhelmed with "dark and sombre" thoughts. "It really seems impossible to get from this spot at present," she wrote in 1829, implying that things could still improve in the future. By 1832, however, she acknowledged that her moral growth might not continue. It was wise to admit, she declared, that she must stop "expecting to grow better." Yet she continued to examine her state of spiritual readiness on a regular basis, clearly hoping for improvement but finding little. "I am one year older, nearer to Eternity, uglier and more infirm," she remarked in 1833. She was not, however, "one bit better" than she had been.[40]

Approaching her final year of life, Logan expressed a heightened sense of urgency. When her son Algernon succumbed to tuberculosis, her expectations of orderly death were destroyed. Unable to accept fully Algernon's death, she found it even more difficult to resign herself to her own impending demise. "I think I have never felt more deficiency," she admitted in 1838. Nevertheless, she struggled to continue her "most important work." "I sadly want to 'set my House in order,'" she recorded wearily one month before her death.[41]

Because of her commitment to the ideal of spiritual growth and moral development in old age, Deborah Logan approached her final years with both joy and anxiety. Apprehension became particularly evident during her last few years when she was beset with both physical and psychological pain. Following the death of her son, she was no longer able to predict the "normal" order of things. Her son's death, unlike her husband's, revealed no pattern of behavior or response that could ameliorate her sense of loss or grief. With Algernon gone, her own death sometimes appeared to her as anticlimactic, no longer requiring urgent moral preparation.

The anxiety dominating so much of Deborah Logan's late life testifies to the inevitable pain associated with approaching death. Yet it also suggests the inadequacies of the Protestant theology of dying as it applied to women. Logan's expectations for constant improvement, for "light" at the end of her journey, failed to materialize in a world seldom yielding to rational order or progress. Although familiar with life's cycle of birth, death, and regeneration, she nonetheless anticipated her final years to be ones of singular improvement and enlightenment. Just as confounding was the reality of the pain of separation and her continuing need to give and receive love. Having devoted three-fourths of a century to the care and nurturance of friends and family, Logan needed the support and comfort of close connections. Yet such earthly ties, she knew, conflicted with the demands of withdrawal at life's end, made so apparent with Algernon's death. She could rationalize neither his death nor the pain she felt from it.

Despite the heavy burden that aspects of Protestant theology imposed on women, the Protestant framework for death offered much to help sustain elderly persons in post-revolutionary America. While anxiety apparently took the upper hand during the last years of her life, Deborah Logan derived hope from her belief in the possibility of growth and improvement in old age that supported her during her most trying hours. Although she continued to doubt her own ability to prepare herself for death, her struggle illustrates the potential strength of this religious framework. Far from abandoning hope as death grew near, she persistently exercised her mental and moral faculties, believing she had life's most critical task ahead of her. It is possible she never became "wise and solid" of herself, as she so eloquently predicted in 1824. But the expectation of an active, ongoing struggle to achieve spiritual and moral perfection gave meaning and direction to Deborah Logan's final years. While her quest brought fear and dismay, it nonetheless set the stage for an active and viable old age.

Although Protestant expectations for death might not have addressed the reality of the feminine experience, women generally acknowledged a belief in feminine fortitude which could overcome even the most difficult trials. Many women perceived their relationship to God as particularly strong and resilient, enabling them to accept death better than men. Believing that her own sex was "strongest in the day of trial," Mary Palmer Tyler contended that such strength derived from women's deeply religious convictions. "Our faith is more firm and reliable," she wrote. "We feel that here is our only sure trust, and His will the best, although we cannot see why. . . ." Strength during times of crisis had enabled women throughout their lives to confront unpleasant, sometimes fearful situations. For this reason, the high expectations imposed on them in the face of death might not have seemed unreasonable or insurmountable.[42]

The death of Elizabeth Inman provides an excellent case in point. When she died in 1785 after a seven-week illness, Inman was eulogized by her niece, notably for the calmness and serenity that surrounded the old woman's death. "The only struggle she appeared to have," wrote the younger woman, "was her attachment to her family. 'My affections still get the better of me,' she would often say." Trying to break the tie with her family while struggling with her own failing health as well, Inman allowed family members to visit her only fifteen minutes each day. Eventually, she "conquered" the painful anticipation of eternal separation from her loved ones. Freed from anxiety over such "affections," she was able to spend her final days surrounded by family and friends. By accepting her situation, Elizabeth Inman could embrace her family at life's end apparently without pain or misery.[43]

But not without great effort. Inman's ability to structure a pattern of withdrawal while on her deathbed—to limit her interaction with her family to fifteen minutes a day—attests to her singular strength and fortitude in the face of death. Although we have no record of the inward battle she waged, her niece's final comments suggest that she indeed achieved a sense of personal integration and unity at the close of life which allowed her to share her final days with those she loved. In the end, she chose not to break her earthly ties but instead learned, through her own strength, how to overcome the fear of separation and face squarely her impending death.[44]

Because death struck young and old alike in early America, expectations about the end of life were of vital interest to people of all ages. The young as well as the elderly contemplated the "transitory" nature of human existence and frequently speculated on their own, perhaps imminent demise. Because of this, men and women drew strength from a religious foundation offering the hope of redemption after death. Since the fears and the hopes associated with death were not age-specific, people of all ages could share their expectations and anxieties about the end of life.

For the old, however, death inevitably seemed closer. The reality of impending death gained force as the infirmities of age advanced. The loneliness of their survival reinforced their perceptions of life and death as irrevocably intertwined, commanding constant vigilance and earnest preparation. For the elderly in post-revolutionary America, old age significantly increased the tenor and intensity of their reflection on death and dying. Anticipating the completion of their spiritual journey within the Protestant tradition, they knew resignation to God's will and withdrawal from earthly ties would ease the transition from this world to the next.

Yet the metaphor of the spiritual journey and the prescription for final preparation were not entirely consistent or compatible with feminine experience. True, women throughout life understood the value of resignation in a society that strictly limited their opportunities and carefully regulated their roles. Most women were not, however, passively "resigned" to their sphere; rather, they openly acknowledged the boundaries of their lives — both cultural and biological — and worked actively within those bounds to maintain productive and useful lives. As death approached, resignation continued to serve as a vehicle for confronting reality, for learning that no one's life is completely under control.

Although the concept of resignation offered women few obstacles in preparation for death, disengagement and withdrawal were tasks which seemed at odds with women's lifelong experience. After years of caretaking, forming bonds with friends and loved ones, and sanctifying the connections between people and generations, women could not easily accept the prospect of withdrawal at the end of life. Separation, of course, was inevitable. Yet disappointment and self-doubt could cast a pall over the final years of women who believed a desire for withdrawal would come naturally at the close of life. Women had to face individually, in their own way and in their own time, the prospect of separation and the necessity of finally letting go. The image of the spiritual journey also offered an ambivalent prospect for women facing death in old age. On the one hand, it provided an outline for spiritual growth, a structure enabling both men and women to gauge their own progress toward enlightenment. It demanded vigilance and self-scrutiny, but it offered in return the hope of a peaceful and everlasting reward at the end of life's journey. Implicit within this concept, however, remained the metaphor of the spiritual pilgrim, the loner who shunned worldly ties in the quest for independent moral progress. Despite their attempts to emulate both the pilgrim and the pilgrim's progress, women could not deny their long lives of interdependency. Neither could they easily find comfort in the singular notion of progress, a concept perhaps more compatible with the masculine sphere.

We are thus faced with the proverbial goblet of wine — either half full or half empty, depending on one's perspective. Unquestionably, aging men and women gained a firm sense of direction and hope from their commitment to Protestant interpretations of dying and death. For aging women, however, the glass sometimes appeared half empty, diminished by a theology which seemed at times to threaten lifelong values. Ultimately, perhaps hindsight is best after all. Only when compared with today's widespread denial of the spiritual implications of death can we appreciate and even admire the demanding task undertaken by these old women facing death. Their determination, their strength, and their hope inspire us today with a much-needed model for facing the end of life.

NOTES

1. May Sarton, *The House by the Sea* (New York: W. W. Norton, 1977), p. 190.

2. This dreary perspective on twentieth-century culture in relation to death is not a denial of Kübler-Ross's findings for individual cases of dying patients. As she tells us, the dying frequently confront and ultimately accept the reality of their condition. Yet popular culture, reinforced at various institutional levels, promotes a vision of death where the dying are often anesthetized from both pain and the reality of their imminent demise; where friends and relatives still attempt to divert patients from thoughts of death; and where the bodies of deceased loved ones are whisked away and manipulated by strangers for profit. More tragically, we all risk becoming spiritually paralyzed by our fear of contemplation in the face of death and our refusal to search for meaning in the way we die as well as in the way we live. See Elisabeth Kübler-Ross, *On Death and Dying* (New York: Macmillan, 1969); David E. Stannard, *The Puritan Way of Death: A Study of Religion, Culture, and Social Change* (New York: Oxford University Press, 1977); and Philippe Ariès, *Western Attitudes towards Death from the Middle Ages to the Present* (Baltimore: Johns Hopkins Press, 1974).

3. For my perspective throughout this chapter, I am particularly indebted to the work of Carol Ochs (especially *Women and Spirituality*), whose insights into the connections between feminine experience and spirituality have greatly clarified

my own understanding of women in this early period. See Ochs, *Women and Spirituality* (Totowa, N.J.: Rowman and Allanheld, 1983).

4. This chapter reflects only the views of Protestant women. As noted above, aging non-Protestant women during this period failed to leave substantial material on their personal responses to old age and death. Heavy non-Protestant immigration to America began only at the end of this period.

5. Thomas Cole has argued that the concept of the spiritual voyage "encouraged individuals of all ages to locate themselves along the route to eternity." According to Cole, this concept, evident as early as John Bunyan's *Pilgrim's Progress* (1678), continued to maintain "a strong incentive to live with the flow of time rather than against it." See Cole, "Past Meridian: Aging and the Northern Middle Class, 1830-1930" (Ph.D. dissertation, University of Rochester, 1980), p. 25. See also Cole and Terri L. Premo, "The Pilgrimage of Joel Andrews: Aging in the Autobiography of a Yankee Farmer," *International Journal of Aging and Human Development* 24:2 (1986-87):79-85.

6. Ochs, *Women and Spirituality,* p. 85.

7. Margaret Bayard Smith to Jane Kirkpatrick, 10 February 1840, Margaret Bayard Smith Papers, LCMD.

8. Robert Jay Lifton, *The Broken Connection: On Death and the Continuity of Life* (New York: Simon and Schuster, 1979).

9. Abigail Adams to John Adams, 16 September 1775, *Familiar Letters of John Adams and His Wife Abigail Adams, during the Revolution,* ed. Charles Francis Adams (Boston: Houghton Mifflin, 1876), p. 97.

10. Mary Andrews to Nancy Shaw, 13 June 1823, Shaw-Webb Family Papers, AAS. See also Hannah Emery to Mary Carter, 16 March 1788, Cutts Family Papers, EI; Margaret Bayard Smith to Samuel Smith, 12 April 1798, Margaret Bayard Smith Papers, LCMD; Mason and Mary Shaw to Nancy Shaw, 27 April 1813, Shaw-Webb Family Papers, AAS; Mary Cutts to Hannah Carter Smith, 11 April 1816, Smith-Carter Family Papers, MHS; Lucy Cargill to niece, 27 October 1829, Waldo Family Papers, AAS. St. Paul advised widows to remain unmarried because they could depend on the special protection of the Lord.

11. Deborah Norris Logan, Diary, 26 August 1822, HSP; Charlotte Chambers Riske to her daughter Mary, March 1821, *Memoir of Charlotte Chambers,* ed. Lewis G. Garrard (Philadelphia: by the author, 1856), p. 131.

12. Abigail Adams to John Quincy Adams, [1813], quoted in Charles W. Akers, *Abigail Adams: An American Woman* (Boston: Little, Brown, 1980), p. 185; Margaret Bayard Smith to Jane Kirkpatrick, 26 October 1838, Margaret Bayard Smith Papers, LCMD. See also Elizabeth Drinker, Diary, 28 September and 15 October 1807, HSP; the poetry of Mercy Otis Warren on the death of her son, in Edmund M. Hayes, "The Private Poems of Mercy Otis Warren," *New England Quarterly* 54 (June 1981):201-24; and Deborah Norris Logan, Diary, 23 October 1836, HSP.

13. Quote from Mercy Otis Warren to Abigail Adams, 19 January 1779, *Adams Family Correspondence,* 3 vols., ed. L. H. Butterfield (Cambridge: Harvard University Press, 1963), 3:152. See also Jane Brainerd to her brother-in-law, 7

November 1839, Hooker Collection, SL; and Elizabeth Murray to her sister, 26 June 1785, James M. Robbins Family Papers, MHS.

14. Ochs, *Women and Spirituality,* p. 77. Margaret R. Miles, in her impressive study of the relationship between language and visual imagery, argues that the recovery of women's history requires "an alternative perspective based on the primacy of physical existence." While male intellectuals recount historical development as uninterrupted continuity "that strangely resembles male physical development," they have "ignore[d] the absolute dependence of human beings on the body, its exigencies, and its natural environment." Yet Miles interprets the female experience as one in direct contrast, that is, one of "irreversible change and discontinuity" rather than, as I argue, one grounded in a cyclical vision of birth, growth, death, and regeneration. See Miles, *Image as Insight: Visual Understanding in Western Christianity and Secular Culture* (Boston: Beacon Press, 1985), pp. 36-37.

15. Deborah Norris Logan, Diary, 16 December 1826, HSP. See also Mercy Otis Warren to Abigail Adams, 22 January 1779, *Adams Family Correspondence,* 3 vols., ed. Butterfield, 3:155; Elizabeth Cranch Norton, Diary, 2 December 1808, Norton Papers, MHS; Rebecca Noyes, Diary, 29 October 1819, CHS; and Lucinda Storrs, Diary, 27 May 1819 and June [1833], CHS.

Late eighteenth-century theologians and physicians agreed that moral faculties extended beyond intellectual functioning in old age. See, for instance, Benjamin Rush, *Medical Inquiries and Observations* (Philadelphia: Thomas Dobson, 1797).

16. Elizabeth Pierce, Journal, 30 March 1826, Poor Family Papers, SL.

17. Sarah Logan Fisher, Diary, 7 December 1785, HSP; Catherine A. Mitchell to Margaret A. Miller, 17 August 1807, Catherine Mitchell Papers, LCMD; Elizabeth Byles to the Reverend Mather Byles, November 1770, Elizabeth Byles Letterbook, HSP. See also Margaret Bayard Smith, Diary, 11 January 1807, Margaret Bayard Smith Papers, LCMD; Deborah Norris Logan, Diary, 24 August 1817, HSP; and F. Chrystie to Rebecca Nicholson, 29 January 1844, Shippen Family Papers, LCMD.

David Stannard contends that eighteenth-century sentimentality profoundly altered the Puritan view of death, creating a more optimistic attitude toward death. See Stannard, *The Puritan Way of Death,* p. 154-55.

18. Rebecca Dickinson, Diary, 8 August 1802, in *A History of Hatfield, Massachusetts, 1660-1910,* ed. Daniel White Wells and Reuben Field Wells (Springfield, Mass.: F. C. H. Gibbons, 1910), p. 207; Mercy Otis Warren, "An Address to the Supreme Being," in Hayes, "Private Poems," p. 223; Margaret Bayard Smith to Jane Kirkpatrick, 10 February 1840, Margaret Bayard Smith Papers, LCMD. See also Rebecca Noyes, Diary, 23 February 1802 and 1827 passim, CHS; Ann R. Page to Elizabeth Adams, November 1805, William B. Randolph Papers, LCMD; and Lucinda Storrs, Diary, 23 February and 13 November 1833, CHS.

19. Robert Lifton has described perceptions of immortality in five general modes: biological, theological, creative, natural, and experiential transcendence. See Lifton, *The Broken Connection,* pp. 18-23.

20. Margaret Bayard Smith to Jane Kirkpatrick, 3 August 1834 and 2 December 1835, Margaret Bayard Smith Papers, LCMD; Rebecca Noyes, Diary, Jan-

uary 1803, 9 May 1807, and 29 October 1819, CHS; Elizabeth Denny Ward to Thomas Ward II, 24 February 1836, Ward Family Papers, AAS. See also Elizabeth Drinker, Diary, 11 April 1795, 19 April and 18 May 1796, and 26 March 1807, HSP; and Deborah Norris Logan, Diary, 7 April 1831, HSP.

21. Ralph Waldo Emerson, quoted in Stannard, *The Puritan Way of Death*, p. 167. Stannard concludes that Mary Emerson's fascination with death was an "extreme product of romantization and sentimentalization of death," which was full-blown in nineteenth-century America. It is my contention, however, that we must try to understand such extraordinary behavior as exhibited by Mary Moody Emerson as an expression of women's distinctive perspective on matters of spirituality and death.

22. Maris Vinovskis, "Angels Heads and Weeping Willows: Death in Early America," *Proceedings of the American Antiquarian Society* 86 (October 1976):273-302, quotations on pp. 289, 292. Sklar's study is described in this article, pp. 290-91.

23. Rebecca Shoemaker, Journal, 30 July 1805, Rawle Family Papers, HSP; Deborah Norris Logan, Diary, 31 December 1827, HSP. See also Elizabeth Jacquelin Ambler Carrington to Nancy ?, 11 March 1823, Letters of Elizabeth Jacquelin Ambler, LCMD.

24. On each birthday, the fifth of December, Elizabeth Smith listed her accomplishments and the state of her preparedness. See her birthday entries from 1822-52 in Elizabeth Smith, Diary, AAS, and compare Alice Izard to Margaret Manigault, 19 January and 1 February 1812, Izard Family Papers, LCMD.

25. Deborah Norris Logan, Diary, 7 March and 16 May 1824, HSP.

26. Mary Callender Mitchell, *A Short Account of the Early Part of the Life of Mary Mitchell* (New Bedford, Mass.: Abraham Shearman, 1812), p. 52. See also Ann Whitall, Diary, 11 January 1762, quoted in J. William Frost, *The Quaker Family in Colonial America: A Portrait of the Society of Friends* (New York: St. Martin's Press, 1973), p. 41; Deborah Norris Logan, Diary, 9 February 1833, HSP; and Sarah Logan Fisher, Diary, n.d. 1784 (13:6-7) and 29 September 1796, HSP.

27. See Elizabeth Drinker, Diary, 11 April 1795, HSP; Mary Andrews to Nancy Shaw, 13 June 1823, Shaw-Webb Family Papers, AAS; and Deborah Norris Logan, Diary, 12 April 1817, 11 April 1822, and 15 June 1823, HSP. Cicero had argued that resignation was a sign of wisdom in age. See Cicero, *De Senectute* 13.82. Carol Ochs interprets the acceptance of boundaries as an element of spiritual growth in *Women and Spirituality*, p. 81.

28. Elizabeth (Ballinger) Mason Collins, *Memoirs of Elizabeth Collins of Upper Evesham, N.J.* (Philadelphia: N. Kite, 1833), p. 121; Rebecca Noyes, Diary, 9 May 1807, CHS. Thomas Cole maintains that minimized preparation for death in the mid-nineteenth century contributed to a growing association of the concept of old age with death. "Repressed fears of death became displaced onto old age," he argues. See Cole, "Past Meridian," p. 156. See also Gordon E. Geddes, *Welcome Joy: Death in Puritan New England*, 2d ed. (Ann Arbor: UMI Press, 1981), pp. 1, 74.

29. David Hackett Fischer, in describing the "emotional distance" between the elderly and the young in early America, fails to address the issue of withdrawal.

See Fischer, *Growing Old,* p. 72. Rather than assume, as Fischer does, that the elderly received little love and affection from young persons, it may be more useful to consider the extent to which old persons *chose* to withdraw from earthly ties in preparation for death.

30. Mary Page to Rebecca Nicholson, 30 May 1828, Shippen Family Papers, LCMD; Margaret Bayard Smith to Jane Kirkpatrick, 17 July 1835, Margaret Bayard Smith Papers, LCMD. Rebecca Shoemaker suggested in 1785 that the eighty-year-old Benjamin Franklin should "disengage himself from every earthly pursuit." See R. Shoemaker to Samuel Shoemaker, 11 November 1785, Shoemaker Papers, HSP; see also ibid., 28 October and 4 December 1785. Women's withdrawal from "earthly ties" as death approached is consistent with the findings of Elisabeth Kübler-Ross who describes the fifth and usually final stage of dying as a period of acceptance. See Kübler-Ross, *On Death and Dying,* pp. 112-37.

The gradual process of withdrawal from close connections considered appropriate for elderly women in post-revolutionary America reveals a phenomenon still familiar to contemporary men and women as they grow old. E. Cumming and W. Henry describe the "disengagement theory" in their seminal and controversial study, where disengagement is defined as an inevitable result of aging, culminating in decreased interaction between the aging person and others in his or her social system. See Cumming and Henry, *Growing Old: The Process of Disengagement* (New York: Basic Books, 1961). While the inevitability of disengagement has been hotly debated, the theory appears particularly valid when applied to death and dying. According to Richard A. Kalish, "The dying individual's sense of loss diminishes as his attachments diminish in importance. That this stage closely resembles the concept of disengagement," he concludes, "is not generally recognized." See Kalish, "Death and Dying in a Social Context," in *Handbook of Aging and the Social Sciences,* ed. Robert H. Binstock and Ethel Shanas (New York: Van Nostrand Reinhold, 1976), p. 486.

31. Abigail Adams to Mary Cranch, 4 April 1798, *New Letters of Abigail Adams, 1788-1801,* ed. Stewart Mitchell (Boston: Houghton Mifflin, 1947), p. 152; Ruth Henshaw Bascom, Diaries, 1 January 1846, AAS. See also Deborah Norris Logan, Diary, 3 July 1812 and 9 February 1833, HSP.

32. Deborah Norris Logan, Diary, 16 May 1824, HSP; Elizabeth Drinker, Diary, 31 December 1794, HSP.

33. Hannah Adams, *A Memoir of Miss Hannah Adams, Written by Herself* (Boston: Gray and Bowen, 1832), p. 72; Elizabeth Denny Ward to grandchildren, n.d., Ward Family Papers, AAS; Sarah Logan Fisher, Diary, 22 August 1785 and 4 June 1793, HSP. See also Deborah Norris Logan, Diary, 3 July 1823, HSP; Rebecca Shoemaker to Samuel Shoemaker, 7 July 1784, Shoemaker Papers, HSP; and Lucinda Storrs, Diary, n.d. 1822, CHS.

34. Rebecca Dickinson, Diary, 12 August 1787, p. 206; Deborah Norris Logan, Diary, 3 November 1831, HSP; Susanna Boylston Adams quoted in Abigail Adams to Mary Cranch, 7 May 1798, *New Letters,* ed. Mitchell, p. 168; Mary McDonald to Mrs. Rossiter, 7 March 1807, McDonald-Lawrence Papers, GHS.

35. Elizabeth Putnam to Samuel Ward, 15 May 1788, Chandler-Ward Family Papers, AAS; Margaret Bayard Smith to Jane Kirkpatrick, 19 December 1839,

Margaret Bayard Smith Papers, LCMD. See also Mary McDonald to Mrs. Rossiter, 1 December 1809, McDonald-Lawrence Papers, GHS; Lucinda Storrs, Diary, [12] March 1833, CHS; and Deborah Norris Logan, Diary, 17 March 1824, 31 December 1832, and 27 March 1838, HSP.

36. Deborah Norris Logan, Diary, 19 October 1815, HSP.

37. Ibid., 18 November 1821.

38. Ibid., 17 March 1822. See also Mercy Otis Warren, "An Address to the Supreme Being," p. 224.

39. Deborah Norris Logan, Diary, 7 March and 16 May 1824, HSP.

40. Ibid., 5 January 1829, 31 December 1832, and 31 December 1833.

41. Ibid., 27 March and 15 June 1838 and 3 January 1839.

42. Mary Palmer Tyler, *Grandmother Tyler's Book: The Recollection of Mary Palmer Tyler (Mrs. Royall Tyler)*, ed. Frederick Tupper and Helen Tyler Brown (New York: G. P. Putnam's Sons, 1925), p. 323. Barbara Welter interprets women's deeply religious ties from a different perspective. "Religion, along with the family and popular taste, was not very important, and so became the property of the ladies," she argues. Post-revolutionary women would have strongly disagreed with Welter's perspective. See Welter, "The Feminization of American Religion," in *Clio's Consciousness Raised: Perspectives on the History of Women,* ed. Mary Hartman and Lois Banner (New York: Harper and Row, 1976), p. 138.

43. Elizabeth Murray to her sister, 26 June 1785, James M. Robbins Family Papers, MHS.

44. According to Carol Ochs, women are aware that "the spiritual struggle is shared and that salvation is the overcoming of separation." It is this interpretation of salvation that may best describe Inman's apparent victory at death. See Ochs, *Women and Spirituality,* p. 3. Some women, of course, simply ignored the tenets of withdrawal. "I may safely say," wrote sixty-eight-year-old Elizabeth Collins, "the older I grow, the more I feel true love towards my friends." See Collins, *Memoirs,* p. 119.

A Pattern of Continuity
and a Vision of Change

American women's history is filled with contradictions. Early colonial women, valued for their bravery as well as their strong backs, nonetheless submitted to the age-old denial of women's rights and privileges under English common law in the "new land." Antebellum women broke new ground as factory employees, teachers, and professional writers, yet most women remained bound within a tightly constricted private sphere. Twentieth-century women made enormous strides in gaining influence over their political and professional lives, but the right to exercise control over their own bodies — and over reproduction in particular — remains largely in the hands of male legislators and judges.

The history of old women reads with much the same ambivalence. Prior to the twentieth century, old age often meant enormous physical debility for the few fortunate (or stubborn) individuals who reached it. Those without property or ample family connections could anticipate hunger and a fair share of misery in their final years. Yet advanced age often brought respect and a certain amount of authority. By contrast, contemporary old women live (for the most part) without fear of destitution at the end of life. Over the past fifty years, aging women and men alike have learned to expect a reasonable amount of economic security. Nonetheless, they have fears: the inability to maintain standards of physical beauty and vigor; the possibility of prolonged yet debilitated old age; the loneliness of survival, devoid of spiritual direction. Today we are only beginning to recognize the full implications of long life for a substantial segment of our population.

From our contemporary vantage point, the experience of old women in the new republic epitomizes the often contradictory nature of feminine historical experience. These strong and resilient women, as we have seen, approached old age head-on, sometimes with a vengeance. Within their sphere, they continued to live and work in well-established ways. Respected by younger generations for their accumulated wisdom and moral fortitude, they served as valuable models for younger women seeking patterns of feminine maturity. Nonetheless, much in their experience seems to deny this model of vigorous aging. Confined by both law and increasingly rigid gender expectations, women in old age showed little enthusiasm for fighting the system, for attacking the legal, social, or political powers that mandated their status. While occasionally acknowledging their reluctance to rely on male support in old age, these women frequently depended on husbands, brothers, or sons for their home or financial security. Pillars of their churches and exemplars of moral and spiritual courage, most old women held no formal positions of power within religious organizations and indeed shied away from public notoriety of any kind. Such an ambiguous heritage poses some obvious problems for twentieth-century women (and men) searching for models of aging that conform to contemporary interpretations of liberated womanhood. (This, indeed, may be one reason why old women are so noticeably absent from accounts of women's history published over the last twenty years.)

There is, of course, little hope of accurately interpreting historical figures — either the great or the obscure — by imposing contemporary standards and expectations. We can, indeed, risk much by concentrating our historical research exclusively on women's past search for autonomy and power outside the home. Such values, held so dearly today, meant little to most women, young or old, in nineteenth-century America. Women's firm belief in the virtues of domesticity and interdependency, not public recognition or independence, served as the foundation of feminine thought and experience throughout the century. As historians, we must endeavor to trace accurately those values and beliefs that influenced the lives of all women, exposing their strengths as well as their weaknesses. As individuals in search of our own past, we should attempt to meet our foremothers on their own terms, drawing from their words and experiences new insights into our own quest for meaning in youth and in old age.

Women in the new republic matured, grew old, and died within a web of connection to the people, beliefs, and traditions that had long given meaning to their lives. This emphasis on the value of connection formed a central component of the concept of woman's sphere as it evolved during this early period. Other aspects of the sphere, however, were clearly less consistent with women's well-being, most noticeably in its well-defined limitations and the rigidity of expectations and standards for women. "Membership" within the sphere was not entirely voluntary; women, by virtue of their gender and social class, were assigned to its ranks and expected to uphold its tenets. Such narrowness cannot belie, however, its strength and durability over time. Nor can its obvious deficits serve as proof of women's relative powerlessness in the nineteenth century. On the contrary, the notion of woman's sphere survived (and thrived) because it was based on the traditional bonds and commitments of womanhood. While the sphere restricted women's opportunities outside the home, it nonetheless confirmed for many women a sense of identity and active engagement in a world cast in feminine profile.

As women grew old, domesticity contributed to and often enhanced their sense of well-being and connectedness. Domestic employment remained essentially unchanged despite advancing age; it was reduced only by diminished household size or declining health. Active childrearing, an increasingly significant component of the domestic sphere, formed the basis for continuing maternal involvement in later life and reinforced active grandmaternal participation as well. Friendships between women, whose foundations were laid early in adolescence, remained vital at the close of life, providing continuing support and nurturance. Expectations of spiritual insight and moral preeminence, those aspects of woman's sphere that most clearly distinguished women's values from those of their male counterparts, were deemed especially appropriate in old age. Significantly, while patterns of domesticity might have contributed enormously to a satisfying and productive old age, marriage per se was no guarantee of contentment. Yet most women who adopted the culture of domesticity and collaborated in the full range of feminine pursuits, as defined by woman's sphere, greeted old age with ease and serenity in the new republic.

Women's separate, private sphere—and the domestic world that flourished within it—promoted a pattern of interdependency that remained critical to women growing old. Perceiving the reciprocal nature of commitment and responsibility, women could anticipate their final years within a framework of shared obligation and trust. The interdependent nature of feminine friendship, for instance, assured women they would have moral support in coping with late-life changes. Reciprocity was especially evident in the attitudes toward filial duty. Aged mothers continued to assist grown daughters and granddaughters with childbearing and childrearing; in return, they expected such lifelong devotion to be rewarded in old age. Because such relationships remained interdependent for as long as health allowed, there was little reason to despair over the proverbial "empty nest." Instead, strong intergenerational ties fostered an ongoing sense of family commitment and unity.

The related themes of interdependency and continuty, so apparent in the writings of older women, appeared as well in the metaphors women most frequently employed to describe the final stage of life. Seasonal images abounded as women attempted to identify themselves within a cyclical pattern of growth, decline, and renewal. The image of a placid and peaceful winter could be comforting indeed if the coming spring was assured for those left behind.

By embracing a continuing, cyclical vision of life, aging women found it easier to identify their role in a larger society that sometimes seemed at odds with the world they knew. This was especially apparent when they were confronted with political and institutional change, which they might indeed support but for which they could not claim credit. Although these women viewed themselves as part of the revolutionary generation, they had good reason to doubt the meaning of revolution in their own lives. Their political and legal status remained virtually unchanged from that known to their own grandmothers. On a day-to-day basis, the impact of Independence might be far less apparent than the continuing influence of *interdependency*. This collaborative, supportive quality of woman's sphere served to buffer the inequities of their revolutionary inheritance and provided security against the possibility of declining status in old age, a possibility which David Hackett Fischer contends was rife in post-revolutionary America.[1]

Some aging women chose not to ignore their revolutionary ties and instead indulged wholeheartedly in reminiscing about a glorified past. Such devotion to their own unique generation, however, tended to separate women from later ideas, groups, and events. Caught in a rapidly changing society, these "relics" of the revolutionary era were often alienated from both the present and the future. Such a retrospective emphasis distorted their perception of time and added an aspect of discontinuity to late life.

Other aspects of their revolutionary heritage proved equally ambiguous. More literate than their prewar mothers and grandmothers, many of these aging women utilized the tools of literacy to expand the dimensions of their old age. More politically aware than earlier generations of women, post-revolutionary women often retained an active, if critical, interest in contemporary activities and events. Yet their expanded awareness sometimes made them vulnerable to the frustrations of limited enlightenment. Even women possessing strong intellectual gifts received little encouragement to pursue nondomestic activities. Women's potential for intellectual growth and recognition in old age was seldom realized in the fifty years following American independence.

Ultimately, it was this confrontation with the individual, autonomous self that incited both challenge and conflict as women grew older. Whether as survivors, outliving friends and family, as relics of a lost generation, or as writers afraid of prominence and public recognition, women on their own were often forced to confront the meaning of their long lives outside the bonds of connection that had shaped their sphere and their own experience. This tension between the connected and the individual self was particularly obvious as women anticipated death. Women long familiar with the traditional (male) metaphor of the pilgrim trodding the last miles of his spiritual journey could not ignore its implications. The pilgrim died alone, without friends or loved ones, without earthly ties. For aging women, such an image of separation and withdrawal might inspire more fear and anxiety than death itself. Some women met this challenge by continuing to locate their spirituality and their sense of self within a vision of continuity and rebirth. Others fared less well, unwilling to modify hopes or lower expectations, unable to integrate self and world.

Then, as now, the issue of autonomy versus connection continued to challenge and perplex the minds and hearts of women. Two hundred years ago, as today, women confronted critical questions of identity, obligation, and meaning. Whether constrained by a female sphere which thwarted women's individual growth, or threatened by a narcissistic culture which fosters competition and individualism at the cost of mutual commitment and caring, women throughout history have known the need for compromise and innovation. In the past, such issues have been closely linked to questions of old age and the completion of life. Today, they are the property of youth, reserved for those early years when choices and decisions must be made. Such issues, in fact, may never be properly addressed until they become the hard questions of a lifetime, the focus of a diligent, introspective search which neither ends in youth nor begins in old age.

Women Growing Old: A Model for the Future

Women in the new republic, like most women in American history, shared an orientation and a system of values which in many ways separated them from the male-defined standards of the "world" outside their sphere. As women aged, they relied on those values to interpret and direct the final course of their lives. As the results of this study indicate, the experience of aging women cannot be understood by simply examining data derived exclusively from aging males. A model for the study of women growing old must include women's self-defined values.

The results of this study suggest at least six elements which reflect areas of meaning and value to aging women in the new republic:

1. *Relationships:* Women's relationships with family and friends formed a central component of their late lives. Within their families, affectionate

ties to daughters and grandchildren became increasingly significant in old age. Female friends remained essential to the well-being of women growing old.

2. *Organic orientation to life:* Women's traditional roles as mother and nurturer, while potentially restrictive in early life, added a critical dimension to the end of life. Their familiarity with patterns of birth, growth, decay, and death tended to reinforce women's understanding and acceptance of old age and, ultimately, death.

3. *Domesticity:* The notion of a "woman's place" at home succeeded in restricting women's activities and limiting their options for centuries. Ironically, in old age, when physical infirmities and diminished strength enforced domesticity, women fared better than men. Comfortable following their daily routine in familiar surroundings in a world of their own making, old women found consolation and peace at home.

4. *Interdependency:* Legally denied rights to property and financial independence, women traditionally relied on others for financial support in old age. Women believed, however, that obligations were reciprocal; they continued to provide "useful" services to friends and kin for as long as possible. Likewise, women considered filial duty appropriate and well deserved as repayment for their own hard work in raising children. Women's status, often described as "dependent," must be understood within the context of mutual obligations as understood by women.

5. *Conservation and transmission of culture:* Aging women responded to both personal and societal change by devoting themselves to the traditions and values of the past. Committed to passing on these values to future generations, women viewed themselves as vital links between past and future. This role enabled them to adapt more smoothly to change in their own status as they grew old.

6. *Spiritual awareness:* This factor dominates the early literature of women growing old and must serve as a central consideration in any model of women and aging. Women's spiritual life proved to be their greatest source of strength and comfort in old age. It was neither passive nor merely compensatory. Spiritual growth demanded full emotional and intellectual commitment. Contemporary historians who devalue the spiritual element of women's lives risk missing altogether a key factor of women's survivorship. In fact, the historical relationship between women's dedication to spiritual growth and their impressive, ever-increasing longevity stands as an exciting and provocative issue yet to be explored.

Sources of meaning for aging women obviously will differ across cultures and over time. The history of American women growing old, for instance, appears in some ways inconsistent with European patterns of feminine aging. Similarly, old women in contemporary American society may find themselves increasingly disengaged from the organic, domestic, and spiritual elements that shaped the lives of their female ancestors. Nevertheless, the aging experience described by post-revolutionary women provides a viable outline for adaptation and survival. For those attempting to envision a new model for an aging society, such patterns represent not only a reminder of the past but also a promise for the future.[2]

NOTES

1. David Hackett Fischer, *Growing Old in America,* 2d ed. (New York: Oxford University Press, 1978).

2. Peter Stearns raises important questions about the nature of women's dependent strategies and their effect on longevity. Stearns does not acknowledge, however, the interdependency of women, family, and friends. This may be a reflection of the cultural differences between aging French women (the subjects of Stearns's article) and American women, as studied here. See Stearns, "Old Women: Some Historical Observations," *Journal of Family History* 5 (Spring 1980):46.

Janet Roebuck addresses the potential consequences of women's ever-increasing longevity and poses intriguing questions concerning the relationship between modernization theory, women's history, and the modernization of old age. See Roebuck, "Grandma as Revolutionary: Elderly Women and Some Modern Patterns of Social Change," *International Journal of Aging and Human Development* 14:4 (1983):261-64.

Selected Bibliography
of Primary Sources

UNPUBLISHED SOURCES

Diaries and Journals

Ruth Henshaw Bascom Diaries, American Antiquarian Society, Worcester, Mass.
Elizabeth Bowen Diary, Essex Institute, Salem, Mass.
Abigail Gardner Drew Diary and Reminiscences, American Antiquarian Society, Worcester, Mass.
Elizabeth Drinker Diaries, Historical Society of Pennsylvania, Philadelphia, Pa.
Sarah Logan Fisher Diaries, Historical Society of Pennsylvania, Philadelphia, Pa.
Grace Growden Galloway Diaries, Historical Society of Pennsylvania, Philadelphia, Pa.
Anna Blackwood Howell Diaries, American Antiquarian Society, Worcester, Mass.
Betsy Graves Johnson Diary, Massachusetts Historical Society, Boston, Mass.
Ann Livingston Diary, Shippen Family Papers, Library of Congress Manuscript Division, Washington, D.C.
Deborah Norris Logan Diaries, Historical Society of Pennsylvania, Philadelphia, Pa.
Rachel Mason Diary, Quaker Collection, Haverford College Library, Haverford, Pa.
Ann Moore Diary, Quaker Collection, Haverford College Library, Haverford, Pa.
Rebecca Noyes Diary, Connecticut Historical Society, Hartford, Conn.
Elizabeth Pierce Journal, Poor Family Papers, Arthur and Elizabeth Schlesinger Library on the History of Women in America, Radcliffe College, Cambridge, Mass.
Patty Rogers Diary, Rogers Family Diaries, American Antiquarian Society, Worcester, Mass.
Rebecca Shoemaker Journal, Rawle Family Papers, Historical Society of Pennsylvania, Philadelphia, Pa.
Elizabeth Smith Diary, American Antiquarian Society, Worcester, Mass.
Lucinda Storrs Diary, Connecticut Historical Society, Hartford, Conn.
Ann Whitall Diary, Quaker Collection, Haverford College Library, Haverford, Pa.

Manuscript Collections and Letters

Elizabeth Jacquelin Ambler Letters, Library of Congress Manuscript Division, Washington, D.C.

Ball Estate–Dupuy Papers, Historical Society of Pennsylvania, Philadelphia, Pa.

Barnard Family Papers, Library of Congress Manuscript Division, Washington, D.C.

Marjorie P. M. Brown Collection, Historical Society of Pennsylvania, Philadelphia, Pa.

Elizabeth Byles Letterbook, Historical Society of Pennsylvania, Philadelphia, Pa.

Chandler-Ward Family Papers, American Antiquarian Society, Worcester, Mass.

Crowninshield Family Papers, Essex Institute, Salem, Mass.

Cutts Family Papers, Essex Institute, Salem, Mass.

Dillwyn Manuscripts, Library Company of Philadelphia/Historical Society of Pennsylvania, Philadelphia, Pa.

Drinker and Sandwith Family Papers, Historical Society of Pennsylvania, Philadelphia, Pa.

Elizabeth Farmer Letterbook, Historical Society of Pennsylvania, Philadelphia, Pa.

Foster Family Papers, American Antiquarian Society, Worcester, Mass.

Grace Growden Galloway Letterbook, Historical Society of Pennsylvania, Philadelphia, Pa.

Hawthorne-Manning Collection, Essex Institute, Salem, Mass.

Hooker Collection, Arthur and Elizabeth Schlesinger Library on the History of Women in America, Radcliffe College, Cambridge, Mass.

Hopkinson Family Papers, Historical Society of Pennsylvania, Philadelphia, Pa.

Abigail Bradley Hyde Letters, Arthur and Elizabeth Schlesinger Library on the History of Women in America, Radcliffe College, Cambridge, Mass.

Izard Family Papers, Library of Congress Manuscript Division, Washington, D.C.

Logan Papers, Historical Society of Pennsylvania, Philadelphia, Pa.

Maria Dickinson Logan Family Papers, Historical Society of Pennsylvania, Philadelphia, Pa.

McDonald-Lawrence Papers, Georgia Historical Society, Savannah, Ga.

May-Goddard Papers, Arthur and Elizabeth Schlesinger Library on the History of Women in America, Radcliffe College, Cambridge, Mass.

Miscellaneous Manuscript Collection, Library of Congress Manuscript Division, Washington, D.C.

Catherine Mitchell Papers, Library of Congress Manuscript Division, Washington, D.C.

Norris Family Letters, Historical Society of Pennsylvania, Philadelphia, Pa.

Norton Papers, Massachusetts Historical Society, Boston, Mass.

Harrison Gray Otis Papers, Massachusetts Historical Society, Boston, Mass.

Robert Treat Paine Papers, Massachusetts Historical Society, Boston, Mass.

Park Family Papers, American Antiquarian Society, Worcester, Mass.

Leonard Moody Parker Papers, American Antiquarian Society, Worcester, Mass.

Benjamin Pickman Family Correspondence, Essex Institute, Salem, Mass.

Pinckney Family Papers, Library of Congress Manuscript Division, Washington, D.C.

Poor Family Papers, Arthur and Elizabeth Schlesinger Library on the History of Women in America, Radcliffe College, Cambridge, Mass.

William B. Randolph Papers, Library of Congress Manuscript Division, Washington, D.C.

James M. Robbins Papers, Massachusetts Historical Society, Boston, Mass.

Rogers Family Papers, American Antiquarian Society, Worcester, Mass.

Catherine Maria Sedgwick Papers, Massachusetts Historical Society, Boston, Mass.

Shaw-Webb Family Papers, American Antiquarian Society, Worcester, Mass.

Shippen Family Papers, Library of Congress Manuscript Division, Washington, D.C.

Shoemaker Papers, Historical Society of Pennsylvania, Philadelphia, Pa.

Singleton Family Papers, Library of Congress Manuscript Division, Washington, D.C.

Margaret Bayard Smith Papers, Library of Congress Manuscript Division, Washington, D.C.

Smith-Carter Family Papers, Massachusetts Historical Society, Boston, Mass.

Smith-Townsend Family Papers, Massachusetts Historical Society, Boston, Mass.

William Thornton Papers, Library of Congress Manuscript Division, Washington, D.C.

Waldo Family Papers, American Antiquarian Society, Worcester, Mass.

Ward Family Papers, American Antiquarian Society, Worcester, Mass.

Mercy Otis Warren Papers, Massachusetts Historical Society, Boston, Mass.

Warren-Winthrop Papers, Massachusetts Historical Society, Boston, Mass.

Washington Family Papers, Library of Congress Manuscript Division, Washington, D.C.

Memoirs and Autobiographies

Louisa Catherine Adams, "The Adventures of a Nobody," Adams Papers III, Massachusetts Historical Society, Boston, Mass.

Elizabeth Perkins Cabot Memoirs, Cabot Family Papers, Arthur and Elizabeth Schlesinger Library on the History of Women in America, Cambridge, Mass.

PUBLISHED SOURCES

Diaries and Journals

Assheton, Susan. "Susan Assheton's Book." Edited by Joseph M. Beatty, Jr. *Pennsylvania Magazine of History and Biography* 55:2 (1931):174-86.

Ayer, Sarah Connell. *Diary of Sarah Connell Ayer, 1805-35.* Portland, Maine: Lefavor-Tower, 1910.

Burney, Frances. *The Diary and Letters of Frances Burney, Mrs. D'Arblay.* 2 vols. Edited by Sarah Chauncey Woolsey. Boston: Little, Brown, 1880.

Cooper, Molly. *The Diary of Molly Cooper: Life on a Long Island Farm, 1768-1773.* Edited by Field Horne. Oyster Bay, N.Y.: Oyster Bay Historical Society, 1981.

Cowles, Julia. *Diary of Julia Cowles: A Connecticut Record, 1797-1803*. Edited by Laura Hadley Moseley. New Haven, Conn.: Yale University Press, 1931.

Dickinson, Rebecca. Diary in *A History of Hatfield, Massachusetts, 1660-1910*. Edited by Daniel White Wells and Reuben Field Wells. Springfield, Mass.: F. C. H. Gibbons, 1910.

Galloway, Grace Growden. Diary. Edited by Raymond C. Werner. *Pennsylvania Magazine of History and Biography* 58 (April 1934):152-89.

Morris, Margaret. *Margaret Morris: Her Journal with Biographical Sketch and Notes*. Edited by John W. Jackson. Philadelphia: The Historical Society of Pennsylvania, 1899.

Nash, Charles Elventon. *The History of Augusta: First Settlement and Early Days as a Town, including the Diary of Mrs. Martha Moore Ballard*. Augusta, Maine: Charles E. Nash, 1904.

Stiles, Ezra. *The Literary Diary of Ezra Stiles*. Edited by Franklin B. Dexter. New York: C. Scribner's Sons. 1901.

Winslow, Anna Green. *The Diary of Anna Green Winslow*. Edited by Alice Morse Earle. Boston: Houghton Mifflin, 1894.

Letters

Adams, Abigail. *Letters of Mrs. Adams, The Wife of John Adams*. Edited by Charles Francis Adams. Boston: Wilkins, Carter, 1848.

———. *New Letters of Abigail Adams, 1788-1801*. Edited by Stewart Mitchell. Boston: Houghton Mifflin, 1947.

Adams, Abigail, and John Adams. *The Book of Abigail and John: Selected Letters of the Adams Family, 1762-1784*. Edited by L. H. Butterfield. Cambridge, Mass.: Harvard University Press, 1975.

Adams, John, and Abigail Adams. *Familiar Letters of John Adams and His Wife Abigail Adams, during the Revolution*. Edited by Charles Francis Adams. Boston: Houghton Mifflin, 1876.

Adams Family Correspondence. Vol. 3. Edited by L. H. Butterfield. Cambridge, Mass.: Harvard University Press, 1963.

Bowne, Eliza Southgate. *A Girl's Life Eighty Years Ago: Selections from the Letters of Eliza Southgate Bowne*. New York: Charles Scribners's Sons, 1887.

Dublin, Thomas, ed. *Farm to Factory: Women's Letters, 1830-1860*. New York: Columbia University Press, 1981.

Franklin, Benjamin. *The Papers of Benjamin Franklin*. Vol. 3. Edited by Leonard W. Labaree. New Haven, Conn.: Yale University Press, 1961.

Mecom, Jane. "Three Jane Mecom-Franklin Letters." *Pennsylvania Magazine of History and Biography* 72 (July 1948):264-72.

Murray, James. *Letters of James Murray, Loyalist*. Edited by Nina Moore Tiffany. Boston: Gregg Press, 1972.

Pinckney, Eliza Lucas. *The Letterbook of Eliza Lucas Pinckney*. Edited by Elise Pinckney. Chapel Hill: University of North Carolina Press, 1972.

Sedgwick, Catherine Maria. *Life and Letters of Catherine Maria Sedgwick*. Edited by Mary C. Dewey. New York: Harper and Bros., 1871.

Warren, Mercy Otis. "Warren-Adams Letters." *MHS Collections* 73 (1925):352-54.

Memoirs and Autobiographies

Adams, Hannah. *A Memoir of Miss Hannah Adams, Written by Herself.* Boston: Gray and Bowen, 1832.

Beecher, Catharine. *Educational Reminiscences and Suggestions.* New York: J. B. Ford, 1874.

Chambers, Charlotte. *Memoir of Charlotte Chambers.* Edited by Lewis H. Garrard. Philadelphia: by the author, 1856.

Collins, Elizabeth (Ballinger) Mason. *Memoirs of Elizabeth Collins of Upper Evesham, N.J.* Philadelphia: N. Kite, 1833.

Ellet, Mary Israel. *Memoirs of Mary Israel Ellet, 1780-1870.* Edited by Herbert P. Gambrell. Doyleston, Pa.: Bucks County Historical Society, 1939.

Fries, Adelaide L., *Road to Salem* [includes Anna Catharine Ernst's memoir]. Chapel Hill: University of North Carolina Press, 1944.

Jemison, Mary. *A Narrative of the Life of Miss Mary Jemison.* Edited by James E. Seaver. Canandaigua, N.Y.: J. O. Bemis, 1824.

Lee, Jarena. *The Life and Religious Experience of Jarena Lee, a Coloured Lady.* Philadelphia: for the author, 1836.

Logan, Deborah. *Memoir of Dr. George Logan of Stenton.* Edited by Frances A. Logan. Philadelphia: Historical Society of Pennsylvania, 1899.

Mitchell, Mary Callender. *A Short Account of the Early Part of the Life of Mary Mitchell.* New Bedford, Mass.: Abraham Shearman, 1812.

More, Hannah. *Memoirs of Hannah More.* Edited by W. Roberts. New York: Harper and Bros., 1835.

Richards, Anna Matlock. *Memories of a Grandmother, by a Lady of Massachusetts.* Boston: Gould and Lincoln, 1854.

Sigourney, Lydia H. *Letters of Life.* New York: D. Appleton, 1866.

Smith, Elizabeth Oakes. *Selections from the Autobiography of Elizabeth Oakes Smith.* Edited by Mary Alice Wyman. Lewiston, Maine: Lewiston Journal Press, 1924.

Tevis, Julia Ann. *Sixty Years in a School-Room: An Autobiography of Mrs. Julia Ann Tevis, Principal of Science Hill Female Academy.* Cincinnati: Western Methodist Book Concern, 1878.

Tyler, Mary Palmer. *Grandmother Tyler's Book: The Recollection of Mary Palmer Tyler (Mrs. Royall Tyler).* Edited by Frederick Tupper and Helen Tyler Brown. New York: G. P. Putnam's Sons, 1925.

Prescriptive Literature and Miscellaneous

Brewster, Martha. *Poems on Diverse Subjects.* New London: T. Green, 1757.

Child, Lydia Maria. *Looking towards Sunset.* Boston: Ticknor and Fields, 1865.

Cicero. *De Senectute.* In *Selected Works*, pp. 211-47. Translated by Michael Grant. Harmondsworth, England: Penguin Books, 1971.

Cowell, Pattie. "Womankind Call Reason to Their Aid: Susanna Wright's Verse Epistle on the Status of Women in Eighteenth Century America." *Signs: Journal of Women in Culture and Society* 6 (Summer 1981):795-800.

Dewees, William P. *A Treatise on the Diseases of Females.* Philadelphia: H. C. Carey and I. Lee, 1826.

"The Fortieth Wedding Day." *The Rose Bud or Youth's Gazette* (Charleston, S.C.),
    6 October 1832.

Gisborne, Thomas. *An Enquiry into the Duties of the Female Sex.* 2d ed. London:
    T. Cadell, 1797.

Hayes, Edmund M. "The Private Poems of Mercy Otis Warren." *New England
    Quarterly* 54 (June 1981):199-224.

Murray, Judith Sargent ["Constantia"]. *The Gleaner, a Miscellaneous Production.*
    3 vols. Boston: I. Thomas and E. T. Andrews, 1798.

Ralph, Joseph. *A Domestic Guide to Medicine.* New York: Leavitt, 1834.

Sigourney, Lydia. *Letters to Mothers.* Hartford, Conn.: Hudson and Skinner, 1838.
————. *Past Meridian.* New York: D. Appleton, 1854.

The Southern Rose (Charleston, S.C.), 25 June 1836.

Stanford, John. *The Aged Christian's Companion.* New York: T. and J. Swords,
    1829.

Index

Note on the Author

Terri L. Premo received her Ph.D. in history from the University of Cincinnati in 1983. She has written numerous articles and papers concerning the history of women growing old, including publications in the *Pennsylvania Magazine of History and Biography* and the *International Journal of Aging and Human Development.* She has served as a research associate at the University of Texas Medical Branch at Galveston and presently teaches women's history at the University of Cincinnati.